REIMAGINING ISRAEL AND PALESTINE IN CONTEMPORARY BRITISH AND GERMAN CULTURE

REIMAGINING ISRAEL AND PALESTINE IN CONTEMPORARY BRITISH AND GERMAN CULTURE

Isabelle Hesse

EDINBURGH
University Press

Edinburgh University Press is one of the leading university presses in the UK. We publish academic books and journals in our selected subject areas across the humanities and social sciences, combining cutting-edge scholarship with high editorial and production values to produce academic works of lasting importance. For more information visit our website: edinburghuniversitypress.com

© Isabelle Hesse, 2024, 2025

Edinburgh University Press Ltd
13 Infirmary Street
Edinburgh EH1 1LT

First published in hardback by Edinburgh University Press 2024

Typeset in 11/15 EB Garamond by
IDSUK (DataConnection) Ltd

A CIP record for this book is available from the British Library

ISBN 978 1 3995 2367 7 (hardback)
ISBN 978 1 3995 2368 4 (paperback)
ISBN 978 1 3995 2369 1 (webready PDF)
ISBN 978 1 3995 2370 7 (epub)

The right of Isabelle Hesse to be identified as author of this work has been asserted in accordance with the Copyright, Designs and Patents Act 1988 and the Copyright and Related Rights Regulations 2003 (SI No. 2498).

CONTENTS

Acknowledgements		vi
Introduction: The Relational Turn in British and German Culture		1
1	Displaced Relationality: Israel as a Mirror for Germany	41
2	Relational Memories: The Holocaust and the *Nakba* in the British Imaginary	71
3	Libidinal Relationality: Humour, the Holocaust and Palestine/Israel in German Culture	95
4	Disrupted Familial Relationality: Ethnicity, Alternative Alliances and Hybridity in Contemporary British Culture	120
5	Relational Coexistence: Donations across Divides and Imagined Kinship in Palestine/Israel	145
Conclusion: Future Relationalities		172
Bibliography		181
Index		202

ACKNOWLEDGEMENTS

This book began to take shape as I started working in the Department of English at the University of Sydney, Australia. It was researched and written on the unceded lands of the Gadigal people of the Eora Nation, and I'd like to pay my respect to elders past, present and emerging and to the knowledge embedded forever within Aboriginal custodianship of Country. My colleagues in English and beyond have been instrumental in the process of writing this book – both in terms of providing feedback on the ideas presented here and through the collegial and intellectual stimulating environment of the Department. For ongoing support, generous advice, corridor and photocopier chats and a great sense of humour I want to thank my current and former colleagues. Thank you in particular to Sarah Gleeson-White, Vanessa Smith, Liam Semler, Beth Yahp, Nicola Parsons, Fiona Lee, Ashley Maher, Rebecca Johinke, Anthony Cordingley, Lee Wallace, Brigid Rooney and Peter Marks. Thank you to my research assistants, Eliza Crespis and Niklas Fischer, and the fantastic team of professional staff in our School whose untiring work behind the scenes supports our work every day, especially Elizabeth Connor, Anna Goschin and Orla McGovern.

Thank you to the School of Arts, Communication and English and the Faculty of Arts and Social Sciences at the University of Sydney, who provided funding and research support for this project, including grants to do research at the National Library in Frankfurt am Main, Germany. I would like to express my profound gratitude to the Parkes Institute for the Study of Jewish/non-Jewish Relations at the University of Southampton, UK, for a visiting fellowship in May and June 2022, which gave me time to read, think and write. I presented parts of Chapter 4 of this book at a seminar hosted by the Parkes Institute, the Department of English, and the Southampton Institute for Arts and Humanities. This chapter benefited from the great questions and insights from the audience and from Devorah Baum, who kindly agreed to be the respondent to my paper. Thank you to Anoushka Alexander-Rose for organising this talk, to Claire Le Foll and George Gilbert for hosting me during my visit, and to Katie Power for technical support.

An earlier version of Chapter 2 was published in *New Formations* 93 (2018) and parts of Chapter 3 were published in *Studies in Travel Writing* 22, no. 2 (2018). I would like to thank the editors of these journals, Jeremy Gilbert and Tim Youngs, for kindly permitting me to reuse this work in my book. Thank you to the team at Edinburgh University Press, especially the editorial team: Louise Hutton, Emma House and Isobel Birks, who are a pleasure to work with and genuinely supportive. I would like to thank the anonymous reviewers of the book proposal and the manuscript for the time they took to read my work and to provide detailed and constructive feedback.

Thank you to my writing group, where many parts of this book were written and rewritten: Avril Alba, Nicholas Bromfield and Elisabeth Valiente-Riedl. Thank you to Jumana Bayeh, Ben Etherington, Laetitia Nanquette and Lynda Ng for introducing me to the intellectual community in Sydney. I owe a big thank you to Anna Bernard, Ziad Elmarsafy, Anna Guttman, Sarah Phillips Casteel and Bryan Cheyette for their support over the years and for continuing to champion my work.

Discussing books and ideas with undergraduate and postgraduate students is always an enlightening and humbling experience, and I'd like to thank the enthusiastic and engaged students that I had the pleasure to teach at the University of Sydney while working on this book. Thank you also to my current and former MPhil and PhD students: Felicia Boyages, Angharad Hampshire, Cyma Hibri, Dashiell Moore, Charlotte Okkes, Angelina Saule and Nicola Travers-Robinson.

Further afield, thank you to Anna Bocking-Welch, Katherine Ebury, James Fraser, Natalija Keck, Eleni Matechou and Sarah Pett. Thank you to my friends back home for always making me feel as if I hadn't been away: Julie Welter, Martina Schiltz, Christine Koener, Sven Fiedler, Marcia Heinen and Sven Schuster. A huge thank you to my mum whose support has played such a key role in my career and whose love of books and reading made me an avid reader from an early age. And thank you to my extended family for their support and good sense of humour.

Finally, thank you to my son Ben and to my husband Jacques. I couldn't have done this without you.

INTRODUCTION: THE RELATIONAL TURN IN BRITISH AND GERMAN CULTURE

'Jew' and 'Arab', rather than representing two independent identities, are in fact inevitably attached, each necessarily configured through or in relation to the other.

– Gil Z. Hochberg[1]

And that is the point: it is a way of thinking: thinking of the future for Palestinians and Jews together; seeing the two identities side by side rather than pitted against each other in a head-to-head conflict.

– Brian Klug[2]

A recent contribution to *The Guardian*'s online edition, entitled 'Life on the Beaches of Tel Aviv and Gaza City – in Pictures', depicts the lives of Israelis and Palestinians 'just 70 km apart' who are living in 'different worlds on opposite sides of a century-old conflict' but 'enjoy some of the same delights'.[3] This series of photographs, which juxtaposed Israelis and Palestinians – in the article they are overlaid and the reader is able to move a slider to reveal more of one or the other image – establishes an important, if implicit, link between Palestinians and Israelis. However, it sets up a problematic mirroring between the situations of people living in Gaza and those living in Israel by carefully editing out any references to Israel's occupation of Gaza and the ways in which life in Gaza is shaped by the ongoing blockade imposed by Israel after its disengagement in 2005 and the election of Hamas in 2006. The effect is to completely erase the power relations between Israeli Jewish people in Israel and Palestinian people in Gaza.[4] In this book, I consider more critical types of relationality that have been established between Israeli Jews and Palestinians in British and German culture, and what it means for British and German literature, TV drama and film to 'see' Palestinian and Jewish 'identities side by side' and to 'think of the[ir] future together,' to use Brian Klug's words from the epigraph. I ask what this 'thinking together' means for each culture's perceptions of Palestinian and (Israeli) Jewish narratives and their interrelations, and for understanding British and German entanglement in the so-called Palestine/Israel conflict,[5] both historically and in the contemporary period.

Reimagining Israel and Palestine in Contemporary British and German Culture proposes a relational approach to discussing Israeli Jewish and Palestinian narratives in works from outside the region, to address a significant comparative and relational turn in representing Israel and Palestine in British and German culture since the 1980s. This turn manifests itself on two levels: one, in depicting Israeli Jewish and Palestinian histories and narratives as relational rather than separate. Two, in representing the links between the current situation in Israel and the Occupied Palestinian Territories and its historical and political roots in Europe, including the roles that Germany and the United Kingdom have played in the region and continue to play in the present. In my use of relationality, I follow Ella Shohat and Robert Stam's application of the concept of the 'relational' in their influential work, *Unthinking Eurocentrism: Multiculturalism and the Media* (2014). They explain that, 'Rather than speaking of cultural/racial groups in isolation, we speak of them "in relation", without ever suggesting that their positionings are identical.'[6] An important aspect of this approach, as they show later on, is that '[r]ather than striv[ing] for "balance"', they 'hope to "right the balance"'.[7] I take a similar approach in that I consider Israel and Palestine as 'in relation', but acknowledge that these relations are marked by the profound power imbalances that govern relations between occupier and occupied. Hence, in this book, I use relationality not only as a critical model that emphasises dialogue and connection but also as a means for uncovering 'opposition and contest',[8] which allows me to theorise the representation and interaction between Israeli Jewish and Palestinian histories and narratives outside of the region while taking into account the power imbalances between Israel and Palestine that define these representations and interactions.

This approach is reflected in the cover image of this book, which is a picture of a part of Colombian artist Doris Salcedo's artwork, *Shibboleth*. For this artwork, Salcedo created a deep fissure in the floor of the Turbine Hall at the Tate Modern in London that stretched from one end of the gallery to the other. Into this fissure, the artist placed a concrete cast of a Colombian rock face with a wire chain-link fence set into the concrete. As Salcedo has explained, the crack in this iconic space reveals a 'colonial and imperial history [that] has been disregarded, marginalised or simply obliterated . . . the history of racism, running parallel to the history of modernity'.[9] Salcedo's work draws attention to the often invisible power relations and their histories that shape the contemporary world, which is compounded by the title of the artwork. A shibboleth is a word, phrase or custom that can be used to determine whether an individual belongs to a particular group, illustrating how ideas of exclusion have not only shaped colonialism but equally how they continue to inform power dynamics in its aftermath. In a similar manner, my book extends our understanding of how Germany's and Britain's histories of colonialism and the Holocaust shape their contemporary engagement with Israel and Palestine, and asks how an emphasis on relationality challenges depictions of Israeli Jewish and Palestinian narratives as separate from each other – a common approach in the European imaginary.

This focus on relationality signals a significant change: in Europe, and in metropolitan culture more widely,[10] the histories of Israel and Palestine are often represented as separate and antagonistic, occluding the many complex relations between Jews and Arabs, Israeli Jews and Palestinians, that have formed since the first arrival of a significant number of Jewish settlers in Palestine in the 1880s. This logic of separation has also animated the use of partition as a framework to analyse Israel and Palestine, which was institutionalised with the 1947 United Nations partition plan.[11] But since the end of the Second Intifada, which saw a major expansion in Jewish settlements, particularly in the West Bank and East Jerusalem, it has become almost impossible to put partition, and the two-state solution, into practice. This difficulty, together with the increasing physical separation of Israeli Jews living in Israel and Palestinians living in the Occupied Palestinian Territories, including through the separation wall surrounding the West Bank and East Jerusalem, has resulted in concepts such as settler-colonialism and apartheid becoming more popular to theorise the relations between Israel and Palestine.[12] These approaches have opened up important critical avenues for thinking comparatively about Israel and Palestine, which contribute to challenging the idea of Israeli exceptionalism as well as transforming the ways in which the Palestinian struggle for liberation and self-determination is framed. However, the emphasis on distance and difference that often accompanies the use of these frameworks can run the risk of reifying the separation between Israeli Jewish and Palestinian people. Instead, building on Raef Zreik's observation that 'one can only "put apart" something that is already together, or conceivable as being together',[13] I use relationality to examine the ways in which Israel and Palestine are brought together in literature, TV drama and film. I also ask what this kind of thinking means for how Germany and the UK engage with and depict Israel and Palestine and their interrelations in the cultural and political sphere.

Relationality has been a key aspect of how (Israeli) Jewish identities and Palestinian identities have been defined since the arrival of the first Jewish settlers in Palestine.[14] As Gil Z. Hochberg emphasises in the epigraph to this introduction, 'Jew' and 'Arab' are not separate identities but are shaped through their relations with each other. What else is often hidden are the relations between Europe and the Middle East, particularly the involvement of major European powers such as Germany and the United Kingdom, and the ways in which Israel and Palestine play a key role in the political and cultural imaginary outside of the Middle East. Bashir Bashir and Leila Farsakh argue that 'the Arab and Jewish questions . . . continue to inform, feed, and kindle conflicts in Europe, the Middle East, and the United States',[15] emphasising the importance of the 'Arab and Jewish questions' and their interrelation for European cultures, which is what this book will develop further through its focus on Germany and the UK. As I demonstrate throughout, using relationality as a framework, and bringing to the fore often overlooked or neglected types of relationality, gives us more nuanced insights into Israeli Jewish and Palestinian narratives and their complex interrelations. This, in turn, raises questions about why authors and directors choose less mainstream approaches to representing these relations, and what this reveals about their works and the cultures that they write from and write for.

The UK and Germany have been chosen as case studies because of the historical roles each country has played in the creation of Israel and due to their ongoing support of the state of Israel. At the same time, both countries have supported Palestinian rights to self-determination and the creation of a Palestinian state at various points throughout history. Moreover, their respective commemorative practices around World War II, which in many ways are diametrically opposed, make them interesting case studies for this book. Britain celebrated World War II as a victory, whereas in Germany the end of World War II was initially seen as '*Stunde Null*' (zero hour) signalling a complete break with the Nazi past, which of course proved impossible. Colonialism also plays a key role in both countries' engagement with Israel and Palestine. The UK was a key colonial stakeholder in the region, including as a mandatory power in Palestine, a role which has only recently started to emerge as a topic of sustained scholarly and cultural inquiry. Germany was not directly involved as an imperial power in the Middle East, but the country's colonial past and its contribution to Orientalist discourses nevertheless play an important role in shaping how Germany engages with both Israel and Palestine. In the contemporary period, both countries have ambivalent relationships with Israel and Palestine, as exemplified through the tension between remembering the Holocaust and critically engaging with Israel and its treatment of the Palestinian people, a tension that we can similarly observe in other countries' engagement with Israel and Palestine.

By using the UK and Germany as case studies with differing types of involvement in colonialism and the Holocaust, this book identifies significant differences in each country's engagement with Israel and Palestine based on their respective histories. At the same time, it draws attention to common trends in the depiction of Israel and Palestine as relational – such as using libidinal relationships to think through both political relations between different countries and the considerations that arise when situating Palestinian and Jewish suffering in a comparative context, especially when invoking the Holocaust – which are applicable to countries beyond the UK and Germany. In order to get a deeper understanding of the power relations between Europe and the Middle East, the next sections will give an overview of the UK's and Germany's political and historical relationships with Israel and Palestine and how the memory of the Holocaust has shaped these relationships, as well as outlining the roles that Palestine and Israel play in each country's cultural and political imaginary, including as signifiers for other concerns.

'The Bible and the Sword': Palestine in the British Imaginary

Barbara Tuchman famously summarised England's reasons for engaging with Palestine as 'Bible and Sword', drawing attention to Palestine as a key religious and imperial issue for the British imagination.[16] Building on this idea, Eitan Bar-Yosef discusses how Victorian literature and culture imagined Palestine as the 'Holy Land', and foregrounds Palestine's ambivalent status as 'exotic', 'strangely familiar' and 'resist[ing] any clear-cut division between Orient and Occident'.[17] Palestine is also one of the case studies for Edward Said's groundbreaking book *Orientalism*, where he argues that the Orient was created by Europe and 'has helped to define Europe (or the West) as its contrasting image, idea, personality, experience'.[18] But Said does not simply posit the Oriental Other as a stable and static category that is used to define a coherent Occidental or European self, rather he emphasises that 'neither the term Orient nor the concept of the West has any ontological stability; each is made up of human effort, partly affirmation, partly identification of the Other.'[19] This approach informs the methodology in my book, as I trace how representations of Israel and the Occupied Palestinian Territories shape and reshape not only German and British audiences' understanding of the Middle East but equally their understanding of Europe, including the cultural and political relationships between Europe and the Middle East.

Britain realised its colonial ambitions in Palestine after the fall of the Ottoman Empire, putting Palestine under British military administration after General Edmund Allenby conquered Jerusalem in the Battle of Jerusalem in December 1917. In 1920, the Mandate for Palestine was officially given to Britain by the League of Nations, but from the outset, the British struggled to reconcile the competing national demands of the Palestinians and the Jews. They made promises to both sides, including in the infamous Balfour Declaration, a letter from the UK Foreign Secretary Arthur James Balfour to Walter Rothschild, dated 2 November 1917, where Balfour stated the following:

> His Majesty's Government view with favour the establishment in Palestine of a national home for the Jewish people, and will use their best endeavours to facilitate the achievement of this object, it being clearly understood that nothing shall be done which may prejudice the civil and religious rights of existing non-Jewish communities in Palestine, or the rights and political status enjoyed by Jews in any other country.[20]

Critics have extensively discussed the wording of this declaration, including the fact that only the civil and religious rights of the non-Jewish communities in Palestine were deemed worthy of preservation, not their political or national rights.[21]

Nevertheless, British support for a Jewish national home in Palestine after 1917 was not always stable but was informed by wider concerns in the region. Toby Greene summarises some of the differing positions as follows: those on the 'far left, saw Zionism as a colonial settler movement and a tool of British imperialism', while others 'saw Zionism positively as a way to transform Jewish society and to bring progress to Palestine.'[22] The latter position confirms that Britain initially considered Zionism as a way to support its imperial interests in the region.[23] This aligns with Britain's perception of Jewish people as useful proxy-colonisers, as demonstrated for example by British Colonial Secretary Joseph Chamberlain, who offered parts of British East Africa as a future Jewish homeland to the World Zionist Congress in 1903. Adam Rovner has argued that this offer would have served Britain's colonial mission, as the 'Jews would be used to populate the Empire and render the dark continent a shade lighter' while 'diverting a Jewish invasion from its own shores'.[24]

On the other hand, Britain was wary of alienating the Arab states in the region, which it saw as important strategic allies. After the Suez crisis in 1956, Britain increasingly 'distance[d] itself from Israel's actions' in an attempt to 'repair its image in the Arab world'.[25] However, during the 1967 war Britain's position was sympathetic to Israel and Israel's rhetoric of self-defence, which alienated the Arab states. On a cultural level, the 1967 war was a turning point in Britain, as elsewhere: Israel's emergence as the winner led to a reconsideration of ideas of victimhood associated with the Jewish state, which were further questioned by Israel's status as an occupying power after 1967. On a political level, the 1967 war did not lead to a pronounced change in the ways in which Britain addressed its historical responsibility in the region.

A more significant turning point occurred after the First Intifada, with Palestine becoming a more important issue on the British Muslim agenda. This also shaped the Labour Party's engagement with Palestine due to their members of parliament representing constituencies with large Muslim populations.[26] Nevertheless, as Toby Greene notes, 'in the Blair era British diplomats were, to a surprising extent, conscious of the historic responsibility Britain carried for the Israeli-Palestinian dispute', but this did not significantly affect British policy in the Middle East during this period.[27] Almost a decade after Tony Blair's term as prime minister finished, then–British prime minister David Cameron visited Israel. Unsurprisingly, his speech to the Knesset, the Israeli parliament, in March 2014 confirmed prevailing sentiments about the British Mandate for Palestine; Cameron emphasised that 'Britain has played a proud and vital role in helping to secure Israel as a homeland for the Jewish people.'[28] Cameron's use of tense is telling, as he uses the present perfect, which implies a continuation between past and present, and thus not only foregrounds Britain's role as a mandatory power but equally its current support for Israel. Absent from this speech is not only the Jewish resistance against the British presence in Mandate Palestine – which in its most extreme manifestation took the form of terrorist attacks by the Zionist paramilitary organisation Irgun and its splinter group, the Stern gang – but equally the failure of Britain as a mandatory power. As Beverley Milton-Edwards puts it:

> the inability of the British authorities to address the dual issue of Zionist and Palestinian national aspirations over the same piece of territory ensured that the period of the mandate (1920–1948) was characterised by continual conflict, revolt and political upheaval.[29]

This offers quite a different perspective on the 'proud and vital role' that Britain played at the time.

In many ways, the British mandate, although mostly absent from the British public sphere, exemplifies Britain's engagement with its colonial past more widely, including in the cultural realm.[30] Although there is Remembrance Sunday, held on the second Sunday in November, which 'commemorate[s] the contribution of British and Commonwealth military and civilian servicemen and women in the two World Wars and later conflicts',[31] there is no remembrance day for the victims of British colonialism, let alone the Palestinians and Israeli Jews who still suffer from the consequences of the British Mandate in Palestine today. Paul Gilroy has described this approach as 'postcolonial amnesia', which is 'the mysterious evacuation of Britain's postcolonial conflicts from national consciousness'.[32] Gilroy takes this further by suggesting that the United Kingdom was not able to mourn the loss of its empire. Instead, since 1945, 'the life of the nation has been dominated by an inability to even face, never mind actually mourn, the profound change in circumstances and moods that followed the end of Empire and the consequent loss of imperial prestige',[33] which explains why – compared to other countries – a critical engagement with the colonial past is still situated at the margins of the British public sphere.

While the British presence in Palestine, short-lived as it was, does not play a major role in British culture, for the British Left, Israel's dispossession and displacement of the Palestinians and its later occupation of the West Bank, the Gaza Strip and East Jerusalem have been instrumental in defining their political agenda and identity. Similar to other European leftist movements (including the German Left, as we will see below), they have had a complex history with the Middle East. They initially supported Zionism as a labour movement, but this position significantly changed in the 1960s as there was a growing identification with anti-imperialist movements.[34] The 1967 occupation of the Palestinian Territories consolidated this idea, and the emergence of grassroots activist groups in the 1970s strengthened it further.[35] As Dave Rich notes, other key factors in the Left's support for Palestine and its criticism of Israel have been anti-racism and human rights, as well as a desire for revolution, as 'sympathy for the Palestinians and opposition to Israel has become the default position for many on the left: a defining marker of what it means to be progressive.'[36] In a similar vein, as Anna Bernard shows through the example of British theatre, one of the appeals of 'the Palestinian struggle' continues to be that it 'presents an "actual revolutionary situation" with imaginable outcomes ... at a time when the possibility of fundamental social change appears to be significantly diminished elsewhere.'[37] Hence, Palestinian aspirations for liberation and statehood become a space for people outside of the region to project a revolutionary desire that is unrealisable at home. As we will see in relation to German writers and directors (discussed in Chapters 1, 3 and 5), this desire for revolution is also linked to a wish to be absolved of responsibility for the Holocaust.

However, at the same time, there is a reluctance in contemporary British culture to critically engage with the Israeli occupation of the Palestinian Territories and Israeli human rights violations, for fear of being accused of anti-Semitism. While there has certainly been a rise of anti-Semitism in the United Kingdom, and there is a need to address hate speech directed against Jewish people as well as neo-Nazism and Holocaust denial, I want to discuss a few examples where anti-Semitism has been used to deflect criticism of Israel, as this is an important political and cultural context for the British works discussed in this book. This tendency has become more prominent in the UK and elsewhere since the start of the Second Intifada. One example is the controversy surrounding Gerald Scarfe's cartoon in *The Sunday Times*, published on Holocaust Memorial Day (27 January 2013), which depicted Benjamin Netanyahu 'cementing' peace with a wall built with Palestinian bodies.[38] More recently, on 12 December 2016, the UK government adopted the International Holocaust Remembrance Alliance's (IHRA) definition of anti-Semitism. Critics – including Jewish and Palestinian critics – have described this definition as being 'worded in such a way as to be easily adopted or considered by western governments to intentionally equate legitimate criticisms of Israel and advocacy for Palestinian rights with antisemitism, as a means to suppress the former.'[39]

This definition was also used to accuse Jeremy Corbyn, then leader of the Labour Party, of anti-Semitism after Corbyn refused to change a code of conduct on anti-Semitism proposed by a subcommittee of the Labour Party. In its original form, this code contextualised and expanded the examples of the IHRA definition, including by stating that criticism of Israel should not be considered anti-Semitic if it pertained to its treatment and occupation of the Palestinian people.[40] Corbyn was the latest in a series of Labour Party members to be dismissed due to accusations of anti-Semitism. His colleague, former mayor of London Ken Livingstone, had to leave the Party in April 2016, after attempting to defend fellow member of parliament Naz Shah. Shah was accused of anti-Semitism after making a series of Facebook posts, including one featuring a map of the United States with Israel transposed onto the middle of the country.[41] But in what many commentators have interpreted as a bizarre justification, Livingstone defended Shah by referring to Adolf Hitler's support for Zionism:

> It's completely over the top but it's not antisemitism. Let's remember when Hitler won his election in 1932, his policy then was that Jews should be moved to Israel. He was supporting Zionism – this before he went mad and ended up killing six million Jews.[42]

What is crucial for my discussion in this book is that Livingstone invokes Hitler, and by extension the Holocaust, to defend his colleague, confirming that the situation in Israel and Palestine cannot be discussed without also referencing the Holocaust. This demonstrates that, in the twenty-first century, the Holocaust still looms large within the European cultural and political imaginary, and shapes perceptions of both Israel and Palestine.

Britain and the Holocaust in the Post-World War II Period

The memory of the Holocaust in the UK, compared to the memory of British colonialism, occupies a more central role.[43] However, similar to other European countries, there was a period of relative silence in the UK in the first decade after the war. This only changed after the trial of Adolf Eichmann in Jerusalem in 1961 and the Auschwitz trials (1963–1967) in Frankfurt, which were accompanied by a large media interest and brought the Holocaust into the public sphere. As Daniel Levy and Natan Sznaider have noted, this made the 1960s and early 1970s a 'turning point for the reception and institutionalization of Holocaust memory'.[44] Following on from this, the late 1970s and early 1980s saw an increase in commemorative events alongside a more sustained engagement with the Holocaust in cultural circles, and as a result, 'memories of the Holocaust came to be regarded simultaneously as unique with reference to the past and universal with reference to the future.'[45]

The idea that the Holocaust is not only an isolated event located in the past, but that it also holds important lessons for the future, laid important groundwork for considering the Holocaust in a comparative context. This includes considering how the racial ideologies underlying the Holocaust can be related to colonial racism, and how remembering the Holocaust as a traumatic event compares to other experiences of persecution and genocide. This approach was consolidated in the late 1990s and early 2000s with the publication of studies such as Levy and Sznaider's *The Holocaust and Memory in the Global Age* (2006) – which was originally published in German in 1999 – and Andreas Huyssen's *Urban Palimpsests and the Politics of Memory* (2003).

Throughout the 1990s the Holocaust and its memory also became increasingly important concerns in British culture. As Tom Lawson and Andy Pearce have argued,

> the changes that had taken place since the 1980s were significant and pronounced enough to suggest a fundamental transformation had occurred. The Holocaust, it appeared, had moved from the margins of British historical culture to become a topic of general interest and intrigue.[46]

The publicity accompanying the fiftieth anniversary of the liberation of Auschwitz in 1996, the opening of the permanent Holocaust exhibition at the Imperial War Museum in London in 2000, and the introduction of a Holocaust Memorial Day in 2001 reflected these changes. Nevertheless, particularly the decision to create an official Holocaust Memorial Day was accompanied by heated discussions, for example between historians David Cesarani and Dan Stone. Whereas the late Cesarani strongly advocated such a memorialisation of the Holocaust,[47] Stone was concerned that a single day of commemoration would not be able to do justice to the horrors of the Holocaust and that there would be a danger of eclipsing other genocides through a focus on the Holocaust.[48] Stone asserted that this memorial day would serve above all to 'shape the country's collective memory with a narrative that will undoubtedly follow the pattern of most mainstream narratives of the Holocaust: catastrophe and redemption. The horror of the Holocaust will be occluded in a celebration of *our* moral superiority.'[49] Paul Gilroy has defined this tendency as 'postimperial melancholia', which involves remembering World War II as a moment of liberation and glory for the UK while being unable to engage with and address the changes in British society that resulted from the decline of the British Empire – part of the 'postcolonial amnesia' that Gilroy mentioned above.[50] In a similar vein, Michelle Gordon has examined how the Holocaust and its violence are used to make British colonial violence seem moderate, arguing that

> explorations of the Holocaust need to be accompanied – not replaced – by greater examination and self-reflection related to British history and violence: we need to move away from an approach that continually portrays Britain as the rescuer and defender of victims of genocide and mass violence.[51]

Hence, contemporary Holocaust memory in the UK has a complex history to grapple with and one that is shaped by, or at least situated in, the shadow of Empire. The British works discussed in this book link the histories of the British Mandate with the Holocaust, including by examining how the Palestinian experience of suffering and displacement can be situated alongside the Holocaust. At the same time, they draw attention to the ways in which Palestinian trauma is a consequence of British imperialism in the region and of Britain's support for a Jewish state. Thus, they contribute to the much-needed work of considering the

Holocaust and colonialism comparatively in the United Kingdom and emphasise the importance of a critical engagement with Britain's involvement in the region, to address the legacies of the British Mandate for both (Israeli) Jewish and Palestinian peoples as well as for British audiences.

The Holocaust and Colonialism in Germany, 1945–Today

Holocaust memory in reunified Germany has been similarly complex, albeit for different reasons, the most obvious being Nazi Germany's role as a Holocaust perpetrator and reunified Germany's attempts to reconcile its Nazi past with contemporary German identity. As a self-proclaimed anti-fascist state, the German Democratic Republic (GDR) did not include National Socialism as part of its history apart from celebrating Communist resistance against fascism.[52] The Federal Republic of Germany (FRG), on the other hand, acknowledged its responsibility for the Nazi crimes, but went through a period of repression in the 1950s where these crimes were mainly attributed to Hitler and a few key Nazi figures. This was followed by a period of rebellion in the 1960s and 1970s, where these assumptions were questioned and instead the discussion 'focuse[d] on individual perpetrators of the war generation',[53] including followers and bystanders. The question of responsibility culminated in the historians' debate of 1987, which started when German historian and philosopher Ernst Nolte published an opinion piece entitled 'Vergangenheit, die nicht vergehen will: Eine Rede, die geschrieben, aber nicht mehr gehalten werden konnte' ('The Past that Will not Pass: A Speech that Could Be Written but Not Delivered') on 6 June 1986. The piece was heavily criticised for offering an 'apologetic' version of the Nazi past, most famously by philosopher Jürgen Habermas, who accused Nolte of relativising the Holocaust.[54] One of the major points of contention of this debate was whether the crimes committed by the Nazis were unique or whether they were comparable to other genocides.

This questioning of the uniqueness of the Holocaust paved the way for considering the Holocaust and colonialism comparatively in a German context. Germany's colonial past was forgotten in the first half of the twentieth century, which critics have explained through the fact that Germany's colonial endeavours were considered insignificant in comparison to empires such as those of France and the UK.[55] Moreover, the events of the Holocaust and

World War II soon overshadowed Germany's colonial past. As a result, sustained scholarly attention to Germany as a colonial power only emerged in the 1960s as part of widespread decolonisation movements. The rise of comparative genocide studies in the 1980s allowed for more sustained scholarly attention to the ways in which the history of (German) colonialism had shaped Nazism, parallels that had already been noted in the 1950s by thinkers such as Hannah Arendt and Aimé Césaire. Together with the memory culture boom of the 1990s, this comparative approach to thinking about genocides contributed to the focus shifting towards the 'contemporary relevance and assigning political, societal or generational meaning to this event [the Holocaust]', as Meike Herrmann notes.[56]

Alongside this opening up of Holocaust memory, Germany saw the rise of a discourse of normalisation, specifically the normalisation of Germany's engagement with the Nazi past. This past, as Bill Niven points out in the context of reunified Germany, 'is everything today's Germany does not want to be. It is from today's perspective, the "opposite", the "anti-normal".'[57] However, at the same time, as Caroline Pearce emphasises, remembering the Holocaust is linked to 'uphold[ing] democratic values' and 'act[ing] as a brake against unwelcome tendencies such as right-wing extremism'.[58] Hence, Pearce suggests that since reunification, Holocaust remembrance has been defined by 'a *dialectic of normality*', which is defined as 'a conflict between the perceived need for remembrance and the desire for "normality"'.[59] However, the recent controversy surrounding the translation of Michael Rothberg's book *Multidirectional Memory* into German, which will be discussed in more detail in Chapter 1, confirms that there are limits to this opening up and that there are still many people in Germany who resist a comparative approach to thinking about the Holocaust.

Germany, Israel and Palestine

The relationships of the GDR and the FRG with Israel were directly linked to the ways in which each country remembered the Holocaust. As a communist and anti-fascist state, the GDR aligned itself with USSR politics, which included an opposition to Israel. As Thomas Fox notes, '[t]he Arab-Israeli conflicts and Israeli conquests constituted important aspects of the official East German discourse on the Holocaust, and the actions of the "Zionist

Aggressor-State Israel" found regular comparison with the Nazis.'[60] In light of this approach, it does not come as a surprise that the GDR was instrumental in defining the Palestine question as one linked to national self-determination rather than simply being seen as a refugee problem. Angelika Timm explains that in 1968, the GDR officially supported the struggle of the Palestinian people for reclaiming its legitimate rights to statehood.[61] Towards the end of the 1980s, however, the GDR started adopting a more moderate line, which critics have attributed to the GDR's political and economic interests in establishing connections with Jewish communities at the time.[62]

The FRG, on the other hand, emphasised its moral obligation from the start, and started to pay reparations to Israel as part of the Luxembourg Agreement in 1952. It took until March 1965, however, for Israel and West Germany to institute official diplomatic relationships. Carole Fink has argued that each country's expectations were quite different, since the FRG wanted to 'establish a normal relationship that focused more on the present and the future than on the past', while Israel emphasised the 'special character' of their relationship, 'insisting that the crimes of Nazi Germany had created a permanent obligation for unconditional support and protection.'[63] The latter approach has often been adopted by German politicians, for example by former West German chancellor Willy Brandt, who during his visit to Israel in 1973 described the relations between Israel and the FRG as 'normal relations with a special character'.[64]

In spite of Israel's expectation of unconditional support for a Jewish homeland, West Germany also supported the Palestinian people. In November 1974, Rüdiger von Wechmar, who was West Germany's permanent representative at the United Nations at the time, demanded the recognition of the Palestinian right to self-determination in front of the General Assembly of the United Nations. West Germany was the first Western state to argue for the Palestinian right to self-determination, which was linked to its internal politics of demanding this right for all its citizens – including those of the GDR, as Sabine Hepperle notes.[65] Another key moment for West German engagement with Israel and Palestine occurred during the 1982 invasion of Lebanon, and the massacre of between 400 and 3,500 Palestinian and Lebanese civilians in the Sabra and Shatila refugee camps. Internationally, this led to a 'discrediting of the Israeli government', alongside a global sense of empathy for the Palestinian people.[66]

In West Germany, the events of 1982 resulted in the German public adopting an 'intensive self-critical questioning of their self-perceptions in relation to the Jewish state'.[67] Five years later, the First Intifada, which pitted stone-throwing Palestinians against heavily armed Israeli soldiers, led to a further interrogation of Israeli politics alongside the emergence of a key distinction between Palestinian terrorists and Palestinian civilian fighters.[68]

In spite of these more nuanced engagements with Palestine and Palestinian people, in contemporary Germany, as elsewhere, identification with Palestine is now mainly linked with people on the left, even though the leftist parties in Germany adhere to the conservative discourse that all the parties in Germany have more or less adopted. This discourse privileges Israel's security, as will be discussed in more detail below. Similar to the British Left, the German Left's relationship with Palestine and Israel since the end of World War II has been complicated. The German Left in the FRG was initially pro-Israel, mainly due to guilt about the Holocaust and because many of them were members of the 1968 generation, who were very critical of, and distanced themselves from, their parents' involvement in Nazism. As a result, Israel was seen above all as the 'homeland of the surviving Jewish victims of the fascist tyranny; and one felt solidarity with these people and their community, who were threatened from the outside', as Martin Kloke observes.[69] However, after the 1967 war, there was a conscious shift away from Israel and towards the Palestinian people within the West German Left, which was linked to the Left's wider identification with anti-imperial and anti-colonial movements.[70] But, since German reunification, as Antje Schuhmann argues, critical engagement with Israel and solidarity with the Palestinians has become an exercise of democratic rights linked to situating oneself within the realm of 'normal' democratic nations, and a part of upholding democratic values: 'in commenting on the sufferings of the Palestinians, [critics of Israel] are affirming the principles of democracy by reclaiming – for the Germans – the basic rights of free speech and uncensored publication.'[71] While Schuhmann is critical of this trend, she does rightly draw attention to many of its key aspects, such as criticism of Israel becoming 'a story of personal liberation from early brainwashing and guilt' which fits into a 'more general genre of redemption narrative, leading to an implied catharsis'.[72] Solidarity with the Palestinian people is thus not only seen as 'catharsis', but can equally be linked to the idea of 'normalisation' in Germany.

Nevertheless, in general, there has been a stronger identification with Israel since reunification in 1990. The fall of the Berlin Wall and the collapse of the Soviet Union led to a large number of Russian Jews moving to Germany, most of whom are in agreement with Israel's right-wing politics.[73] Moreover, during the Second Intifada, Germany started to 'adopt the Israeli line on the question of security',[74] which can be seen for example, in then-Chancellor Angela Merkel's visit to Israel in 2008, where she proclaimed in front of the Knesset that, 'The security of Israel is of German national interest and as such not negotiable.'[75] Describing German engagement with Israel after the Second Intifada, Pól Ó Dochartaigh argues that

> by offering essentially uncritical support for an Israel that is engaged in actions that have been repeatedly condemned as illegal, Germany has abandoned its belief in 'never again' in favour of a right-wing Israeli doctrine [never again to the Jews] which is even rejected by many Israelis. Germany seeks to compensate for its adoption of racist, *anti*-Semitic doctrines some 70 years ago by allying itself to racist, *philo*-Semitic doctrines today.[76]

Germany's guilt about the Holocaust thus often precludes a productive – read: critical – engagement with Israel in mainstream German society. This was confirmed more recently in a 2021 article for *Die Zeit*, where Fabian Wolff argued that in Germany, loving Israel

> is not only of national interest but already part of the German soul, especially of those Germans that dictate cultural and political discourses. Those Germans hope that unconditionally loving Israel and fighting anti-Semitism will result in a type of transcendence of German guilt.[77]

Support for Israel is clearly linked to overcoming the guilt of the past and can almost be considered an act of atonement for the Holocaust. This connection was also the subject of a recent article, which used the Achille Mbembe controversy in 2020 as means to unpack the complicated relationships between Germany, Israel and Palestine.[78] Mbembe, a renowned Cameroonian postcolonial critic, was scheduled to give the opening address at the 2020 *Ruhrtriennale*, a triannual music and arts festival in the Ruhr area, but he was uninvited due to his works being denounced as questioning the right of Israel to exist and comparing South African apartheid with the Holocaust.[79] This is one of many examples where Holocaust guilt translates into a hypervigilance against criticism addressed to Israel, which is often dismissed as anti-Semitism.[80] Hence, for Germany's memory politics, Palestine constitutes 'a dangerous challenge . . . a thorn in Germany's atonement plans, and therefore necessary to be repressed'.[81]

The anonymous author of the article that makes this salient point links the idea of Palestine as an obstacle to German memory politics to a recent phenomenon that Leandros Fischer has termed 'German pride'. Fischer argues that this is the result of an 'attempt to forge a positive national identity' in reunified Germany, an identity based on 'uncritical support for a supposedly threatened Israel', which in turn allows people to transcend guilt for the Holocaust.[82] Support for Israel thus becomes part of a 'normalised' German identity and is seen as a way of 'overcoming' the Nazi past. This idea is developed further by the anonymous author who argues that, 'This German pride is a new, national and redeemed project, fully centred on Israel and founded on making invisible the colonial violence of the Israeli state means for Palestinians', and that it 'is projected both onto Israel as well as onto the now growing Jewish community in Germany'.[83] Hence a renewed philo-Semitism, an approach to engaging with Jewish people that was also prominent in the immediate post–World War II years, is seen both as atonement for the Holocaust and as part of the new German identity after reunification, playing a key role in the ways in which Germany engages with Israel and its treatment of the Palestinians.

This engagement is further shaped by the emergence of '[t]he figure of the anti-Semitic Muslim', which as German Palestinian academic Anna-Esther Younes has shown, has led to the perception of the 'Palestinian' as someone who 'incites and propels anti-Semitism and manipulates other Muslims, Arabs, Turks, refugees and so on, to do the same'.[84] While there has certainly been a rise in anti-Semitism in Germany and this is an issue that should be taken seriously and investigated,[85] the conflation of anti-Semitism and pro-Palestinian sentiments has led to Germany actively 'domesticating its Palestinian, Muslim, and/or pro-Palestinian inhabitants and international guests by policing their political activities, cultural work, and scholarship.'[86] Germany's guilt about the Holocaust is thus displaced onto Palestine and Palestinians and manifests as an inability to critically engage with Israel's occupation of the Palestinian

Territories and the suffering of Palestinian people since 1948. As a result of this displacement of guilt, support for Palestine and the Palestinian people is often wrongly equated with a negation of the Holocaust and Germany's responsibility for the Nazi past.

The German works discussed in this book demonstrate on different levels this fear of criticism of Israel being conflated with anti-Semitism, and challenge the assumption that any critical engagement with Israel automatically devalues Holocaust memory. Instead, they explore the ways in which Germany can remember the Holocaust and support a Jewish state, while taking into account the suffering of the Palestinians since 1948 and Palestinian aspirations for liberation and statehood. While some of these works are more successful than others in situating the memory of the Holocaust alongside solidarity with the Palestinians, all of them draw attention to the need for doing so, even if, paradoxically, they do so by failing to successfully juxtapose these two concerns.

Israel and Palestine as Signifiers in the Contemporary Period: Towards a Model of Critical Relationality

Given its prominent role in politics from outside the region, it is not surprising that encounters between Israeli Jewish and Palestinian people preoccupy the European cultural imaginary, nor that increasingly, the so-called conflict, as well as Israel and Palestine as ideas, are used as 'signifiers' for other concerns. These concerns can be related to a long history of European stereotypes and colonial fantasies about Jews and Palestinians. German–Palestinian relations, as George Lavy has emphasised, 'have been shaped partly by the phenomenon of Germany's peculiar past relationship with western "colonialism and imperialism"'.[87] Lavy further confirms that German–Palestinian relations have been influenced by 'the romantic European conception in the nineteenth and early twentieth centuries of ancient Arab culture', which is a typical Orientalist point of view but which equally shows how colonial ideologies and Orientalism have shaped Germany's contemporary postcolonial engagement with the Middle East.[88] This aligns with Martin Braach-Maksvytis's description of the relationship between West Germany and Israel as one of 'proxy-colonialism' until 1967, as especially in popular culture, Israel was represented as a 'terra incognita' where the Jewish people were fighting against a 'hostile' Arab world.[89] In West Germany, general support for Israel in the mid-twentieth century was linked to a 'glowing adulation for the "valiant" Jewish pioneers' and their civilising mission of the 'backward' Orient.[90]

In contrast to these stereotypes, which position the 'Arab' as 'other', Jewish people, and Israeli Jewish people, are essentially perceived as 'Western' and/or 'white', even though they are geographically located in the Middle East. Arabs, as well as Palestinians, on the other hand, are seen as 'Eastern' and 'backward': as Edward Said points out, 'if the Arab occupies enough space for attention, it is as a negative value', including as 'the disrupter of Israel's and the West's existence, or in another view of the same thing, as an insurmountable obstacle to Israel's creation in 1948.'[91] Hence, if Palestinians are given any agency, it is usually a negative agency, pitting them as the main antagonist to Israel and the 'West'. This aligns with how Palestinians have been seen as 'terrorists' since the late 1960s and 1970s, which was reinforced by the conflation between Islam and terrorism after 11 September 2001, as Anna Bernard has shown.[92] After the Second Intifada, another common image of the Palestinian emerged, namely that of the 'abject victim', which, as Laleh Khalili argues, is not only circulated by non-governmental organisations (NGOs) in their humanitarian campaigns but also adopted by Palestinians themselves 'in order to appeal to the larger international audience'.[93] Neither the image of the victim nor the terrorist allows for much agency, while at the same time occluding Palestinian aspirations for self-determination and their resistance against an occupying power. These are the ideas and stereotypes that many of the works discussed in this book challenge, thus providing a more comprehensive and nuanced portrait of the individual lives and aspirations that make up the abstract idea of Palestine. This is important since, as Beshara Doumani has argued, taking into account Palestinians as individuals is necessary for 'building coalitions across international and psychological boundaries'.[94]

The First Intifada (1987–1993) paved the ways for building these types of coalitions as it played a key role in changing international perceptions of the power dynamics at stake, including in relation to Israeli Jewish victimhood and Palestinian rights to self-determination. As Sami K. Farsoun argues,

> For the first time, the long-cherished Western perception of a little, beleaguered Israel facing the Arab Goliath was reversed. Having been portrayed dramatically on television screens worldwide, Israel's harsh policies toward Palestinians elicited

widespread criticism. Long demonized by Israel and its supporters, Palestinians under occupation suddenly became humanized, and the intifada restructured the parameters of the Palestine question and the Arab-Israeli conflict.[95]

The uprising challenged received ideas about Israeli/Jewish victimhood and Palestinians as terrorists, and opened up avenues for critically engaging with Israel and its treatment of the Palestinian people in Israel and the Occupied Palestinian Territories. Moreover, since the 1980s, the Palestinian cause has become a symbol of oppression, colonisation and anti-globalisation and has been linked to different political causes, such as the anti-apartheid movement, the dangers of globalisation and the disappearance of democracy, as Helga Tawil-Souri amongst others has argued.[96] Hence, the 1980s laid important groundwork for the emergence of more critical engagements with Israel in British and German culture in the twenty-first century.

It is worth noting that all but one of the works discussed in this book were published after the Second Intifada: it took the 1993 Oslo Accords and the Second Intifada to significantly increase the number of works published about Israel and Palestine outside of the region that offered a critical engagement with Israel's occupation. This change in approach also needs to be read in light of the establishment of, and public support for, the Boycott, Divestment and Sanctions (BDS) movement, which was launched in 2005 by several Palestinian civil society bodies and has garnered strong international support, including by public figures such as Alice Walker, Judith Butler, Kamila Shamsie and the late Stephen Hawking. This movement has not only contributed to making the Palestinian cause visible to international audiences but has equally made it more acceptable to critically engage with Israel as an occupying power. This, in turn, has opened up important avenues for comparative work that situates Israel and Palestine alongside each other.

A key aspect of situating Israel and Palestine alongside each other in this book is the development of a theoretical approach that I term 'critical relationality'. My starting point is relationality as a way to theorise how identities – both individual and collective – are defined in relation to others and significantly shaped by encountering others, following theories of selfhood developed in postcolonial and cultural feminist studies. For example, Sara Ahmed argues that 'the subject's existence cannot be separated from the others who are encountered', and hence any encounter between the self and the stranger 'suggests that identity does not simply happen in the privatised realm of the subject's relation to itself. Rather, in daily meetings with others, subjects are perpetually reconstituted.'[97] Throughout this book, I will extend and develop these ontological conceptions of relationality by drawing on theories from memory studies, which offer productive models for comparative engagement through their emphasis on commonalities between different memories; Palestine/Israel studies, which advocate for examining Israel and Palestine and their histories in dialogue with each other; and world literature and world cinema studies, which foreground the importance of considering the connections between different contexts while paying attention to the power differentials that define these connections. Before moving on, I want to give a brief overview of these different fields and the ways in which their theorisations of relationality inform my own methodology.

Discussions about the scope for comparisons with the Holocaust, which gained momentum at the end of the twentieth century, paved the way for sustained engagement with comparative memory studies, especially those that take Holocaust memory as their starting point or as a point of reference, and led to a number of works that proposed comparative and non-competitive models of memory. One of the most famous ones is Michael Rothberg's theory of multidirectional memory, which was developed in Rothberg's 2009 book of the same name. Examining how the memory of the Holocaust can be situated within a comparative framework with discourses of colonisation and decolonisation, Rothberg defines multidirectional memory as 'subject to ongoing negotiation, cross-referencing and borrowing', and he emphasises the reciprocal relationship between different types of memories.[98] In a similar vein, Maxim Silverman proposes the concept of palimpsestic memory as a means to think through the relationship between past and present. This memory, Silverman argues, 'takes the form of a superimposition and interaction of different temporal traces to constitute a sort of composite structure, like a palimpsest, so that one layer of traces can be seen through, and is transformed by, another.'[99] Like Rothberg, Silverman emphasises the reciprocal relationship between different memory 'traces', suggesting that a new structure emerges from this relationship. However, this dialogue between different types of memories has mainly focused on Jewish memories – particularly the memory of the Holocaust – and colonialism, to the exclusion of an in-depth discussion of

Palestinian memories and histories. While Rothberg argues that multidirectional memory is indeed able to avoid a competition between memories, as even 'hostile invocations of memory' can still result in a balanced account of different memories,[100] I demonstrate throughout this book that these power imbalances are difficult to redress, and thus they engender exactly the type of competition between memories that Rothberg claims can be avoided.

A similar comparative and relational turn can be observed in Palestine/Israel studies. This turn emphasises the need to read (Israeli) Jewish and Palestinian histories together while paying attention to the power differentials that have governed and continue to govern relations between these communities and their histories. Zachary Lockman – following Perry Anderson, who advocated the need for a relational history 'that studies the incidence – reciprocal or asymmetrical – of different national or territorial units and cultures on each other'[101] – emphasises the importance of using 'relational history' in the context of Palestine/Israel. This type of history, according to Lockman, is

> rooted in an understanding that the histories of Arab and Jews in modern (and especially mandatory) Palestine can only be grasped by studying the ways in which both of these communities were to a significant extent constituted and shaped within a complex matrix of economic, political, social, and cultural interactions.[102]

I am interested in how British and German authors and directors emphasise this idea by depicting the histories of 'Arabs' and 'Jews' as interdependent, and how they relate these histories to British and German politics in the region.

Literary and cultural studies scholars working on Israel and Palestine have also adopted a relational approach to discussing Israeli and Palestinian works, for example through comparative readings of Israeli and Palestinian literature and culture.[103] Moreover, this relational turn manifests itself in a theorisation of the relations between Israeli and Palestinian literature and 'Jews' and 'Arabs/Palestinians' as ideas. Gil Z. Hochberg's 2007 book *In Spite of Partition: Jews, Arabs, and the Limits of Separatist Imagination* examines the ways in which Israeli and Palestinian literature depicts 'Jews' and 'Arabs' as mutually shaping each other's identities. More recently, Lital Levy has discussed how Israeli and Palestinian writers have created a dialogue between Hebrew and Arabic, establishing 'a dynamic space of literary and cultural interaction even in the absence of a corresponding political space'.[104] In *Reimagining Israel and Palestine in*

Contemporary British and German Culture, I build on these non-separatist approaches to examine the 'Jew' and the 'Arab', and extend the scope of previous work by asking how authors and directors from outside the region engage with the idea of (Israeli) Jewish and Palestinian identities as connected. I also consider how the works discussed in this book imagine literary and cinematic spaces for critically engaging with the intersections of Palestinian and Israeli Jewish narratives, as well as the ways in which Europe and the Middle East are depicted as connected on a cultural and political level.

Hence, it is important to examine not only how the realities on the ground in Israel and the Occupied Palestinian Territories pit (Israeli) Jews and Palestinians as enemies, but equally how this opposition is cemented in the European imaginary through antagonistic portrayals in media and culture. In order to further unpack these relationships between Europe and the Middle East, I situate my work in relation to studies that have examined the links between Europe and its 'others', namely the 'Jew' and the 'Arab', to theorise how and why Germany and the UK engage with Israel and Palestine. Gil Anidjar examines 'Arabs' and 'Jews' as separate signifiers in the European imaginary, and argues for the importance of focusing on Europe as 'the site, uncertain and fragmented that it is, from which the two figures emerge as enemies.'[105] Farsakh and Bashir's edited collection *The Arab and Jewish Questions* similarly traces the history of separation between 'Arabs' and 'Jews' in Europe. In their introduction, they note that, 'The complicated processes of splitting Arabs and Jews and delinking the Jewish and Arab/Muslim questions are deeply entrenched in contemporary mainstream Western political thought.'[106] Farsakh and Bashir relate this separation to the ways in which imperialism and the Holocaust have created – and indeed needed – different types of others. These include Jewish others, who have often been seen as Europe's internal others, especially since the Enlightenment period, when Jewish people were asked to assimilate to European – read Christian – societies. Muslims have been Europe's internal others since the ninth century but their historical presence has often been forgotten in a Europe that defines itself in opposition to Islam, and which is shaped by Orientalism and Orientalist stereotypes about Muslim people.[107]

Since the September 11 attacks in 2001, Muslim others – and Arab is often used as a synonym for Muslim in Europe – have been turned into external others. Brian Klug, for example, examines how the figure of the Palestinian has become an external other in France. Klug argues that both Europe and Israel use 'a shared foundational myth of rebirth' after the Holocaust and World War II, but that this myth conveniently excludes the fact that this 'is the starting point of catastrophe for a third party, the Palestinian people, and their continuing dispossession.'[108] As Klug convincingly goes on to show, this constitutes the 'repression of an inconvenient truth, for the Nakba disrupts the sanguine reunion between a repentant Europe and its age-old internal Other: the Jew.'[109] Hence, the *nakba* or catastrophe of 1948 – the dispossession and displacement of around 750,000 Palestinians as part of the lead up to and the creation of Israel – and the continued suffering of the Palestinians is perceived as an obstacle to the vision of a new Europe. As we saw earlier in relation to Germany, Palestine can become a 'thorn' in a country's memory culture, an effect which is also due to a common conflation between Palestinian and Arab identities in the European imaginary. This conflation in turn establishes a link between Palestinians and Muslims, and thus with Islamophobia.

My theorisation of the connections between Israel and Palestine, and the Middle East and Europe, builds on and extends the relational work proposed in memory studies and Palestine/Israel studies discussed above, and brings it into dialogue with recent work in world literary studies and world cinematic studies that emphasises the connections between the local and the global. Drawing on postcolonial studies and world-systems theory, the Warwick Research Collective proposes the deliberately hyphenated term 'world-literature', which emphasises the ways in which literature is shaped by different contexts, including what they call 'barometric indications of invisible forces acting from a distance on the local and the familiar'.[110] Similarly, if we consider world cinema as a theoretical category that encourages 'ceaseless problematisation', as Stephanie Dennison and Song Hwee Lim do, this allows us to ask what its purpose is, what 'mechanisms of power' it is shaped by and which audiences are addressed and potentially empowered.[111] Using a 'worldly' approach to examining literature, TV and film – with a conscious nod to Edward Said's discussion of texts as 'worldly' and specifically his emphasis on the power dynamics that govern textual presences in the world – *Reimagining Israel and Palestine in Contemporary British and German Culture* extends our understanding of how imagining Palestine and Israel advocates thinking together Palestine and Israel as real and imagined places in European culture. At the same time, it serves as a way to reassess both Israel's and Palestine's relationships with the UK and Germany.[112] In this sense Israel and Palestine as geographical and imaginary spaces can be read as 'worlded', following Eric Hayot's discussion of the clear links between the aesthetic world created inside a cultural work and the world outside, arguing that aesthetic worlds are 'always a relation to and theory of the lived world, whether as a largely preconscious normative construct, a rearticulation, or even an active refusal of world-norms'.[113] I am interested both in how authors and directors 'rearticulate' the ways in which Israel and Palestine and their narratives are represented in German and British culture and how they 'refuse' those representations, especially through an emphasis on these narratives as relational rather than separate.

In a similar vein, Shu-mei Shih has emphasised that a key aspect of reading world literature is comparison, which 'is not the juxtaposition' of different locations, 'but their relationality in the context of world history'.[114] Applied to representations of Israeli Jewish and Palestinian narratives in British and German culture, a comparative relational approach encourages us to be mindful of how the local and the global intersect in order to support the circulation of different memories and histories. Moreover, it asks us to consider how these modes of circulation confirm, but potentially also contest, received ideas about the power differentials that govern encounters between Israeli Jews and Palestinians, which often emphasise Jewish victimhood. In this context, it is not only essential to compare Israel and Palestine but equally Germany and the United Kingdom to identify wider trends in representing the cultural and political relations between Israel and Palestine, and Europe and the Middle East, as well as unpacking the political and cultural complexities that accompany relational representations in literature, TV drama and film. I choose to include a wide range of media – text and screen – and genres – fiction, documentary and travel writing – for two reasons. One, to explore how cultural works are shaped by different forms of production, distribution and reception, and are read and received differently in terms of the claims they make, and are seen to make, on 'truthfully' representing Israel and Palestine. Two, to show how relationality permeates British and German culture at all levels, whether this is low-brow, middle-brow or high-brow culture, testifying to the importance of this idea in German and British imaginaries in the twenty-first century.

By offering comparative close readings on how relationality is expressed through aesthetic strategies and narrative tropes in the selected literature, TV drama and film, this book provides a snapshot of how a relational history of Israel and Palestine has been depicted in Germany and the UK in the last 30 years, and how this extends our understanding of the relationship between Israel and Palestine as circulated in the European imaginary as well as the relations between Europe and the Middle East. In the body chapters that follow, I examine relationality both as a trope and as a methodology, focusing on displaced relationality (Chapter 1), libidinal relationality (Chapter 2), relational memories (Chapter 3), disrupted relationality (Chapter 4) and relational coexistence (Chapter 5). While these types of relationality, as we will see below, encourage a comparative approach to examining Israeli Jewish and Palestinian histories and narratives, they also offer a critical lens that allows us to reassess how past, present and future relations between Israel and Palestine – and Palestine/Israel, Germany and the UK – are imagined in the contemporary period. Hence, they enable us to consider how Palestine and Israel as geopolitical and imaginary spaces reveal wider political, historical and cultural issues in Germany and the United Kingdom. These issues include concerns about nationalism, anti-Semitism and racism, as well as concerns about how to engage with difficult histories and their legacies, as we will see throughout *Reimagining Israel and Palestine in Contemporary British and German Culture*.[115]

Chapter 1, entitled 'Displaced Relationality: Israel as a Mirror for Germany', examines how Andres Veiel's documentary *Balagan* (1993) and Ina Dentler's novel *Zerbrochenes Deutsch: Zweimal Berlin-Haifa* (*Broken German: Two Times Berlin-Haifa*; 2014) use Israel to think through the ways in which the Holocaust has been remembered in Germany since the First Intifada, and how this has shaped Germany's relationship with Israel and Palestine. Israel, and its relations with Palestinians, functions as a space or mirror for both artists to displace their anxieties about how the Holocaust is remembered in Germany geographically, and in Dentler's case also temporally. Through this 'displaced relationality', Veiel – and to a lesser extent Dentler – creates the necessary distance to address Germany's coming to terms with its Nazi past after reunification and the ways in which the Holocaust, and Germany's relationships with Israel and Palestine, should be engaged with in the twenty-first century. Hence, in their works, both Veiel and

Dentler emphasise that Holocaust memory should not only look backwards, but also needs to address present and future concerns.

In the second chapter, 'Relational Memories: The Holocaust and the *Nakba* in the British Imaginary', I extend the idea of 'displaced relationality' by moving to the British context to examine how the Holocaust and the Palestinian *nakba* are represented in a comparative context. Using Peter Kosminsky's miniseries *The Promise* (2011) and Marina Lewycka's book *We Are All Made of Glue* (2009) as case studies, this chapter shows how 'relational memories' – which are memories that create links between events that might seem unconnected and/or are often depicted as such – provide a comparative framework for examining Jewish and Palestinian suffering. I argue that, together with Kosminsky's and Lewycka's juxtaposition of the British Mandate with the current situation in Israel and the Occupied Palestinian Territories, this comparative approach challenges accepted narratives of the Holocaust, the creation of the state of Israel and the *nakba* as separate events, as well as foregrounding the United Kingdom's responsibility as a colonial power alongside its continued involvement in the region.

The works discussed in the third chapter, entitled 'Libidinal Relationality: Humour, the Holocaust and Palestine/Israel in German Culture', are Theresa Bäuerlein's *Das war der gute Teil des Tages* (*That Was The Good Part of the Day*, 2008) and Markus Flohr's *Wo samstags immer Sonntag ist* (*Where Saturday Is Always Sunday*, 2011). They consider the idea of a rapprochement between Germany and Israel, and reflect on Germany's 'special' relationship with Israel and the ways in which this has precluded a productive engagement with Israel's treatment of the Palestinian people. I show that the trope of the libidinal relation between German and Israeli Jewish characters, together with the use of humour, allows Bäuerlein and Flohr to create a framework for critical engagement with the connections between Germany and Israel. However, this chapter also draws attention to the limitations of these relations through the failure of the libidinal relation between a German and an Israeli Jewish character in Flohr's book, and the inability to critically engage with Israel's occupation of Palestine in Bäuerlein's novel.

Using the concept of 'disrupted familial relationality', which is defined as disrupting traditional kinship models as metaphors for the nation, the works examined in the fourth chapter – Claire Hajaj's novel *Ishmael's Oranges* (2014) and Hugo Blick's miniseries *The Honourable Woman* (2014) – depict Jewish-Palestinian marriage and friendship as well as Jewish-Palestinian children to challenge perceptions of Jewish and Palestinian suffering as separate and to imagine alternative alliances. By focusing on disrupted families – including disrupted relations between parents and children and disrupted relations across divides – I argue that Hajaj and Blick consider how families and the ideologies that they transmit contribute to the exclusion of those that are seen as outside the collective national or ethnic community. Instead, they foreground Palestinians and their narratives of suffering, and their displacement and dispossession at the hands of Israel, as well as Palestinian aspirations to statehood. In this way, both artists encourage their audiences to reflect on the power differentials that govern these contexts, including those between Israel, Palestine and international powers. These imbalances are often occluded in discussions that emphasise a kinship approach on a national and international level, including those that use being part of the 'family of nations' as a justification for Israel's treatment of the Palestinian people and to obscure Israel's role as a settler-colonial and occupying power, alongside the UK's involvement as a mandatory power in Palestine at the start of the twentieth century.

The fifth chapter, 'Relational Coexistence: Donations Across Divides and Imagined Kinship in Palestine/Israel', considers how German authors and directors establish a 'relational coexistence' – a coexistence between (Israeli) Jewish and Palestinian characters that models relations between Israel and Palestine that take into account each community's history of suffering and displacement and emphasises the relations between these histories. Werner Sonne's novel *Wenn ich dich vergesse, Jerusalem* (*If I Forget You, Jerusalem*, 2008; translated into English as *Where the Desert Meets the Sea*, 2019) and Leon Geller and Marcus Vetter's documentary *Das Herz von Jenin* (*The Heart of Jenin*, 2008) do this using blood and organ donations across divides. These function as a critical means to challenge ideas of kinship and universal humanity and the possibilities of coexistence between Israeli Jews and Palestinians in a shared state, possibilities that take into account the power imbalances between Palestinians and (Israeli) Jews before 1948 and after the Second Intifada. In this chapter I develop the concept of 'relational coexistence' to challenge ideas of Israeli Jews and Palestinians as antagonists. At the same time, the concept draws attention to the German desire to imagine a solution to Israel's occupation of the Palestinian territories and Palestinian aspirations for statehood. In this context, the emphasis on relationality and coexistence is linked to a desire to be absolved of Holocaust guilt.

The conclusion offers a critical outlook on the future of relationality by focusing on (Israeli) Jewish and Palestinian artists working in the diaspora, especially those that consider relations across the Israel-Palestine divide, such as Israeli Jewish artist Oreet Ashery and Palestinian artist Larissa Sansour. Focusing on their co-authored mixed genre work *The Novel of Nonel and Vovel* (2009) I examine the more speculative genres that are becoming increasingly popular in Palestinian and Israeli culture. I ask how these genres might facilitate ways of transcending the political impasse between Israeli Jewish and Palestinian relations in the present by focusing on speculative relationalities that are situated in the future rather than in the present or the past.

In this book, I use critical relationality as a methodology that not only emphasises connection but, more importantly, constitutes a means for challenging mainstream ideas of (Israeli) Jewish and Palestinian narratives as separate. This, in turn, enables me to theorise the representation and interaction between Israeli Jewish and Palestinian narratives outside of the region in a way that takes into account the significant power imbalances that shape encounters between Israeli Jews and Palestinians and the mediation of their narratives in Europe. Critical relationality also encourages us to rethink the ways in which British and German culture and politics engage with Jewish and Palestinian narratives, including the central role of the Holocaust and Jewish victimhood in this space. Finally, this approach extends our understanding of how Israel and Palestine function as symbols in the contemporary period beyond Israel, Palestine and their diasporas, both as individual signifiers but also as images of relationality through their relationships with each other.

Notes

1. Gil Z. Hochberg, *In Spite of Partition: Jews, Arabs, and the Limits of Separatist Imagination* (Princeton: Princeton University Press, 2007), 2.
2. Brian Klug, 'An Emblematic Embrace: New Europe, the Jewish State, and the Palestinian Question,' in *The Arab and Jewish Questions: Geographies of Engagement in Palestine and Beyond*, ed. Bashir Bashir and Leila Farsakh (New York: Columbia University Press, 2020), 63.

3. Associated Press, 'Life on the Beaches of Tel Aviv and Gaza City – in Pictures,' *The Guardian*, 3 November 2021, https://www.theguardian.com/artand-design/2021/nov/03/life-on-the-beaches-of-tel-aviv-and-gaza-city-in-pictures.
4. Throughout this book, I use the term 'Israeli Jewish' to foreground how 'Israeli' is often conflated with the idea of Israeli Jewishness at the expense of the Palestinians living in Israel. I use 'Israeli' to refer to the state or to organs representing the state, or when it is not possible to verify if the term also applies to Israeli Palestinians.
5. The term 'conflict' has been rightly criticised for suggesting that it posits Israel and Palestine as equally empowered and for not directly referencing the occupation of the Palestinian people and their land (see, for example, John Collins, *Global Palestine* (London: Hurst, 2011), 19). I limit the use of this term to instances where it reflects a common perception in British and German culture. Throughout, I also critically interrogate how the term has been circulated in Europe and beyond.
6. Ella Shohat and Robert Stam, *Unthinking Eurocentrism: Multiculturalism and the Media* (London: Routledge, 2014), 6.
7. Shohat and Stam, *Unthinking Eurocentrism*, 10.
8. Anna Bernard, *Rhetorics of Belonging: Nation, Narration, and Israel/Palestine* (Liverpool: Liverpool University Press, 2013), 13.
9. Doris Salcedo, quoted in Martin Herbert, *The Unilever Series: Doris Salcedo: Shibboleth* (London: Tate Publishing, 2007), 2. Exhibition Brochure.
10. I use the term 'metropolitan' to refer to 'Western' audiences, including North American, British and Australian audiences.
11. Works in literary studies have engaged with the ways in which partition creates a separatist framework for examining opposing sides while considering the types of narrative solutions that literature and culture envision to these divisions and inequalities. See, for example, Joe Cleary, *Literature, Partition and Nation-State: Culture and Conflict in Ireland, Israel and Palestine* (Cambridge: Cambridge University Press, 2002), Hochberg, *In Spite of Partition*, and Anna Bernard, 'Forms of Memory: Partition as a Literary Paradigm,' *Alif: Journal of Comparative Poetics* 30 (2010): 9–33, https://www.jstor.org/stable/27929845.
12. For an overview of the 'settler-colonial turn,' see Rachel Busbridge, 'Israel-Palestine and the Settler Colonial "Turn": From Interpretation to Decolonization,' *Theory, Culture & Society* 35, no. 1 (2018): 91–115, https://doi.org/10.1177/0263276416688544, and David Lloyd, 'Settler Colonialism and the State of Exception: The Example of Palestine/Israel,' *Settler Colonial Studies* 2, no. 1 (2012): 59–80, https://doi.org/10.1080/2201473x.2012.10648826. A recent special issue for *Interventions*, entitled 'Settler-Colonialism in Palestine,' which was published in

2019, argued for the importance of using settler-colonialism as a way to 'think... beyond the classic two-state solution', and 'approaching liberation and decolonization from perspectives other than classic national anticolonial frames', including by focusing on 'local modes of indigenous struggles for decolonization' (Francesco Amoruso, Ilan Pappé and Sophie Richter-Devroe, 'Introduction: Knowledge, Power, and the "Settler Colonial Turn" in Palestine Studies,' *Interventions* 21, no. 4 (2019): 462, https://doi.org/10.1080/1369801X.2019.1581642). Raef Zreik includes an interesting discussion of how we might apply the framework of apartheid to the three major groups of Palestinians – those living in the Occupied Territories, those who are citizens of Israel, and those in the diaspora – and what the limitations of using this approach are in each context (Raef Zreik, 'Palestine, Apartheid, and the Rights Discourse,' *Journal of Palestine Studies* 34, no. 1 (2004): 70, https://doi.org/10.1525/jps.2004.34.1.68).
13. Zreik, 'Palestine, Apartheid, and the Rights Discourse,' 70.
14. As Hagar Kotef argues in *The Colonizing Self: or, Home and Homelessness in Israel/Palestine*, Israeli Jewish ideas about belonging and home are inevitably shaped by their relations with Palestinians. For example, Kotef emphasises that in a settler-colonial context the construction of an Israeli Jewish home and an Israeli Jewish national identity has led to the destruction of Palestinian homes (Hagar Kotef, *The Colonizing Self: or, Home and Homelessness in Israel/Palestine* (Durham, NC: Duke University Press, 2020), 2).
15. Bashir Bashir and Leila Farsakh, 'Introduction: Three Questions that Make One,' in Bashir and Farsakh, *Arab and Jewish Questions*, 16–17.
16. Barbara W. Tuchman, *Bible and Sword; England and Palestine from the Bronze Age to Balfour* (New York: New York University Press, 1956), xiv.
17. Eitan Bar-Yosef, *The Holy Land in English Culture 1799–1917: Palestine and the Question of Orientalism* (Oxford: Clarendon Press, 2005), 4, 9.
18. Edward Said, *Orientalism* (New York: Vintage Books, 1994), 1–2.
19. Said, *Orientalism*, xvii.
20. Avi Shlaim, *Israel and Palestine: Reappraisals, Revisions, Refutations* (London; New York: Verso, 2009), 4–5.
21. See, for example, Shlaim, *Israel and Palestine*, 3–24. Moreover, the Balfour Declaration negated the promises of their own homeland that the British made to the Arab people in exchange for their support against the Ottoman Empire as outlined in a series of letters between Hussein Ibn Ali, the emir of Mecca, and Sir Henry McMahon, the British high commissioner in Egypt in 1915–16. At the same time as these letters were exchanged, the British were already secretly

drawing up the Sykes-Picot agreement, which defined how the Ottoman Empire would be divided between the British and the French, making clear that their promises to the Arab people were null and void from the start.

22. Toby Greene, *Blair, Labour, and Palestine: Conflicting Views on Middle East Peace After 9/11* (New York: Bloomsbury Academic, 2013), 35.
23. Gardner Thompson, *Legacy of Empire: Britain's Support of Zionism and the Creation of Israel* (London: Saqi Books, 2019), xii.
24. Adam Rovner, *In the Shadow of Zion: Promised Lands Before Israel* (New York: New York University Press, 2014), 47, 53. In a similar vein, A. J. Sherman has pointed out that Palestine was thought of as 'a strategic base and an anchor of British interests in the Middle East' (A. J. Sherman, *Mandate Days: British Lives in Palestine, 1918–1948* (New York: Thames and Hudson, 1998), 190).
25. Greene, *Blair, Labour, and Palestine*, 17.
26. Greene, *Blair, Labour, and Palestine*, 32.
27. Greene, *Blair, Labour, and Palestine*, 25.
28. Government of the United Kingdom, 'David Cameron's Speech to the Knesset in Israel,' 12 March 2014, last modified 13 March 2014, https://www.gov.uk/government/speeches/david-camerons-speech-to-the-knesset-in-israel.
29. Beverley Milton-Edwards, *Contemporary Politics in the Middle East*, 3rd ed. (Cambridge; Malden: Polity Press, 2011), 40.
30. A Palestine memorial was erected at the National Memorial Arboretum at Alrewas, in Staffordshire, UK, in 2001 but this was not widely reported in the news. In the cultural realm, there was a surge in British Jewish novels in the late 1990s and early 2000s, which engage with the British Mandate in Palestine from a Jewish perspective, such as Bernice Rubens's *The Sergeants' Tale* (2003) and Linda Grant's *When I Lived in Modern Times* (2000). Further examples include Marina Lewycka's novel *We Are All Made of Glue* (2009) and Peter Kosminsky's miniseries *The Promise* (2011), which I discuss in Chapter 2, as well as Claire Hajaj's novel *Ishmael's Oranges* (2014) and Hugo Blick's TV drama *The Honourable Woman* (2014), which are the focus of Chapter 4.
31. Department for Culture, Media and Sport, Helen Grant, and the Rt Hon. Sajid Javid MP, *Policy Paper: 2010 to 2015 Government Policy: National Events and Ceremonies*, 27 February 2013, updated 8 May 2015, https://www.gov.uk/government/publications/2010-to-2015-government-policy-national-events-and-ceremonies.
32. Paul Gilroy, *After Empire: Melancholia or Convivial Culture?* (Abingdon: Routledge, 2004), 97.

33. Gilroy, *After Empire*, 98.
34. For an overview of the British Left's relationship with Zionism, see Paul Kelemen, *The British Left and Zionism: History of a Divorce* (Manchester: Manchester University Press, 2012).
35. Dave Rich, *The Left's Jewish Problem: Jeremy Corbyn, Israel and Anti-Semitism* (London: Biteback Publishing, 2016), 1.
36. Rich, *The Left's Jewish Problem*, xviii.
37. Anna Bernard, 'Taking Sides: Palestinian Advocacy and Metropolitan Theatre,' *Journal of Postcolonial Writing* 50, no. 2 (2014): 165–6, https://doi.org/10.1080/17449855.2014.883174.
38. Gerald Scarfe's cartoon is available as part of this blog post: Phil Weiss and Annie Robbins, 'Robust debate? Murdoch apologizes for London "Times" cartoon of Netanyahu as bloody obstructionist,' *Mondoweiss*, 29 January 2013, https://mondoweiss.net/2013/01/apologizes-netanyahu-obstructionist.
39. Free Speech on Israel, 'FSOI supports global Jewish initiative against demonising criticism of Israel,' 17 July 2018, https://freespeechonisrael.org.uk/globaljewishstatement/#defn.
40. The full text of this code can be accessed here: Lee Harpin, 'Read Labour's New Definition of Antisemitism,' *The Jewish Chronicle*, 5 July 2018, https://www.thejc.com/comment/analysis/jeremy-corbyn-labour-definition-antisemitism-1.466626.
41. Academic Norman Finkelstein first posted this map on his website (Norman G. Finkelstein, 'Solution for Israel-Palestine Conflict,' *Website of Norman G. Finkelstein*, 4 August 2014, https://www.normanfinkelstein.com/solution-for-israel-palestine-conflict). Shah's accusation of anti-Semitism is exemplary of a rhetoric often employed by Israel's supporters to dismiss accusations against the Jewish state, whereby they conflate anti-Zionism and anti-Semitism. For a discussion of this conflation, see Judith Butler, *Parting Ways: Jewishness and the Critique of Zionism* (New York: Columbia University Press, 2012) and Jacqueline Rose, *The Question of Zion* (Princeton: Princeton University Press, 2005).
42. Ken Livingstone, 'Naz Shah "not anti-Semitic",' interview by Vanessa Feltz, *BBC News*, 28 April 2016, http://www.bbc.com/news/uk-politics-36163432.
43. For an overview of Britain's engagement with the Holocaust since the post-war period see, for example, Andy Pearce, *Holocaust Consciousness in Contemporary Britain* (New York; London: Routledge, 2014).
44. Daniel Levy and Natan Sznaider, *The Holocaust and Memory in the Global Age*, trans. Assenka Oksiloff (Philadelphia: Temple University Press, 2006), 17.
45. Levy and Sznaider, *Holocaust and Memory in the Global Age*, 17.

46. Tom Lawson and Andy Pearce, 'Britain and the Holocaust: An Introduction,' in *The Palgrave Handbook of Britain and the Holocaust*, ed. Tom Lawson and Andy Pearce (Cham: Palgrave Macmillan, 2020), 20.
47. David Cesarani, 'Seizing the Day: Why Britain Will Benefit from Holocaust Memorial Day,' *Patterns of Prejudice* 34, no. 4 (2000): 61–6, https://doi.org/10.1080/003132200128811008.
48. Dan Stone, 'Day of Remembrance or Day of Forgetting? Or, Why Britain Does Not Need a Holocaust Memorial Day,' *Patterns of Prejudice* 34, no. 4 (2000): 53–9, https://doi.org/10.1080/003132200128810991.
49. Stone, 'Day of Remembrance or Day of Forgetting?,' 57; original emphasis.
50. Gilroy, *After Empire*, 98.
51. Michelle Gordon, 'Selective Histories: Britain, the Empire and the Holocaust,' in Lawson and Pierce, *Palgrave Handbook of Britain and the Holocaust*, 225, 238.
52. Stefan Berger, *Germany* (London: Hodder Headline, 2004), 202.
53. Siobhan Kattago, *Ambiguous Memory: the Nazi Past and German National Identity* (Westport, Connecticut; London: Praeger, 2001), 42.
54. Jürgen Habermas, 'A Kind of Settlement of Damages (Apologetic Tendencies),' trans. Jeremy Leaman, *New German Critique*, no. 44 (1988): 25–39, https://doi.org/10.2307/488144. All translations from German are my own unless otherwise indicated. A later key debate, which has often been seen as another *Historikerstreit*, was the 1996 Goldhagen debate, which discussed the extent to which Germans could be held accountable for what they did during the Nazi regime. Bill Niven has described this debate as being 'marked by an intriguing discrepancy between public and historiographical memory', and suggested that it 'also led to a greater awareness of the holocaust and the extent of German involvement' (Bill Niven, *Facing the Nazi Past: United Germany and the Legacy of the Third Reich* (London; New York: Routledge, 2002), 117).
55. Sebastian Conrad, *German Colonialism: A Short History*, trans. Sorcha O'Hagan (Cambridge: Cambridge University Press, 2012), 1, 10.
56. Meike Herrmann, 'Spurensuche in der dritten Generation. Erinnerung an den Nationalsozialismus und Holocaust in der jüngsten Literatur,' in *Repräsentation des Holocaust im Gedächtnis der Generationen*, ed. Margrit Fröhlich, Yariv Lapid and Christian Schneider (Frankfurt: Brandes und Apsel, 2004), 139.
57. Niven, *Facing the Nazi Past*, 5.
58. Caroline Pearce, *Contemporary Germany and the Nazi Legacy: Remembrance, Politics and the Dialectic of Normality* (Basingstoke: Palgrave Macmillan, 2008), 2.
59. Pearce, *Contemporary Germany and the Nazi Legacy*, 2; original emphasis.

60. Thomas C. Fox, *Stated Memory: East Germany and the Holocaust* (New York: Camden House, 1999), 13.
61. Angelika Timm, *Hammer, Zirkel, Davidstern: Das gestörte Verhältnis der DDR zu Zionismus und Staat Israel* (Bonn: Bouvier, 1997), 273.
62. Timm, *Hammer, Zirkel, Davidstern*, 391.
63. Carole Fink, *West Germany and Israel: Foreign Relations, Domestic Politics, and the Cold War, 1965–1974* (Cambridge: Cambridge University Press, 2019), 127; original emphasis.
64. This wording has also been used by Johannes Rau, former President of Germany, who emphasised in 2000 that the relations between Germany and Israel will 'always be special' (Brandt and Rau quoted in Markus A. Weingardt, *Deutsche Israel- und Nahostpolitik: Die Geschichte einer Gratwanderung seit 1949* (Frankfurt: Campus, 2002), 11, 223).
65. Sabine Hepperle, *Die SPD und Israel. Von der großen Koalition 1966 bis zur Wende 1982* (Frankfurt: Peter Lang, 2000), 223.
66. Kinan Jaeger, *Quadratur des Dreiecks: die deutsch-israelischen Beziehungen und die Palästinenser* (Schwalbach: Wochenschau Verlag, 1997), 169.
67. Jaeger, *Quadratur des Dreiecks*, 3.
68. Jaeger, *Quadratur des Dreiecks*, 195. This distinction had been blurred by the activities of Black September, a militant Palestinian splinter group, who were behind attacks such as the one during the 1972 Olympic Games in Munich, where eleven Israeli athletes were killed.
69. Martin Kloke, 'Zwischen Lobpreisung und Verteufelung: Die Haltung der deutschen Linken gegenüber Israel,' in *Israel in den neunziger Jahren und die deutsch-israelischen Beziehungen*, ed. Karl Schmitt and Michael Edinger (Jena: Universitätsverlag Jena, 1996), 56.
70. Peter Ullrich, 'Antisemitismus, Antizionismus und Kritik an Israel in Deutschland. Dynamiken eines diskursiven Feldes,' in *Jahrbuch für Antisemitismusforschung 23*, ed. Stefanie Schüler-Springorum (Berlin: Metropol Verlag 2012), 109.
71. Antje Schuhmann, 'Whose Burden? The Significance of the Israel-Palestine Conflict in German Identity Politics,' in *Nationalist Myths and Modern Media: Contested Identities in the Age of Globalization*, ed. Jan Herman Brinks, Stella Rock, and Edward Timms (London: I. B. Tauris, 2006), 170.
72. Schuhmann, 'Whose Burden?', 168.
73. Sa'ed Atshan and Katharina Galor, *The Moral Triangle: Germans, Israelis, Palestinians* (Durham, NC: Duke University Press, 2020), 63–4.
74. Daniel Marwecki, *Germany and Israel: Whitewashing and Statebuilding* (London: C. Hurst & Co., 2020), 212.

75. Jürgen Hardt, 'Israels Sicherheit ist für uns nicht verhandelbar,' *CDU/CSU*, 30 June 2020. https://www.cducsu.de/presse/pressemitteilungen/israels-sicherheit-ist-fuer-uns-nicht-verhandelbar.
76. Pól Ó Dochartaigh, 'Philo-Zionism as a German Political Code: Germany and the Israeli-Palestinian Conflict Since 1987,' *Debatte: Journal of Contemporary Central and Eastern Europe* 15, no. 2 (2007): 250–1, https://doi.org/10.1080/09651560701508547.
77. Fabian Wolff, 'Nur in Deutschland,' *Die Zeit*, 2 May 2021, https://www.zeit.de/kultur/2021-04/judentum-antisemitismus-deutschland-israel-bds-fabian-wolff-essay.
78. Anonymous, 'Palestine Between German Memory Politics and (De-)Colonial Thought,' *Journal of Genocide Research* 23, no. 3 (2021): 374–82, https://doi.org/10.1080/14623528.2020.1847852. The author of the article asked to remain anonymous 'for fear of career-threatening retribution', as the editors of the special issue explain (Ulrike Capdepón and A. Dirk Moses, 'Introduction,' *Journal of Genocide Research* 23, no. 3 (2021): 372, https://doi.org/10.1080/14623528.2020.1847851). The fact that the author felt they could not reveal their identity when writing this article as they were working in Germany and saw any criticism of Israel as detrimental to their career is another case in point of how the policing of Palestinian solidarity and critical engagements with Israel permeates the German public, but also the academic, sphere.
79. Martin Eiermacher, 'Eine echte Causa,' *Die Zeit*, 22 April 2020, https://www.zeit.de/2020/18/achille-mbembe-antsemitismus-vorwurf-israel.
80. There have been a number of major controversies in Germany since reunification that exemplify this. A prominent literary example was the outrage generated by the publication of the late Günter Grass's 2012 poem '*Was gesagt werden muss*' ('What Needs to be Said'), where he denounced Israel as a nuclear power but also criticised how Germany often condones Israel's actions due to its Nazi past (Günter Grass, '*Was gesagt werden muss*,' *Spiegel Online*, 4 April 2012, https://www.spiegel.de/kultur/gesellschaft/dokumentation-gedicht-was-gesagt-werden-muss-von-guenter-grass-a-825744.html). For an overview of how Grass's poem has been received and how German and British academics have responded to this see, for example, Stuart Taberner, '*Was gesagt werden muss*: Günter Grass's "Israel/Iran" Poem of April 2012,' *German Life and Letters* 65, no. 4 (2012): 518–31, https://doi.org/10.1111/j.1468-0483.2012.01586.x. This approach was given further clout by the decision of the German parliament in May 2019 to officially condemn the BDS movement as anti-Semitic (Deutscher Bundestag, 'Bundestag verurteilt Boykottaufrufe gegen Israel,' 17 May 2019, https://www.bundestag.de/dokumente/textarchiv/2019/kw20-de-bds-642892).

81. Anonymous, 'Palestine Between German Memory Politics and (De-)Colonial Thought,' 378.
82. Leandros Fischer, 'Deciphering Germany's Pro-Israel Consensus,' *Journal of Palestine Studies* 48, no. 2 (2019): 33, https://doi.org/10.1525/jps.2019.48.2.26.
83. Anonymous, 'Palestine Between German Memory Politics and (De-)Colonial Thought,' 378.
84. Anna-Esther Younes, 'Fighting Anti-Semitism in Contemporary Germany,' *Islamophobia Studies Journal* 5, no. 2 (2020): 252, https://doi.org/10.13169/islastudj.5.2.0249.
85. On 18 January 2018, the German parliament voted to set up the position of Commissioner for Jewish Life in Germany and the Fight Against Anti-Semitism. In December 2022, the Federal Government approved the 'National Strategy against Anti-Semitism and for Jewish Life' in Germany.
86. Anonymous, 'Palestine Between German Memory Politics and (De-)Colonial Thought,' 377. Another recent example of this was the criticism levelled at the organisers of the 2022 Documenta, an international art exhibition, in Kassel, Germany. They were accused of showing works by artists that supported the BDS movement and later on, accusations emerged that the exhibition contained anti-Semitic images ('Documenta-Gesellschafter benennen Expertengremium zur Aufarbeitung,' *Der Spiegel Online*, 1 August 2022, https://www.spiegel.de/kultur/documenta-expertengremium-soll-antisemitismus-skandale-aufarbeiten-a-3e03b833-0b5f-4216-ae1e-04ef75b0126d).
87. George Lavy, *Germany and Israel: Moral Debt and National Interest* (London: Frank Cass, 1996), 24.
88. Lavy, *Germany and Israel*, 24. Nina Berman, in her discussion of how the Middle East has been depicted in Germany between 1000 and 1989, identifies a 'specific archive of images – from religious enemy to noble heathen, from debauched, violent, and hypersexed Arab to wise and amiable Oriental' that has persisted across time (Nina Berman, *German Literature on the Middle East: Discourses and Practices, 1000–1989* (Ann Arbor: University of Michigan Press, 2011), 16).
89. Martin Braach-Maksvytis, 'Germany, Palestine, Israel, and the (Post)Colonial Imagination,' in *German Colonialism: Race, the Holocaust, and Postwar Germany*, ed. Volker Langbehn and Mohammad Salama (New York: Columbia University Press, 2011), 297.
90. Braach-Maksvytis, 'Germany, Palestine, Israel, and the (Post)Colonial Imagination,' 294.
91. Said, *Orientalism*, 286.

92. Anna Bernard, 'Another Black September? Palestinian Writing after 9/11,' *Journal of Postcolonial Writing* 46, no. 3 (2010): 349–58, http://dx.doi.org/10.1080/17449855.2010.482409.
93. Laleh Khalili, *Heroes and Martyrs of Palestine: The Politics of National Commemoration* (Cambridge: Cambridge University Press, 2007), 204, 206.
94. Beshara Doumani, 'Palestine versus the Palestinians? The Iron Laws and Ironies of a People Denied,' *Journal of Palestine Studies* 36, no. 4 (2007): 60, https://doi.org/10.1525/jps.2007.36.4.49.
95. Sami K. Farsoun and Naseer H. Aruri, *Palestine and the Palestinians*, 2nd ed. (New York: Routledge, 2018), 12. The late Bart Moore-Gilbert made a similar point, but he argued that this perception started to change in 1982 and was cemented during the onset of the First Intifada (Bart Moore-Gilbert, 'Palestine, Postcolonialism and Pessoptimism,' *Interventions* 20, no. 1 (2018): 9, https://doi.org/10.1080/1369801X.2016.1156555).
96. Helga Tawil-Souri, 'Media, Globalization, and the (Un)Making of the Palestinian Cause,' *Popular Communication* 13, no. 2 (2015): 151, https://doi.org/10.1080/15405702.2015.1021470.
97. Sara Ahmed, *Strange Encounters: Embodied Others in Post-Coloniality* (London: Routledge, 2000), 7.
98. Michael Rothberg, *Multidirectional Memory: Remembering the Holocaust in the Age of Decolonization* (Stanford: Stanford University Press, 2009), 3.
99. Maxim Silverman, *Palimpsestic Memory: The Holocaust and Colonialism in French and Francophone Literature and Film* (New York: Berghahn, 2013), 3.
100. Rothberg, *Multidirectional Memory*, 11.
101. Perry Anderson, 'Agendas for Radical History,' *Radical History Review* 36 (1986): 36, https://doi.org/10.1215/01636545-1986-36-26.
102. Zachary Lockman, *Comrades and Enemies: Arab and Jewish Workers in Palestine, 1906–1948* (Berkeley; Los Angeles; London: University of California Press, 1996), 8. This emphasis on relational histories can also be seen in recent historical works in this area, such as Grace Wermenbol, *A Tale of Two Narratives: the Holocaust, the Nakba, and the Israeli-Palestinian Battle of Memories* (Cambridge: Cambridge University Press, 2021) and Yair Auron, *The Holocaust, Rebirth and the Nakba: Memory and Contemporary Israeli-Arab Relations* (Lanham: Lexington Books, 2017).
103. See, for example, Ammiel Alcalay, *After Jews and Arabs: Remaking Levantine Culture* (Minneapolis: University of Minnesota Press, 1992); Bernard, *Rhetorics of Belonging*; Cleary, *Literature, Partition and Nation-State*; Rachel Feldhay Brenner, *Inextricably Bonded: Israeli Jewish and Arab Writers Re-Visioning*

Culture (Madison: University of Wisconsin Press, 2003); and Isabelle Hesse, *The Politics of Jewishness in Contemporary World Literature: The Holocaust, Zionism and Colonialism* (London: Bloomsbury Academic, 2016).
104. Lital Levy, *Poetic Trespass: Writing Between Hebrew and Arabic in Israel/Palestine* (Princeton: Princeton University Press, 2014), 4.
105. Gil Anidjar, *The Jew, the Arab: A History of the Enemy* (Stanford: Stanford University Press, 2003), xxv.
106. Bashir and Farsakh, 'Three Questions that Make One,' 10.
107. Bashir and Farsakh, 'Three Questions that Make One,' 11.
108. Klug, 'Emblematic Embrace,' 57.
109. Klug, 'Emblematic Embrace,' 57.
110. Sharae Deckard et al., *Combined and Uneven Development: Towards a New Theory of World-Literature* (Liverpool: Liverpool University Press, 2015), 17.
111. Stephanie Dennison and Song Hwee Lim, 'Introduction: Situating World Cinema as a Theoretical Problem,' in *Remapping World Cinema: Identity, Culture and Politics in Film*, ed. Stephanie Dennison and Song Hwee Lim (London: Wallflower Press, 2006), 9.
112. Said has argued that texts 'have ways of existing that even in their most rarefied form are always enmeshed in the circumstance, time, place, and society – in short, they are in the world, and hence worldly' (Edward Said, *The World, the Text and the Critic* (London: Vintage, 1991), 35, 48).
113. Eric Hayot, *On Literary Worlds* (Oxford; New York: Oxford University Press, 2012), 44–5.
114. Shu-mei Shih, 'Theory in a Relational World,' *Comparative Literature Studies* 53, no. 4 (2016): 723, https://doi.org/10.5325/complitstudies.53.4.0722.
115. I agree with critics such as Gargi Bhattacharyya and Helga Tawil-Souri, who caution against the risk of commodifying Palestine by using it as a metaphor for other contexts. Bhattacharyya, for example, has argued that 'serving as a cipher for the aspirations and alliances of others brings greater attention to the Palestinian struggle, but this is achieved at the cost of bearing the symbolic burden of other struggles and issues' (Gargi Bhattacharyya, 'Globalizing Racism and Myths of the Other in the "War on Terror",' in *Thinking Palestine*, ed. Ronit Lentin (London: Zed Books, 2008), 48). While there is a danger of Palestine 'bearing the symbolic burden of other struggles', in this book, I make sure to give prominence to Palestinian aspirations and issues before considering how Palestine might additionally be read as a metaphor for concerns in the United Kingdom and Germany.

1

DISPLACED RELATIONALITY: ISRAEL AS A MIRROR FOR GERMANY

The Holocaust has been one of the defining aspects of post–World War II identity in Germany. While the introduction of this book focused on the broad strokes of the development of Holocaust memory in Germany, in this chapter, I want to take a closer look at how Holocaust memory has shaped German identity since reunification and how this has impacted on Germany's political and cultural relations with both Israel and Palestine. Meike Herrmann has argued that since 1990, Holocaust discourse has been marked by an increasing opening up and internationalisation, emphasising that rather than examining the Holocaust as a historical event, the focus is now on 'its contemporary relevance' and reading the Holocaust in relation to political, social and generational concerns.[1] Moreover, as Herrmann observes, the emphasis has shifted from coming to terms with the past to addressing questions of remembering and commemorating this past.[2] Constantin Goschler agrees with this position, emphasising that the 1990s represented 'a transition from a communicative memory of those who experienced the Holocaust to the cultural memory of the descendants'.[3] As part of this transition from personal to cultural memory,

> guilt was no longer denied or subdivided through complicated intellectual manoeuvres ... rather guilt had become historical and as such could be willingly accepted and did not constitute a challenge to personal identity or to the collectivity of the political community.[4]

Goschler highlights how this shift from the personal experience of the generation of people living through World War II and the Holocaust, to those generations whose memory is second- or third-hand, has shaped a German understanding of guilt as something that is located in the past rather than in the present. For the purpose of this chapter, I follow Anne Fuchs's use of generations when discussing contemporary German literature, which applies the term 'first generation' to authors who directly experienced World War II. The second generation are those born after the war who 'hav[e] few or no personal memories of the Third Reich', but who might have been involved in the student rebellions of 1968.[5] Both of the artists discussed in this chapter – director Andres Veiel and writer Ina Dentler – can be situated in the latter category and exemplify critical engagement with the idea of guilt as being situated in the past. At the same time, we can read their works as reflecting on how the Holocaust as a past event shapes Germany's present relations with Israel and Palestine.

Linked to the temporal distance and compartmentalisation of guilt that Goschler foregrounds is a German tendency to identify with the victims of the Holocaust after 1968. Aleida Assmann has explained that for the generation of 1968, the identification with the Jewish victims of the Holocaust was useful

> to break with their own families and to move from a contaminated historical environment into a morally faultless world. The means of this wonderful rescue through identity conversion was the memory culture with whose help one was hoping for a deliverance from German guilt.[6]

In addition to feeding into a narrative of deliverance where redemption is seen as necessary to overcome the past, identifying with the victims changes the ways in which people look at perpetrators. In this context, guilt is transferred onto others and thus, it becomes separate from one's own identity, as Ulrike Jureit argues.[7] Discussing Jureit's concept of perceived victims (*gefühlte Opfer*),[8] Assmann suggests that identification with the victims does not erase one's own identity but rather encourages 'empathy' and an 'emotional connection' with the victims.[9] Instead of identification, Assmann proposes that German memory culture is 'oriented towards victims'.[10] While this is an important semantic distinction to make, for the purpose of this chapter I want to emphasise that feeling a connection with the Jewish victims of the Holocaust often impedes critical engagement with Germany's Nazi past. Jureit foregrounds that one of the reasons for this lack of critical engagement is that a memory culture that is focused on identifying with the victims 'is primarily concerned with defining oneself on the morally correct side'.[11] This is part of a wider trend that defines countries who have been paying reparations for past wrongs. As John Torpey argues, 'Efforts to rectify past wrongs have thus arisen in part as a substitute for expansive visions of an alternative human future.'[12] Hence, focusing on how the Nazi past shapes contemporary German identity can preclude engagement with the present and the future, including contemporary debates about xenophobia, anti-Semitism and Israel's treatment of the Palestinian people, to which a number of controversies discussed in this book testify.

One of these examples, and indeed a very recent one, was the controversy caused in 2021 when Michael Rothberg's important work *Multidirectional Memory* was translated into German. Critics accused Rothberg of relativising the Holocaust by not considering it as a unique event.[13] This approach in turn precluded the comparative approach to discussing the Holocaust with German colonial history, including the Herero and Nama genocide (1904–1907) in German South West Africa (now Namibia). This controversy confirms that in Germany the Holocaust is still considered as a unique event, to the point that it cannot be used to think comparatively about Nazism and colonialism. Moreover, and importantly for the purpose of this chapter, remembering the Holocaust as a unique event, and considering it as not comparable to other genocides and instances of discrimination and displacement, plays a key role in Germany's engagement with both Israel and Palestine.

If German memory culture considers the Holocaust as a unique event and is shaped by a sense of empathy with Jewish victimhood in order to situate itself on the 'morally correct side', then it is easier for Germany to align itself with Israel's security discourse, especially a discourse that uses victimhood to justify the necessity for occupying Palestine. Atonement for the Holocaust and responsibility for safeguarding Israel as a Jewish state are inseparable from any German engagement with the Holocaust and, as Kinan Jaeger noted already in 1997, loaded words such as '"atonement," "ethics" and "responsibility" are considered integral parts of the self-perception of German-Israeli relations.'[14] This often uncritical support for Israel, and by extension for Zionism as a movement for the creation and preservation of a Jewish state, can be linked to philo-Zionism, a phenomenon whose origins Pól Ó Dochartaigh has described as follows:

> Germany seeks to compensate for its adoption of racist, anti-Semitic doctrines some 70 years ago by allying itself to racist, philo-Semitic doctrines today.... Since this form of philo-Semitism relates specifically to Israeli policy rather than to the Jews as a whole, it is in fact, a counterpart not to anti-Semitism but to anti-Zionism.[15]

Adopting philo-Semitism as an ideology that is uncritical of Israel, together with a philo-Semitism that expresses itself as an identification with, or at least empathy for, the Jewish victims of the Holocaust and which continues to see Jewish people in Israel as victims, does not leave much room for considering Palestinian suffering and Palestinian rights to self-determination. However, as Ó Dochartaigh has argued, the language of philo-Zionism used in this context 'focuse[s] primarily not on Israel or Jews but on Germany'.[16] The two works discussed in this chapter, Andres Veiel's documentary *Balagan* (1993) and Ina Dentler's novel *Zerbrochenes Deutsch: Zweimal Berlin-Haifa* (*Broken German: Two Times Berlin-Haifa*; 2014) use Israel to think through the ways in which the Holocaust has been remembered since the First Intifada and how this has shaped Germany's relationship with Israel and Palestine. This might seem like the philo-Zionism that Ó Dochartaigh criticises above, but Veiel and, to a lesser extent, Dentler create the necessary distance to engage with these ideas more clearly and critically, which allows them to move beyond Israel as a simple space of projection for Germany. I argue that they achieve this through what I call 'displaced relationality' since in both works Israel, and its relations with Palestinians, functions as a space or a mirror for the artists to displace their anxieties about how the Holocaust is remembered in Germany geographically and, in Dentler's case, also temporally.

By using Israel's engagement with the Holocaust and how this affects its relations with Palestinians and their memory of the *nakba* as a mirror for Germany, Veiel not only addresses the relations between Israel and Palestine in his documentary but also clearly links these relations to German history, specifically how Germany's guilt about the Holocaust prevents critical engagement with Israel. *Balagan* can thus be seen as an attempt to think through the relationships between Germany, Israel and Palestine from a critical distance by displacing these relationships geographically, an approach which is presented as a model for comparative memory in Germany. Dentler's novel displaces relationality temporally by juxtaposing the protagonist Anja with her great-aunt Toni, who moved to mandatory Palestine in 1934, in order to think through Anja's engagement with Israel and Palestine in the contemporary period, including her relationship with her Israeli Jewish cousin. This doubling is used to address Germany's coming to terms with its Nazi past after reunification and the ways in which the Holocaust, and Germany's relationships with Israel and Palestine, should be addressed in the twenty-first century. Hence, in their works, as we will see below, both Veiel and Dentler emphasise that Holocaust memory should not only look backwards but needs to address present and future concerns.

Using these two contrasting examples, not only in terms of their conclusions and the degree of critical engagement they represent with Israel but equally in terms of genre and aesthetic merit, this chapter traces the development of the relationship between the Holocaust, Israel and Palestine from the First Intifada to the twenty-first century, and examines the role that identifying, or at least empathising with, Jewish victimhood plays in this context.[17] However, the chapter also draws attention to some of the limitations of displacing relationality, especially if it leads to more conservative rather than more critical engagement with Germany's relationship with Israel, as we will see in relation to Dentler's novel.

The *Balagan* of Comparative Memory: The Holocaust and the *Nakba* in Israel and Germany

German director Andres Veiel's award-winning documentary *Balagan*, which was screened at the 1994 Berlinale, follows the production of Israeli Jewish playwright David Maayan's play *Arbeit macht frei vom Toitland Europa* (*Work Liberates from Deathland Europe*) by the Akko Theatre Company, a mixed Israeli-Palestinian theatre group in Israel.[18] *Balagan* is one of the early works of Veiel, who is nowadays renowned as an acclaimed documentary filmmaker and is one of Germany's most successful directors. In contrast to the mainstream position in Germany at a time when reunified Germany was redefining its identity and emphasising the normalisation of the past, Veiel's work asks to what extent the Holocaust has been normalised in German culture. This challenge is achieved by drawing attention to the silences of Holocaust commemorations, including comparative approaches to the Holocaust, which Veiel models by situating Israeli Jewish victimhood and Palestinian rights to self-determination alongside each other. This critical engagement with the relationship between the Holocaust and the *nakba*, and Israel and Palestine, was seen in very few other works at the time – and has similarly been a less popular approach since.[19]

The focus of Veiel's documentary is on Israel and its commemoration of the Holocaust and how this shaped Israeli Jewish relationships with Palestinians at the end of the First Intifada. Nevertheless, one of Veiel's key aims in making his documentary 'was his own attempt at coming to terms with the Holocaust'.[20] Veiel's father and grandfather were part of the German invasion of the Soviet Union, codenamed Operation Barbarossa, and Veiel, who was born in 1959, considers himself a 'typical representative of the second generation', including in terms of how his family's involvement in World War II was silenced at home.[21] When Veiel worked with the Akko Theatre Company, he met other people from the second generation who had experienced the silence of their parents and grandparents – but of course, those were people whose families were victims rather than perpetrators of the Holocaust.[22] What Veiel finds appealing in examining Holocaust memory in Israel is how openly this is discussed and criticised. Making *Balagan* was thus a key aspect of exploring what the Holocaust and Israel's occupation of and discrimination against Palestinians 'meant for [Veiel's] biography'.[23]

Making this documentary was not only important for Veiel's individual identity but equally for Germany's collective engagement with the Nazi past. As Veiel has explained, German and Jewish people 'have all been damaged by history . . . But the necessity to deal with that damage is greater in Israel. There the Holocaust is a black hole, a silence that swallows us.'[24] Veiel's documentary addresses the silence that surrounded the Holocaust in Israel in the early 1990s. This was not necessarily a literal silence, but a metaphorical one, in that there was often an absence of critical engagement with how Holocaust memory, especially one focused on how Ashkenazi Jewish or European Jewish suffering, occludes other memories of suffering and displacement, such as those of Mizrahi Jews and Palestinians. As Dalia Ofer has argued, since the 1980s, the Holocaust is increasingly in demand and Israelis miss the paramount message: the universal meaning of the catastrophe and the moral threat to a society that makes wide-scale use of force in its political relations towards the 'other', whether a minority group or an enemy.[25]

One of the key aspects of Veiel's documentary is to show how a focus on the Holocaust in Israeli culture has occluded engagement with Palestinian suffering, especially in the context of the *nakba*. Using Israel as a mirror to think through how the Holocaust should be engaged with and commemorated in Germany allows Veiel to draw attention to the situation of the Israeli Palestinians and the relationship between the *nakba* and the Holocaust. Moreover, this approach implicitly addresses the centrality of Palestine and Palestinian suffering and rights not only for Israeli Jewish but also for German discourses about the Holocaust, by modelling the ways in which Palestinian and Israeli Jewish experiences can be juxtaposed and addressed concomitantly rather solely focusing on the Jewish experience of the Holocaust and excluding Palestinian suffering. Thus, the Holocaust as a 'black hole' that swallows the Germans, as mentioned in Veiel's quotation above, not only establishes a clear link between Holocaust memory in Israel and Germany and foregrounds how these countries and their cultural and political relations are inextricably linked; it equally shows how this black hole makes critical engagement with Israel, and its settler-colonial occupation of the Palestinians, difficult, if not impossible, both in Israel and in Germany.

The work involved in untangling these relations is reflected in the title of Veiel's documentary, *Balagan*, which is the Yiddish and Hebrew word for mess. British Jewish writer Linda Grant reflects on the meaning of this concept in her book *The People on the Street: A Writer's View of Israel*. She writes that, 'a *balagan* is more than a mess. A *balagan* is a mess that verges on the uncontrollable. It is chaos, disorder, the throwing up of your hands, because what the hell can you or anybody do about this *balagan*?'[26] Grant's definition of *balagan* comes close to how Veiel uses the concept to frame his documentary, especially in the sense of something 'uncontrollable'. For Veiel, however, it is also a productive chaos, even if solving it might be impossible. In Veiel's documentary the concept of *balagan* can be related to the three main subjects that he discusses: one, the memory of the Holocaust in contemporary Israel; two, relationships between Israeli Jews and Israeli Palestinians in the wake of the First Intifada; and three, Germany's engagement with the Holocaust. In order to examine the first two subjects, the documentary combines footage from the performance of *Arbeit macht frei vom Toitland Europa* with interviews with the three main actors. The actors represent the major groups that make up contemporary society in Israel: Madi Smadar Maayan, a second-generation Holocaust survivor whose parents are from former Czechoslovakia; Moni Yosef, a religious Iraqi Jew; and Khaled Abu Ali, an Israeli Palestinian from the village of Sakhnin in the Northern Galilee.

The third subject, Germany's relationship with the Holocaust, is addressed more implicitly. Unlike in other works discussed in this book (and chapter), contemporary Germany does not appear as a location nor as a topic of discussion in Veiel's documentary. Veiel does not feature as a director or character in the documentary and neither does he provide any voiceovers apart from responding once to a comment that Madi makes. In his analysis of *Balagan*, Tobias Ebbrecht-Hartmann argues that Germany is only 'present' as a 'bizarre-eerie' source for the 'orchestration of an Israeli-Palestinian identitarian and emotional chaos'.[27] Some scenes from *Arbeit macht frei vom Toitland Europa* are indeed used in an uncanny manner to make the audience uncomfortable, but I argue that this is done in order to distance the German audience from identifying with a sense of Jewish victimhood. Moreover, the distinction that Ebbrecht-Hartmann does *not* make is the one between Nazi Germany as the location and perpetrator of the genocide of, amongst others, the Jewish people, and contemporary Germany and its engagement with the Nazi past. The absence of contemporary Germany in favour of Nazi Germany in the documentary mirrors the central role that remembering the Holocaust played in West Germany and continues to play in reunified Germany. It also demonstrates the extent to which the memory of the Nazi past has now become a ritual of commemoration, resulting in a lack of in-depth engagement with the Holocaust and the legacies of Germany's Nazi past in the present and the future.[28]

As a remedy to locating the lessons of the Holocaust in a distant past, Veiel suggests that 'our only chance is to work on it, to go into all of the contradictions. It's like a relay race. You take the baton that is handed to you, even if it burns. You can't run away from history.'[29] Indeed, through its confronting nature, Veiel's documentary makes it very hard for his audiences to 'run away from history'. After a pastoral opening shot of a village by the sea and impressions of village life comes a shot of a dark passageway next to lit-up windows (which could be read in a Freudian way as a path into the subconscious). This leads the audience into a room where a naked man is beating himself with a baton, an interesting link to Veiel's idea of the 'baton' of history being passed down the generations. As we come to understand later in the documentary, this opening shot, taken from Maayan's play, represents the ways in which people have been 'beating themselves up' with the memory of the Holocaust in Israel.

However, if we consider this scene in relation to the ways in which the Holocaust has been remembered in Germany, and the situation of the scene in a documentary that is presumably aimed at German audiences, it can be read as a comment on how the Holocaust in Germany dominates the ways in which people define their identity.[30] It pre-empts Martin Walser's 1998 statement in which he criticised the fact that, in Germany, Auschwitz – as a symbol for the Holocaust – is an 'always readily available means to intimidate [people] or as a moral cudgel'.[31] Walser suggests that Germany beats itself up too much about Auschwitz, which results in an inability to critically engage with its own history but also with contemporary issues such as its political position in relation to Israel and Palestine, a position that is marked by ambivalence.[32] One example is Germany's response to the First Intifada, where the government sent a letter of protest to Israel one week into the uprising, but otherwise did not take a clear position since it 'did not want to endanger its relations with Israel nor its ties with the Arab states'.[33] Moreover, as David Maayan, the director of the Akko Theatre Company, notes, because the Germans start from the past, rather than the present, to engage with contemporary manifestations of prejudice and racism, 'they are really stuck on that guilt-complex from the Holocaust: They never open these doors. And until they open those doors, very wide, they will not grow further.'[34] Made in 1992, this comment still resonates thirty years later, when many aspects of German memory culture have stagnated, including comparative approaches to remembering. Moreover, there is a sense that Germany cannot develop further if it focuses too much on the past rather than considering the lessons and legacies of the Holocaust that could be used to develop a critical approach to the present and the future.

Linked to this idea, Madi Smadar Maayan, one of the actors in the play, says in a voiceover early on in the film that the Holocaust has become 'the opium for the masses in Israel',[35] a nod to Karl Marx's famous dictum that religion is the opium of the people. Esther Benbassa made a similar point when she argued that, 'Over the years, on a foundation provided by the millennial history of Jewish suffering, the Holocaust itself has been erected into a new secular religion without a God.'[36] Madi's statement in the documentary is overlaid with images of her serene face as she looks out of the window, imitating the perceived soothing effect created by using the Holocaust as an explanation for wider issues. More poignantly, it emphasises how in Israeli society – and the same argument can be made in the context of German society – a focus on the Holocaust can result in escapism, as a way for not engaging with other social and political concerns. Madi goes on to explain that what they are doing in their play is blasphemy, 'to take something that is sacred and go against it, to make a big *balagan* in [*sic*] this sacred thing'.[37] The *balagan* that they make of the Holocaust not only relates to how they portray the Holocaust, including by drawing on the grotesque, but equally emerges in their discussion of the relationship between the Palestinian people and the Holocaust in Israel. Both of these are controversial topics in Germany where the mainstream position is that the Holocaust can only be represented as a unique event, not used in a comparative context.

In Maayan's play and the excerpts from it that Veiel includes in his documentary, the relationship between the Holocaust and the *nakba* is complicated by giving Israeli Palestinian actor Khaled Abu Ali's character, who is also named Khaled, the role of 'expert on destruction', which involves explaining to the audience how the concentration camps worked.[38] First, this decision interrogates who is entitled to speak about the Holocaust and its history; and second, as we will see below, it creates links between the Holocaust and the Palestinian *nakba*. Khaled confesses to the audience of the play that he did not know anything about the Holocaust before doing research at Yad Vashem, Israel's Holocaust museum. He tells them that he spent an entire day there and he 'was upset and cried' and 'did not want to leave. What upset [him] most was remembering a sentence [his] teacher said in school: "It's a pity Hitler did not kill the whole Jewish people".'[39] Khaled's experience is confirmed by Sarah Ozacky-Lazar, who notes that, 'the average Arab high school graduate has a limited knowledge of the Holocaust.'[40] Moreover, the textbooks that are used are not adapted to a Palestinian context but 'emphasize the Jewish point of view and not universal lessons',[41] which in turn makes it hard for Palestinian students to engage with the event. As a result of this pedagogical approach, as Abu Ali has discussed in an interview, he sees more thorough education as a key aspect of resolving the animosity between Israeli Jews and Israeli Palestinians: 'Right now, Palestinians learn in school that the Jews are their enemy, and in Jewish schools they are taught [likewise]. If we didn't have all this brainwashing, we could absolutely for sure, live very well together.'[42] He emphasises the need to know the other side's history and to acknowledge the suffering that both (Israeli) Jews and Palestinians have experienced. This can also be applied to a German context, not only in relation to Jewish history but equally to Palestinian history and the connections between those histories, which are important to be taught and thought about together.[43]

Nevertheless, using a Palestinian actor in the play to explain a Jewish catastrophe does not always work in the way that is intended by the theatre group. While in an interview Abu Ali explains that 'hearing about the details of what happened to the Jewish people during that period [the Holocaust] from an Arab with a definite Arab accent . . . invariably adds a poignancy to the subject for Israeli theatregoers',[44] the message that the audience takes from this approach is at times slightly different. For example, in the documentary, one of the audience members points at Khaled and says that,

> He is one of the righteous of the world. This very man. He left his village and went to the Yad Vashem memorial. He stayed there a whole day, and now he tells us everything. Us, the Jews. He is righteous, no matter whether he's an Arab or a Hottentot.[45]

Although slightly over the top, this statement puts Khaled in the category of 'the righteous among the nations', a description used by the State of Israel to honour non-Jewish people who helped Jewish people during the Holocaust. Khaled's act of researching and engaging with the Holocaust is seen as recognising the suffering of the Jews during World War II, and diverges from discourses in the Arab world which negate the Holocaust.[46] But the comment from the audience member does not acknowledge that the Palestinian people have also suffered displacement and dispossession, as they consider the history of Israel to be one exclusively shaped by Jewish suffering. The play, however, criticises this perspective when Moni's character tells Khaled: 'Shut up Arab! They ruin everything!'[47] Madi, in her role as Selma, intervenes and says that, 'Personally, I have nothing against you. I even have some friends in the Arab sector. But you're comparing our tragedy with your filth. That's too much.'[48] This emphasis on the impossibility of comparison mirrors Shira Stav's observation that, 'A common Israeli response to this comparison is, "There is no comparison!" The very comparison between the Holocaust and the life and fate of the Palestinian refugees is considered "monstrous".'[49]

However, as Khaled Abu Ali has noted in an interview, this refusal to acknowledge Palestinian suffering is not the only reaction of audiences: some had cried in the past when he explained the Holocaust to them, 'because of the suddenly acute realization, in hearing a Palestinian recounting the horrors of the past, that Arabs are now experiencing harsh suffering in their country'.[50] In addition to including footage from *Arbeit macht frei vom Toitland Europa* that addresses the issue of comparison and encourages audiences to make this link, Veiel subtly emphasises the comparison by preceding the scene with filming Madi, who recounts visiting her father's family home in former Czechoslovakia when she was seven years old. She tells the camera that her father did not want to enter the house since there was another family living there now. This echoes the experience of many Palestinians who left their homes in 1947 and 1948 during the war that led to the establishment of Israel. When they later went back to visit their houses, they found another, usually Jewish, family living in their home. Focusing on Palestinian experiences of suffering and victimhood and creating this comparative framework for examining them alongside Jewish experiences is not only important for Israeli Jewish audiences but also for German viewers, in order to move away from an exclusive focus on Jewish victimhood that prevents an acknowledgement of other experiences of suffering.

The fact that Palestinian suffering is often eclipsed by Jewish suffering during the Holocaust explains why, in the documentary, Khaled Abu Ali does not tell his family and friends what the play is about until the end of the documentary. When he does, he emphasises the idea of relationality and kinship, saying that, 'The Jewish actors are like brothers to me. I'm not working for Jews in a theatre but the theatre belongs to us.'[51] He emphasises that he is not their 'token Arab' but that it is a collaborative project where everyone is valued equally. Against Omar Barghouti's dismissal of collaborative activities that foster dialogue, since '[t]hose who think they can wish away a conflict by suggesting only some intellectual channels of rapprochement, détente, or "dialogue" are crucially seeking only an illusion of peace, and one that is devoid of justice at that',[52] Abu Ali suggests that 'the people I work with would never kill a Palestinian. They're for peace and good relationships between Jews and Arabs.'[53] However, one of Abu Ali's friends is doubtful about the possibility of Israeli–Palestinian relations as he says that he has 'never before heard of Jews liking Arabs'.[54] This comment emphasises how the ways in which Palestinians have been treated by Israeli Jews in the past makes it hard for them to believe in amicable relationships in the present.

The documentary is similarly very sceptical about a rapprochement between Israeli Jews and Palestinians, which emerges through Veiel's interviews with Moni Yosef and Khaled Abu Ali. Moni explains in Hebrew that

> Khaled . . . is not just a colleague, but also a friend. I've been working with him at this theatre for nine years. Sometimes he bothers me, sometimes I bother him. . . . During our film work I thought about the following: People on the outside, like you or the audience in Berlin, you see Khaled as an Arab living and working with Jewish Israelis. But he is Israeli too.[55]

He addresses the common misconception that only Jewish people are Israelis, and draws attention to how this misconception excludes Palestinians living in Israel. Interestingly, when Moni says, 'People on the outside, like you', he points and looks at the camera, thus specifically addressing his comment to Veiel as the director as well as to audiences outside of Israel and Palestine. Moni emphasises that he finds it ridiculous and simplistic to divide people along ethnic lines, categorising them as 'Jews' or 'Arabs'.

While initially Moni seems very open and progressive in his views, the audience increasingly see the limits of his beliefs about the practical aspects of coexisting with Palestinians. For example, after a shot showing Moni lying in a hammock, dribbling a basketball, with his toddler in the background, he says in English that, 'The Holocaust was a children's game compared to what will happen if the Arabs one day occupy Israel.'[56] This statement reiterates fears about Palestinians wanting to kill Israeli Jews, which is heightened by the inclusion of the child and by juxtaposing the projected genocide with the idyllic picture of Moni and his son relaxing in a peaceful setting.

Contrasting with these suspicions and the distance they create between Israeli Jews and Palestinians, the play, and the documentary, end with a naked embrace between the characters Selma and Khaled. Rebecca Rovit has observed that 'their union suggests many couplings besides that of the sexes: past and present, victim and oppressor, Arab and Jew, or perhaps, two victims equal in their victimization.'[57] However, as Rovit implies here, this is a reading that is confined to the play itself rather than being applicable to Israeli–Palestinian relations more widely. Abu Ali's discussion of this final moment in an interview confirms Rovit's interpretation. He says that this was 'the strongest, most difficult and painful part in the production for [him]' since

> [a]t that point, our two holocausts, because we are living in the same deeply troubled country, become one. The hug makes me feel peace has arrived. But then, after the show, when I am in Israel and go outside, nothing has changed. And I find myself waiting for the next performance so I can experience again, for at least one brief moment, that feeling of peace.[58]

What Veiel's documentary shows is that the embrace between Israeli Jew and Israeli Palestinian, and by extension the coexistence of the memory of the Holocaust and the *nakba*, is confined to the space of the play and the documentary. Veiel can certainly be commended for 'open[ing] a window and let[ing] in some fresh air' and 'leav[ing] the usual discursive trails' linked to how Germany has engaged with the Holocaust,[59] showing that a critical engagement with the Holocaust in Germany is not only possible but necessary. However, the confinement of this ending to the fictional space of artistic productions can be read in light of how the Holocaust not only precluded engagement with Palestinian suffering in the 1990s, but also how it still does so in many ways today, both in Israel and in Germany. Nevertheless, by displacing the relationality between Israel and Palestine and their respective memories of suffering, Veiel provides the necessary distance for his audiences to critically engage with ideas of Jewish and German victimhood as well as Germany's relationship with both Israel and Palestine. This, in turn, allows them to imagine what a comparative approach to thinking about Israel and Palestine and the relationships between their histories and narratives might look like, and what the implications for Holocaust memory in Germany would be.

Doubles and Mirroring: The Holocaust, Germany and Israel in *Zerbrochenes Deutsch: Zweimal Berlin-Haifa*

Ina Dentler's novel *Zerbrochenes Deutsch: Zweimal Berlin-Haifa* (*Broken German: Two Times Berlin-Haifa*; 2014) is part of an interesting trend that arose in the 2010s in Germany, whereby authors who do not have a direct link with Israel and Palestine started writing about and engaging with this geopolitical context in their works.[60] This trend illustrates how Israel and Palestine are becoming more mainstream topics in German popular culture, at the same time as it exposes – as we will see below but also in Chapter 3 – some of the limitations of critically engaging with Israel and its treatment of the Palestinian people during and after the Second Intifada.

Dentler's book is set in 2004 and 2005, ten years after Veiel's documentary and at the end of the Second Intifada, which as discussed in the general introduction to this book resulted in Germany aligning itself with very conservative Israeli approaches to its security discourse. The novel engages with the possibility of overcoming Germany's Nazi past, especially through achieving redemption by identifying with Jewish victims. This redemption is aligned with 'repairing' relations between Germany and Israel, which is implied in the title of the novel: 'Broken German', a phrase which is used in the book by the Israeli Jewish character Oshrat to describe her linguistic command of German.[61] This idea of something that has been broken, and indeed shattered, can be applied to Israel's relationship with Germany, including the descendants of German Jewish people in Israel and their perceptions of Germany, as we will see below. However, we can also read this title as a comment on the ways in which the Nazi past has 'broken' contemporary Germany's relationship with its identity and with Israel (and implicitly but less prominently in Dentler's novel, with Palestine) through Nazi Germany's role as a perpetrator of the Holocaust.

Like Veiel, Dentler belongs to the second generation of Germans engaging with the Holocaust, while her protagonist Anja can in many ways be seen as a typical member of the third generation, which – especially since the late 1990s, as Fuchs has argued – is shaped by a 'huge investment in issues of genealogy, family tradition and heritage'.[62] Compared to Veiel's documentary, Dentler's novel is situated at the more lowbrow end of cultural productions, as its writing style and the development of the narrative are not what one would consider of high literary value. Nevertheless, *Zerbrochenes Deutsch* uses interesting strategies for depicting the relationships between Germany, Israel and Palestine, which makes it worthwhile as a case study for this chapter. While Veiel's documentary displaces relationality geographically, Dentler's novel displaces relationality temporally to develop her readers' understanding of German–Israeli relations in the contemporary period. Dentler juxtaposes her protagonist Anja, a thirty-year-old woman living in Berlin in 2004, with her great-aunt Toni, who lived in Berlin until 1934 when she left for Palestine with her Jewish husband Erik due to the rise of anti-Semitism and the increasing number of restrictions imposed on Jewish people in Germany. This comparison encourages Anja, alongside Dentler's readers, to consider Germany's contemporary engagement with the Holocaust and Israel by establishing strong links between 1930s and 2000s Germany – Nazi Germany and reunified Germany. This doubling is important since 'doubling in literature usually symbolizes a dysfunctional attempt to cope with mental conflict', as Robert Rogers has argued.[63] The 'mental conflict' at hand is Germany's coming to terms with its Nazi past and the ways in which the Holocaust should be addressed in the twenty-first century, especially alongside narratives of Palestinian suffering. In this sense, Anja's great-aunt Toni can be read as a double of a kind typical in German literature in that she 'is at once an historical figure, re-presenting past times, and a profoundly anti-historical phenomenon, resisting temporal change by stepping out of time and then stepping back in as a revenant.'[64] While Toni is not depicted as a ghost in the novel, she certainly represents Germany's past, including its past before the Holocaust, and how Germany has been 'haunted' by the Holocaust – as well as the ways in which Germany might atone for, and potentially be absolved of, its Holocaust. This becomes evident when Anja not only retraces her great-aunt Toni's footsteps in Germany and Israel, but also decides, like her aunt, to settle in Israel, as we will see below.

Retracing the past in order to understand the present is an approach that informs the writing of the third generation, a generation that needs to 'work through' the 'transgenerational legacy' of the Holocaust.[65] This emerges in Dentler's novel, as in many other German works, such as the 2013 miniseries *Unsere Mütter, unsere Väter* (broadcast in English under the title *Generation War*), and in the German public and cultural sphere more generally, through the question of what one's family did during World War II. This question arose with the generation of 1968, which took their parents to task for being members of the Nazi party as well as for being followers and bystanders during the Holocaust. In Dentler's novel, Anja's exploration of her family history, including her family's involvement in the Holocaust, starts when she meets her aunt Oshrat and her cousin Uri from Israel. Oshrat and Uri have come to Berlin to retrace the life of Oshrat's mother – Anja's great-aunt Toni – in Berlin during the Nazi regime before she left for Palestine. Encountering her Israeli Jewish family is key for Anja to understand her own relationship with the German past. This includes considering how previous generations, such as her grandmother Friedl, who represents the first generation that experienced the Holocaust directly, and her mother, who is a representative of the 1968 generation that rebelled against their parents' complicity with Nazism, have engaged with the Holocaust. Oshrat and Uri's quest to find out more about Toni's life in Berlin results in Anja finding out more about her family's past. As Kylie Giblett argues, in third-generation German literature about Holocaust perpetrators, the quest is used by protagonists 'to uncover the "truth" about their family history in the face of fragmentary and conflicting evidence', which in turn is important for the third generation 'to identify the implications of their family origins for their own identity narratives'.[66] In Dentler's novel, Anja's coming to terms with her family history is triggered by reading Toni's diary entries, which Anja finds in a cookbook that Toni gave to Oshrat and which Oshrat passes on to her. Through detailed descriptions of the ways in which Jewish people in Germany were increasingly restricted and discriminated against in 1930s Nazi Germany and entries on how Toni and Erik were ostracised by their non-Jewish friends, Anja gets a better sense of how German society treated Jewish people during this time. Moreover, she finds out that Friedl, her grandmother and Toni's mother, was anti-Semitic and did not approve of Toni's relationship with Erik, which leads to Anja reflecting on her family's role in supporting the exclusion of Jewish people from German public life.

This reading of the diaries can be situated within the larger context of the quest that drives Dentler's narrative. Anja's quest, which is effective in creating parallels between Toni's and Anja's narratives, also involves physically visiting some of the places in Berlin that shaped the lives of Toni, her boyfriend (and later husband) Erik, and Erik's Jewish family. This revisiting of key locations where Erik's and Toni's lives took place is not only an important part of Anja's attempt to retrace her family's history, but equally emphasises the need for an everyday awareness of spaces in Germany that have been shaped by Jewish lives and histories – one that is not only limited to spaces explicitly marked as such.[67] This more critical impulse is lessened when Anja and her Israeli Jewish family visit the Jewish cemetery in Tröbitz in the state of Brandenburg, which leads Anja to reassess her family's involvement in the Second World War. Anja reflects that, 'Under Hitler there had been followers . . . as well as perpetrators in her family',[68] and then mentions her grandfather, whom she has never met, but who was in the *SS*. However, it is important to note that the relatively more official site of the cemetery resulted in this confession and reflection, rather than the more private spaces associated with Toni's and Erik's lives in Berlin.

A key aspect of this confession is that it confirms that Anja still experiences guilt, or rather responsibility, for the Nazi past as she is relieved that her cousin and love interest Uri 'doesn't hold [her] generation responsible for the past'.[69] While Uri might suggest that Germany has done enough *Vergangenheitsbewältigung* (coming to terms with the past, literally translated as 'grappling with the past'), this is not a mainstream position in Germany or elsewhere. Michael Elm has emphasised that 'Auschwitz' – which seems to stand in as a metonym for the Holocaust in Elm's reading – 'requires a reflection far beyond personal guilt', which has resulted in 'German identity [being] challenged and haunted, driven theoretically by the need to take on a post-conventional shape'.[70] According to Elm, this 'post-conventional' shape 'implies an obligation to reflect one's own social and cultural origin, to question normality as a convention'.[71] However, I would suggest that in Dentler's novel, bringing together Germany, Israel and Palestine can be seen as a 'post-conventional' move, at least initially, as it not only addresses personal guilt but also reflects on collective responsibility, including through the figure of Toni as a haunting presence or double for Anja.

Toni's function as a double, and the quest narrative associated with reconstructing Toni's and Erik's lives in Nazi Germany, lead Anja to discover parallels with her relationship with Uri. While Anja and Uri's relationship might not be marked by the anti-Semitism that Toni and Erik experienced in 1930s Germany – and indeed it is interesting that Dentler does not address the issue of anti-Semitism in contemporary Germany – Anja emphasises that being in a relationship with an Israeli Jew forces her to reflect on her family's involvement in the Holocaust as well on as her own views of Israel and its treatment of the Palestinian people. This is confirmed in Uri's statement that, '[I]n order to be happy in Israel, it is not enough to love me. You don't only have to connect with me but also establish a link with the land.'[72] Uri explains that moving to Israel will require Anja to come to terms with Israel's actions and policies, including its discrimination against the Palestinians. Implicit in this statement is the suggestion that Anja needs to adopt philo-Zionism as an ideology in order to achieve this goal.[73] However, as Anja mentions early on, she 'was startled by the realisation that she was not ready at all to form an opinion' about the situation in Israel and Palestine.[74] She links this to the ways in which 'in the public sphere and in school they had been increasingly talking about Israel and Jewish people for almost 60 years, but hardly impartially or openly'.[75] It is important that Anja emphasises how Israel as a topic of discussion in Germany is shaped by Germany's 'partiality', which, on one hand, could be read as a nod towards Nazi Germany's role as a perpetrator of the Holocaust, but, on the other hand, references Germany's partiality towards Israel and the ways in which Israel cannot be engaged with critically in the German public discourse.

Anja initially counteracts this tendency when Uri shows her a video about a Palestinian suicide bomber and explains that it is his job as a helicopter pilot in the Israeli army to prevent terrorist attacks. Anja comments that, 'While translating, Uri's voice had merged in a strange way with that of the suicide bomber.'[76] The conflation of Uri's voice and that of the suicide bomber raises doubts about whether Israel's actions against Palestinians are justifiable through its security discourse, as Israel's actions are, at least momentarily, conflated with the actions of the Palestinian people. As a result of Uri explaining what he does for a living, Anja realises that she has created an idealised image of her Israeli Jewish boyfriend, which aligns more generally with how West Germany and later reunified Germany have perceived Israel and its 'colonisation' of Palestine: 'She had suppressed the image of the pioneer, the conqueror, and the settler. She had been blind to the unlucky bird, the messenger of war and death.'[77] Up to that point, Anja had not critically engaged with Israel's role as an occupying power, or considered Uri's job as a pilot in the Israeli army, who is in charge of killing Palestinian targets, but she now realises that both of these identities clash with her beliefs as a pacifist and as someone who is sympathetic to the Palestinian cause.

Shortly after, Anja sees an interview with an Israeli Jewish sniper on TV. When the man is asked whether he considers himself a murderer, he responds by saying that he is only doing his job. But he does concede that when he goes home to his family, he still thinks about his victims, saying that, 'They sit in my head. They press on my heart. I can't get rid of them.'[78] This exemplifies the popular Israeli figure of the 'shooting and weeping' soldier, who injures or kills Palestinian people and then expresses regret. However, as Alon Gan has argued, this trope has been criticised since 'the process of purification through weeping' is seen as 'a substitution for taking action against injustice'.[79] Anja's interpretation of the scene is slightly different, as she is relieved that the sniper is represented as human rather than as a machine. Nevertheless, she concludes that she does not want to be the wife of a sniper, which leads her to tell Uri that 'our circumstances, our political convictions, they are too different for us to live together'.[80] This emphasis on their differences constitutes a clear rejection of Germany's endorsement of Israel's security discourse since the Second Intifada, and offers a more critical perspective on it, especially if an endorsement would translate into the harming and taking of Palestinian lives. However, Anja – instead of sustaining this more critical perspective on Israel's treatment of the Palestinian people – concedes that 'her knowledge of the Israeli-Palestinian conflict was too superficial to understand what Uri's opinions are based on'.[81] While it is admirable to acknowledge the limitations of one's knowledge, this comment mainly appears to be an excuse for not engaging in depth with both sides and their respective histories.

After the death of her grandmother Friedl – Toni's sister, and the only living representative of the first generation in Anja's family – Anja decides to visit Oshrat and Uri in Israel in order to get a better understanding of the country. Her grandmother's death not only frees Anja from her caring duties, but can also be read as releasing Anja from the need to always and exclusively engage with Israel through the prism of the Holocaust. But as we will see below, rather than leading to more critical engagement with Israel, this visit results in Anja adopting a more conservative approach that aligns with Israel's security discourse. Anja's journey is motivated by finding out more about Toni's life in Palestine and later in Israel, mirroring Oshrat and Uri's journey to Berlin. It further emphasises the motif of the quest, and the importance of piecing together Toni's life for Anja to be able to understand her own identity. Anja wonders 'which one of her current beliefs would hold up to' living in Israel, but then goes on to say that 'she was tired of the arguments for or against Israel or Palestine. What did she know?'[82] As this statement already indicates, Dentler does not want to continue exploring Anja's critical stance. Instead, by depicting her as 'being tired' of all the arguments, Dentler – alongside Anja herself – dismisses any thorough engagement with Israel's settler-colonial occupation of Palestinian peoples and lands.

This is confirmed when Anja arrives in Israel and Dentler only exposes her to conservative views of Israel's politics in the Occupied Palestinian Territories. These include those of Uri's father Ben, a former army general, whose grandfather immigrated to Palestine as part of the first *aliyah* in 1887 to escape the pogroms in Russia, and his son Zvi, Uri's eldest brother, who lives in a kibbutz. While she is visiting the kibbutz, Ben and Zvi discuss the situation in Israel, and Ben tells Anja that, 'The fight over the same land will never end . . . Even if we were prepared to relinquish a large part of the land, this would never be enough for Hamas.'[83] Ben reduces Israel's occupation of the Palestinians to an issue of land. While land is a key aspect of the occupation, this focus on it omits the fact that Israel is also an occupying power in Gaza, the West Bank and East Jerusalem, as well as treating Palestinians in Israel as second-class citizens. Moreover, Ben very problematically conflates Palestine and Palestinians with Hamas, an Islamist fundamentalist organisation, which confirms stereotypes about Palestinians as 'fanatics' and 'terrorists'. Ben's son Zvi agrees, and asks why the Palestinians left Palestine in the first place, a question that is often used to justify why Palestinians no longer have access to their lands and properties. As we will see in relation to other texts discussed in this book, for example in Chapters 2 and 5, this question omits the role that the Israeli leadership and paramilitary organisations played in Palestinian departures from their homes in the lead-up to the establishment of Israel, including by creating a sense of fear through violence and killings.

Ben and Zvi also discuss the right of return, which is a major bone of contention for both Israeli Jewish and Palestinian people. For Palestinians it is paramount to be able to return to their lands, both for those in the diaspora and those that are internally displaced. For Israeli Jews, the Palestinian right of return is problematic as it constitutes a threat to the Jewish majority in Israel and is thus equated with a threat to Jewish security – security which, according to some, can only be guaranteed in a state that is predominantly made up of Jewish people.⁸⁴ This is the main reason why Ben and Zvi agree that the Palestinian people cannot be allowed to return and even Oshrat, who seemed left-wing and in favour of peace throughout the novel, agrees with this position.⁸⁵ Unfortunately, instead of critically engaging with Israeli society and presenting a wider range of different opinions towards Palestinians, Dentler rehearses mainstream conservative and right-wing arguments against making any concessions to the Palestinians. She does not include a perspective in her novel that draws attention to the settler-colonial nature of Israel's occupation in the West Bank and its control of Gaza. This settler-colonial attitude is exemplary of the wider philo-Zionism that shapes the novel, especially the second half.

The novel's philo-Zionism is linked to the idea of redemption that emerges through Anja's quest in Israel. Anja visits Haifa and Nahariya, where Toni lived, to retrace her aunt's steps as well as to establish a connection with Israel through Toni. Anja emphasises that, 'Only at Toni's grave would they reach the end of their joint search for clues.'⁸⁶ This can be read as part of a redemptive narrative that allows Anja to follow in Toni's footsteps to settle in Israel and be in a German–Jewish relationship.⁸⁷ The novel ends with Anja suggesting that she wants to try finding a place for herself in Israel, saying that,

> She didn't want to be an occasional visitor to Israel. She wanted to live with Uri in Toni's city Haifa, but for the time being without a marriage certificate, close to Oshrat and the entire *mischpoche* [Hebrew for family]. – In dialogue with Toni this could be successful.⁸⁸

While Anja's engagement with her family's history and her interest in Israeli Jewish culture are certainly commendable for not just being token gestures, this ending is problematic for several reasons. First, it mirrors the philo-Semitism that emerged in post-war Germany and aligns with philo-Zionism. Both of these approaches to coming to terms with Jewish and Israeli culture are aimed at defining Anja's identity and sense of belonging, thus confirming arguments that German engagement with Israel is about Germany rather than about Israel. Second, it suggests that relations between Germany and Israel can be repaired, at the expense of the Palestinians and their suffering as well as their aspirations. This reflects, on one hand, accepted representations of the histories of the Holocaust and Israel, and on the other hand the history of Palestine – and treats them as separate and unrelated.

Relational Endpoints

The two works discussed in this chapter conclude on very different notes, giving a snapshot of how German–Israeli–Palestinian relations have developed since the First Intifada. While both end on a note of relationality – in Veiel's documentary the embrace between an Israeli Jewish and an Israeli Palestinian actor, and in Dentler's novel the relationship between a German and an Israeli Jewish character – the suggested duration of this relationality differs quite significantly. Veiel confines the moment to the space of David Maayan's play and his own documentary, positioning it as wishful thinking that cannot exist in an outside world marked by political divisions and occupation. While Germany is not explicitly mentioned at the end of the documentary, it is clear that the impossibility of the embrace extends to Germany as a geopolitical and commemorative space and the impossibility of embracing both Israeli Jewish and Palestinian histories of suffering – predicting the work of later authors such as Dentler in interesting ways. Dentler's ending, contrary to Veiel's, suggests that there is a possibility for Germany to come to terms with its Nazi past and find redemption by immersing itself in Israeli Jewish culture, but at the expense of a sustained critical engagement with Israel and by occluding Palestinians and their history.

Interestingly, by juxtaposing these two works, which were published twenty years apart, there is a sense that Germany has regressed in terms of its ability to critically engage with Israel and its occupation of Palestine. While Veiel's documentary can certainly not be read as indicative of a mainstream tendency after the First Intifada, it is important to consider how some of the critical approaches to Israel subsided after the end of the Second Intifada and at a time when Israel's military operations in Gaza have prominently featured on the news in Germany and elsewhere.[89] This will be unpacked further in Chapter 3 in relation to third-generation German writers and their depictions of Israel and Palestine, but also situated in a comparative context by examining in Chapters 2 and 4 how British literature and TV series that came out after the Second Intifada engage with Israel and Palestine.

In the next chapter, entitled 'Relational Memories: The Holocaust and the *Nakba* in the British Imaginary', I extend the idea of 'displaced relationality' by moving to the British context to examine how the Holocaust and the Palestinian *nakba* are represented in a comparative context. Using Peter Kosminsky's miniseries *The Promise* (2011) and Marina Lewycka's book *We Are All Made of Glue* (2009) as case studies, this chapter shows how 'relational memories' – memories that create links between events that might seem unconnected and/or are often depicted as such – provide a comparative framework for examining Jewish and Palestinian suffering. I argue that, together with Kosminsky's and Lewycka's juxtaposition of the British Mandate with the current situation in Israel and the Occupied Palestinian Territories, this comparative approach challenges accepted narratives of the Holocaust, the creation of the state of Israel and the *nakba* as separate events. It also foregrounds the United Kingdom's responsibility as a colonial power, alongside its continued involvement in the region.

Notes

1. Herrmann, 'Spurensuche in der dritten Generation,' 139–40.
2. Herrmann, 'Spurensuche in der dritten Generation,' 142.
3. Constantin Goschler, *Schuld und Schulden: Die Politik der Wiedergutmachung für NS-Verfolgte seit 1945* (Göttingen: Wallstein, 2005), 415.
4. Goschler, *Schuld und Schulden*, 415.
5. Anne Fuchs, *Phantoms of War in Contemporary German Literature, Films and Discourse: The Politics of Memory* (Basingstoke: Palgrave Macmillan, 2008), 5.
6. Aleida Assmann, *Das neue Unbehagen an der Erinnerungskultur: Eine Intervention* (München: C. H. Beck, 2013), 61–2.
7. Ulrike Jureit, 'Opferidentifikation und Erlösungshoffnung: Beobachtungen im erinnerungspolitischen Rampenlicht,' in *Gefühlte Opfer: Illusionen der Vergangenheitsbewältigung*, by Ulrike Jureit and Christian Schneider (Stuttgart: Klett-Cotta, 2011), 29–30. This is an interesting continuation of the perception of German people as victims of Nazism, which emerged in the post-war years (see, for example, Berger, *Germany*, 170) and led to a similar distancing from perpetrators, followers and bystanders.
8. I translate the German word '*gefühlt*' as 'perceived' rather than 'felt', as some other people have done, to emphasise that it is a sense of perceived victimhood rather than something that is directly experienced.
9. Assmann, *Das neue Unbehagen*, 63.
10. Assmann, *Das neue Unbehagen*, 66.
11. Jureit, 'Opferidentifikation,' 52.

12. John Torpey, *Making Whole What Has Been Smashed: On Reparation Politics* (Cambridge, MA: Harvard University Press, 2006), 16.
13. See, for example, Tobias Rapp, 'Macht uns das Gedenken an den Holocaust blind für andere deutsche Verbrechen ?,' *Der Spiegel*, 12 February 2021, https://www.spiegel.de/geschichte/holocaust-macht-uns-das-gedenken-blind-fuer-andere-deutsche-verbrechen-a-00000000-0002-0001-0000-000175304219; Thomas Schmid, 'Die Holocaust-Frage,' *Die Welt*, 28 February 2021, https://www.welt.de/kultur/literarischewelt/plus226821125/Multidirektionale-Erinnerung-Die-Holocaust-Frage.html; Claudius Seidl, 'War der Holocaust eine koloniale Tat?' *Frankfurter Allgemeine Zeitung*, 1 March 2021, https://www.faz.net/aktuell/feuilleton/streit-um-gedenkkultur-war-der-holocaust-eine-koloniale-tat-17217645.html.
14. Jaeger, *Quadratur des Dreiecks*, 3.
15. Ó Dochartaigh, 'Philo-Zionism as a German Political Code,' 250–1.
16. Ó Dochartaigh, 'Philo-Zionism as a German Political Code,' 251.
17. There are other more recent works that employ the idea of perceived victimhood but they do not link this to Israel or Palestine. See, for example, Iris Hanika's novel *Das Eigentliche* (*The Essential*, 2010).
18. As Freddie Rokem notes, making a documentary about the play was Israeli Jewish playwright Ashler Tlalim's idea. Tlalim proposed this project to a German TV channel, who accepted the proposal but decided to give the assignment to Veiel (Freddie Rokem, *Performing History: Theatrical Representations of the Past in Contemporary Theatre* (Iowa City: University of Iowa Press, 2000), 58). Tlalim later made his own documentary, whose title *Don't Touch my Holocaust* can be read as a critical nod to Veiel making the documentary that he initially proposed.
19. Other examples include Robert Krieg's documentary *Intifada – Auf dem Weg nach Palästina* (*Intifada – On the Way to Palestine*, 1989) and German Jewish writer Angelika Schrobsdorff's work, especially her memoirs about living in Jerusalem, such as *Jerusalem war immer eine schwere Adresse* (*Jerusalem Has Always Been a Difficult Address*, 1989) and *Wenn ich dich je vergesse, oh Jerusalem . . .* (*If I Ever Forget Thee, Oh Jerusalem . . .*, 2004).
20. Ken Shulman, 'Youth and the Legacy of the Holocaust,' *The New York Times*, 15 January 1995, https://www.nytimes.com/1995/01/15/movies/film-youth-and-the-legacy-of-the-holocaust.html.
21. Mariam Niroumand, 'Ein Encounter, eine Art Entlastung,' *TAZ*, 21 April 1994, https://taz.de/Ein-Encounter-eine-Art-Entlastung/!1566321/. The second generation has often been described as '*Kinder des Schweigens*' (children of silence) as they did not hear much about the Holocaust from their parents, at school, or elsewhere.

22. Veiel encountered suspicion from both sides, with Palestinian people thinking he was working for the Israeli secret police and Israeli Jewish people being sceptical about his motives for engaging with the Holocaust. As Ken Shulman notes, Moni Yosef, one of the actors of the play, criticised Veiel for filming in the Occupied Palestinian Territories and told Veiel that he 'was just a German looking for exoneration... That [he] was trying to point a finger at the Jews' (Shulman, 'Youth and the Legacy of the Holocaust').
23. Niroumand, 'Ein Encounter.'
24. Shulman, 'Youth and the Legacy of the Holocaust.'
25. Dalia Ofer, 'The Past that Does Not Pass: Israelis and Holocaust Memory,' *Israel Studies* 14, no. 1 (2009): 22–3, https://www.jstor.org/stable/30245842.
26. Linda Grant, *The People on the Street: A Writer's View of Israel* (London: Virago, 2006), 38.
27. Tobias Ebbrecht-Hartmann, *Übergänge: Passagen durch eine deutsch-israelische Filmgeschichte* (Berlin: Neofelis Verlag, 2014), 209.
28. For a discussion of the ritualisation of Holocaust memory in Germany see, for example, Assmann's *Das neue Unbehagen*, 76–81.
29. Shulman, 'Youth and the Legacy of the Holocaust.'
30. The closing credits of the documentary tell the audience that the play was performed in Berlin in April 1992 as part of the exhibition '*Jüdische Lebenswelten*' (Jewish Lifeworlds). For a review of the Berlin performance of the play, see Rebecca Rovit, 'Emerging from the Ashes: The Akko Theatre Center Opens the Gates to Auschwitz,' *The Drama Review* 37, no. 2 (1993): 161–73.
31. Martin Walser, 'Dankesrede von Martin Walser zur Verleihung des Friedenspreises des Deutschen Buchhandels in der Frankfurter Paulskirche am 11. Oktober 1998,' in *Friedenspreis des Deutschen Buchhandels 1998. Ansprachen aus Anlaß der Verleihung* (Frankfurt: Börsenverein des Deutschen Buchhandels, 1998).
32. Walser's speech ignited a heated debate between Walser and Ignatz Bubis, then chairman of the Central Council of Jews in Germany, a debate that has often been described as one of the most significant discussions since the *Historikerstreit* of the late 1980s. Bubis accused Walser of encouraging German people to look away and to forget about the Holocaust (for a discussion of this see, for example, Amir Eshel, 'Vom eigenen Gewissen: Die Walser-Bubis-Debatte und der Ort des Nationalsozialismus um Selbstbild der Bundesrepublik,' *Deutsche Vierteljahrsschrift für Literaturwissenschaft und Geistesgeschichte* 74, no. 2 (2000): 333–60, https://doi.org/10.1007/BF03375544).
33. Sebastian Kunze, 'Deutschland, Israel und der Nahost Konflikt,' in *Deutschland, die Juden und der Staat Israel: Eine politische Bestandsaufnahme*, ed. Olaf Glöckner and Julius H. Schoeps (Hildesheim: Georg Olms Verlag, 2016), 255.

34. Linda Joffee, 'An Interview With the Akko Theater's Artistic Director,' *The Christian Science Monitor*, 18 August 1992, https://search-proquest-com.ezproxy1.library.usyd.edu.au/docview/291196332/fulltext/F99DA54126F548CEPQ/1?accountid=14757.
35. Andres Veiel, dir., *Balagan*. Featuring Madi Maayan, Khaled Abu Ali and Moni Yosef, 1993. Streamed via Vimeo, https://vimeo.com/ondemand/balagan [00:04:00–00:04:04].
36. Esther Benbassa, *Suffering as Identity: The Jewish Paradigm*, trans. G. M. Goshgarian (London: Verso, 2010), 106.
37. Veiel, *Balagan*, [00:04:07–00:04:14].
38. In order to distinguish between the character and the actor, I will use the first name Khaled to refer to the character in the play and the last name, Abu Ali, or the full name, Khaled Abu Ali, to refer to the actor.
39. Veiel, *Balagan*, [01:26:05–01:26:44].
40. Sarah Ozacky-Lazar, 'Holocaust Memory among Palestinian Arab Citizens in Israel: Personal Sympathy and National Antagonism,' in *Holocaust Memory in a Globalizing World*, ed. Jacob S. Eder, Philipp Gassert and Alan E. Steinweis (Göttingen: Wallstein Verlag, 2017), 148. This is confirmed in Samira Alayan's research on how the Holocaust is represented in Palestinian textbooks, see Samira Alayan, 'The Holocaust in Palestinian Textbooks: Differences and Similarities in Israel and Palestine,' *Comparative Education Review* 60, no. 1 (2016): 80–104, https://doi.org/10.1086/684362.
41. Ozacky-Lazar, 'Holocaust Memory among Palestinian Arab Citizens in Israel,' 148.
42. Linda Joffee, 'Acting Stint Transforms Arab's View of Israelis,' *The Christian Science Monitor*, 18 August 1992, https://search-proquest-com.ezproxy1.library.usyd.edu.au/docview/291194727/fulltext/673250E5D5F04B5FPQ/1?accountid=14757.
43. This approach is also encouraged in Stefanie Landgraf and Johannes Gulde's 2011 documentary *Wir weigern uns Feinde zu sein* (*We Refuse to Be Enemies*), which follows twelve German students between the ages of sixteen and twenty-two who travel to Israel and the Occupied Palestinian Territories to learn more about the geopolitical context. In preparation for their trip, they use a history book that was developed by PRIME (Peace Research Institute in the Middle East) as part of a project entitled 'Learning Each Other's Historical Narratives' in Palestinian and Israeli schools. Understanding the other side's history and narrative is seen as key to changing attitudes on both sides but also, interestingly, in this documentary, to changing German students' approaches to both Israel and Palestine.
44. Joffee, 'Acting Stint Transforms Arab's View of Israelis.'

45. Veiel, *Balagan*, [00:33:19–00:33:47].
46. For an overview of Arab engagement with the Holocaust, see Gilbert Achcar, *The Arabs and the Holocaust: The Arab-Israeli War of Narratives*, trans. G. M. Goshgarian (London: Saqi, 2010).
47. Veiel, *Balagan*, [01:11:53–01:11:55].
48. Veiel, *Balagan*, [01:12:14–01:12:28].
49. Shira Stav, 'Nakba and Holocaust: Mechanisms of Comparison and Denial in the Israeli Literary Imagination,' *Jewish Social Studies* 18, no. 3 (2012): 89, https://www.jstor.org/stable/10.2979/jewisocistud.18.3.85.
50. Joffee, 'Acting Stint Transforms Arab's View of Israelis.'
51. Veiel, *Balagan*, [01:19:51–01:20:00].
52. Omar Barghouti, *Boycott, Divestment, Sanctions: The Global Struggle for Palestinian Rights* (Chicago: Haymarket Books, 2011), 103.
53. Veiel, *Balagan*, [01:20:28–01:20:40].
54. Veiel, *Balagan*, [01:20:50–01:20:52].
55. Veiel, *Balagan*, [00:05:00–00:05:44].
56. Veiel, *Balagan*, [00:49:33–00:49:45].
57. Rovit, 'Emerging from the Ashes,' 168.
58. Joffee, 'Acting Stint Transforms Arab's View of Israelis.'
59. Stefan Reinecke, 'Laudatio anlässlich der Verleihung des Konrad-Wolf-Preises 2005,' in *Andres Veiel: Edition der Filmemacher* – DVD booklet (Berlin: Neue Visionen Medien, 2006), 18.
60. Some of these are of dubious literary value and laced with Orientalist stereotypes about Palestinians, such as Pit Bernie's *So könnte es gehen* (*It Could Work This Way*, 2017) but there are works of higher literary value, including a number of travelogues, some of which will be discussed in Chapter 3. There is of course also German Jewish writing on Israel and Palestine, such as Lena Gorelik's *Hochzeit in Jerusalem* (*Wedding in Jerusalem*, 2007) and Michel Bergmann's *Herr Klee und Herr Feld* (*Mr Klee and Mr Feld*, 2014), alongside a growing body of works by Israeli Jewish authors living in Germany and writing in German, such as Tomer Gardi's *Broken German* (2016) and Tomer Dotan-Dreyfus's *Birobidschan* (2023).
61. Oshrat mistakenly uses the word '*zerbrochen*', which in German means 'shattered', while the more commonly used word to describe imperfect command of a language would be '*gebrochen*'.
62. Fuchs, *Phantoms of War*, 6.
63. Robert Rogers, *The Double in Literature: A Psychoanalytic Study* (Detroit: Wayne State University Press, 1970), vii.

64. Andrew J. Webber, *The Doppelgänger: Double Visions in German Literature* (Oxford: Clarendon Press, 1996), 10.
65. Fuchs, *Phantoms of War*, 24.
66. Kylie Giblett, '"Was ich nicht sehen kann muss ich erfinden": Third generation narratives of Nazi Herkunft in Tanja Ducker's "Himmelskörper" and Marcel Beyer's "Spione",' *Limbus: Australisches Jahrbuch für germanistische Literatur- und Kulturwissenschaft* 11 (2018): 178, 181, https://doi.org/10.5771/9783968218588-175.
67. The most prominent example of this would be the '*Stolpersteine*', which are small brass stones embedded in the pavement of many major German cities, marking where Jewish people that were killed by the Nazis lived. This commemorative project has now been extended to cities across Europe and Russia.
68. Ina Dentler, *Zerbrochenes Deutsch: Zweimal Berlin-Haifa* (Berlin: AphorismA, 2014), 217.
69. Dentler, *Zerbrochenes Deutsch*, 98.
70. Michael Elm, 'The Making of Holocaust Trauma in German Memory: Some Reflection about Robert Thalheim's Film *And Along Come Tourists*,' in *Being Jewish in 21st-Century Germany*, ed. Haim Fireberg and Olaf Glöckner (Berlin: De Gruyter, 2015), 35.
71. Elm, 'The Making of Holocaust Trauma,' 35.
72. Dentler, *Zerbrochenes Deutsch*, 281.
73. This is not a very nuanced view of Israeli society as it glosses over the many Israeli Jewish people living in Israel who actively oppose Israel's treatment of the Palestinians and for whom critical engagement with Israel is compatible with being (Israeli) Jewish.
74. Dentler, *Zerbrochenes Deutsch*, 34.
75. Dentler, *Zerbrochenes Deutsch*, 34.
76. Dentler, *Zerbrochenes Deutsch*, 184.
77. Dentler, *Zerbrochenes Deutsch*, 186. Anja previously used the nickname 'raven' for Uri but now she links this name with the German term '*Unglücksrabe*', which translates as 'unlucky raven'. While this term usually describes someone who has bad luck, Anja here foregrounds the association between ravens and death.
78. Dentler, *Zerbrochenes Deutsch*, 227.
79. Alon Gan, 'The Tanks of Tammuz and The Seventh Day: The Emergence of Opposite Poles of Israeli Identity after the Six Day War,' *The Journal of Israeli History* 28, no. 2 (2009): 162, https://doi.org/10.1080/13531040903169727.
80. Dentler, *Zerbrochenes Deutsch*, 229.
81. Dentler, *Zerbrochenes Deutsch*, 237.

82. Dentler, *Zerbrochenes Deutsch*, 217.
83. Dentler, *Zerbrochenes Deutsch*, 290.
84. This is one of the key ideas that post-Zionist critics challenge; see, for example, Ephraim Nimni's edited collection *The Challenge of Post-Zionism: Alternatives to Israeli Fundamentalist Politics* (London: Zed Books, 2003).
85. This reflects a commonly held belief among those Israeli Jews that are considered pro-peace and left-wing, such as famous Israeli Jewish writer David Grossman, who has described 'accepting the right of return' as 'a dangerous move for Israel as a Jewish state, and as a political entity' (David Grossman, *Writing in the Dark: Essays on Literature and Politics*, trans. Jessica Cohen (London: Bloomsbury, 2009), 100).
86. Dentler, *Zerbrochenes Deutsch*, 276–7.
87. This narrative of redemption seems to include Anja seeing herself as – not unproblematically – contributing to 'solving' the animosity between Israeli Jews and Palestinians through her job as a children's book writer and illustrator. This stance is problematic since it reduces a colonial occupation and the dispossession and displacement of the Palestinians to misunderstandings that could be solved through dialogue.
88. Dentler, *Zerbrochenes Deutsch*, 342.
89. A recent study found that remembering and engaging with the Holocaust continues to be a key issue for German–Israeli Jewish relations, which in turn affects German–Palestinian relations (Jenny Hestermann, Roby Nathanson and Stephan Stetter, *Deutschland und Israel heute: Zwischen Verbundenheit und Entfremdung*. Gütersloh: Bertelsmann Stiftung, 2 September 2022, https://doi.org/10.11586/2022125). For an ethnographic study of how the Holocaust and the *nakba* affect the relations between Germans, Palestinians and Israeli Jews in contemporary Germany, see Atshan and Galor, *Moral Triangle*.

2

RELATIONAL MEMORIES: THE HOLOCAUST AND THE *NAKBA* IN THE BRITISH IMAGINARY

The Holocaust has become a recurrent metaphor in contemporary culture and it is often co-opted for purposes as varied as animal rights, nuclear catastrophes and exposing censorship.[1] Drawing on the Holocaust as a universal metaphor is not unproblematic, as can be seen in the case of PETA's 'Holocaust on your Plate' campaign in 2003. Their comparison between the treatment of animals in factories and Jewish people in concentration camps was widely criticised in the public sphere, for example by the Anti-Defamation League and the United States Holocaust Memorial Museum. However, some critics have defended PETA's use of these images by arguing that this comparison also exposes the fact that 'structures of domination are "interlocking"' and that 'the fates of subordinated groups are linked'.[2] They foreground the benefits of comparison in order to draw attention to the ways in which different forms of oppression and discrimination are connected, which aligns with the world studies approach to comparison that I mentioned in the introduction to this book, and which I discuss further below. For now, I would like to emphasise that these contrasting reactions align with a key issue that arises when considering the Holocaust as a universal trope, as Andreas Huyssen points out: '[O]ne must always ask whether and how the trope enhances or hinders local memory practices and struggles, or whether and how it may help and hinder at the same time.'[3] Using the Holocaust as a trope is certainly problematic, but a thoughtful comparison can contribute to drawing attention to the connections between different histories of marginalisation and suffering. This approach is at the heart of recent work in comparative memory studies, including in the works of Michael Rothberg, Maxim Silverman, and Bashir Bashir and Amos Goldberg.

One obvious problem when using a comparative approach to engage with Jewish and Palestinian suffering, especially in the European imaginary, is that the Holocaust often eclipses the *nakba*. Nur Masalha, following Ilan Pappé, has called this 'memoricide', since 'Zionist methods have not only dispossessed the Palestinians of their own land; they have also attempted to deprive Palestinians of their voice and their knowledge of their own history'.[4] In addition to these conscious attempts to erase the Palestinian *nakba* from Israeli Jewish and Palestinian history, using the Holocaust and the *nakba* in a comparative context can result in the *nakba* being, as Shira Stav observes, transformed into an 'internal event of Jewish history'.[5] Hence, the *nakba* is often only examined as part of Jewish history and as such is deemed lesser in comparison with Jewish suffering during the Holocaust.

The problems arising from such comparative models are addressed in Michael Rothberg's work on multidirectional memory, which I started discussing in the introduction to this book. While in theory Rothberg's model of multidirectional memory can be read as non-competitive and not creating a 'hierarchy of suffering',[6] in practice, the Holocaust – and the concomitant conflation between Jewishness and victimhood – is still perceived, and used, as a validation of exclusive Jewish rights to territorial sovereignty in Israel. This, in turn, often eclipses the Palestinian history of suffering and their claims to a national homeland in a European context. In a 2011 article, Michael Rothberg revisited the concept of multidirectional memory and its specific application to the context of Israel and Palestine, arguing that in order for multidirectional memory to work in a non-competitive manner, it needs to 'include a differentiated empirical history, moral solidarity with victims of diverse injustices, and an ethics of comparison that coordinates the asymmetrical claims of those victims'.[7] Rothberg emphasises the importance of contextualising the Holocaust alongside the event that it is situated in a comparative context with, and of addressing the power imbalances that shape encounters between different memories.

In many ways, this approach foreshadows the work of Bashir Bashir and Amos Goldberg, who advocate the need to move beyond a competition between different memories and narratives related to the Holocaust and the *nakba*, and the associated discourses of victimhood. These discourses of victimhood are often seen as essential for creating empathy and support for their respective nation-building projects – in the case of the Jewish people, ongoing support for Israel and in the case of the Palestinian people, support for an independent Palestinian state – while at the same time, and conversely, these discourses are intrinsically linked to ideas of power. This is why Bashir and Goldberg propose a 'new grammar' which offers 'another register of history and memory – one that honors the uniqueness of each event, its circumstances and consequences, as well as their differences, but also offers a common historical and conceptual framework within which both narratives may be addressed.'[8] While they draw attention to the benefits of using a comparative framework for discussing Jewish and Palestinian experiences of suffering, they emphasise the need to contextualise these experiences by taking into account the specific historical and political circumstances that create and shape this suffering.

Building on this work, in this chapter I use the framework of 'relational memories' – which is a comparative framework that allows the creation of links between events that might seem unconnected and/or are often depicted as such – to bring together studies on how to compare the memories of the Holocaust and the *nakba*, alongside theories in world studies, especially those that use comparison as a theoretical approach. Shu-mei Shih emphasises how comparison 'sets into motion historical relationalities between entities brought together for comparison', which in turn reveal 'workings of power'.[9] This framework, I argue, not only allows us to compare Jewish and Palestinian narratives of suffering and to take into account significant power imbalances between these experiences, but also shows how uncovering historical relations between different locations 'inevitably implicates multiply interconnected orbits of culture, politics, and economy in their dynamic interaction',[10] as Shih continues to argue.

This chapter will trace the 'multiply interconnected orbits' that manifest themselves when memories of the Holocaust and the *nakba* intersect with the memory of the British Mandate in the United Kingdom. Peter Kosminsky's TV miniseries *The Promise* (2011) and Marina Lewycka's novel *We Are All Made of Glue* (2009) use the Holocaust as a metaphor to make Palestinian experiences accessible to their British audiences. At the same time, they foreground the Palestinian history of suffering during the *nakba*, as well as, in Kosminsky's case, the discrimination against Palestinians living in Israel and the oppressive conditions that Palestinian people in the West Bank and Gaza experience due to Israel's occupation and blockade of Gaza. I have chosen Kosminsky's and Lewycka's works as case studies in this chapter because they create a comparative framework for representing the Holocaust and the *nakba* by drawing attention to the relations between these histories and how they are remembered in the United Kingdom, while linking these histories to British involvement in Palestinian and Israeli politics since the British Mandate. Together with Kosminsky's and Lewycka's juxtaposition of the British Mandate with the current situation in Israel and the Occupied Palestinian Territories, this comparative approach challenges accepted narratives of the Holocaust, the creation of the state of Israel and the *nakba* as separate events. Moreover, the two works open up a critical space to consider some of the blind spots and grey zones of much contemporary engagement with Israel and Palestine in British culture, including the conflation between the Holocaust and Jewish victimhood, and the often neglected relationship between the British colonial presence in Palestine and Israel's occupation of Palestine today.

From the British Mandate to Twenty-first-Century Gaza: Relational Memories in Peter Kosminsky's *The Promise*

British writer, filmmaker and producer Peter Kosminsky is known for not shying away from addressing complicated or sensitive political issues in his work, as can be seen in his TV drama *Warriors* (1999) about British peacekeepers in Bosnia in 1992/1993 and his 2007 serial *Britz* about the radicalisation of second-generation Muslims in Britain. Inspired by a letter he received from a British veteran who had seen *Warriors* and asked if Kosminsky could make a similar film about the British military in Palestine, *The Promise* critically engages with the British presence in the last days of the Mandate, specifically from August 1945 to May 1948.[11] In an interview, Kosminsky has described this period as follows: '[A]s the departing colonial power, [Britain] was charged with seeing both communities to independence in good order. In Palestine . . . we left chaos, political confusion, bloodshed and war.'[12] The failure of the British Mandate is a key concern in *The Promise*, but through its juxtaposition with Israel and Palestine in 2005, Kosminsky demonstrates the legacies of this 'political confusion' in the contemporary period, especially at the end of the Second Intifada. This approach subverts a general tendency in the UK, which Paul Gilroy has described above as 'the mysterious evacuation of Britain's postcolonial conflicts from national consciousness'.[13] Kosminsky, however, resists locating the British Mandate in a distant past without connection to the present situation in Israel and the Occupied Palestinian Territories, as we will see below.

In *The Promise*, bringing back 'Britain's postcolonial conflicts' is achieved by combining the perspective of Len Matthews (Christian Cooke) and his eighteen-year-old granddaughter Erin (Claire Foy), who reads about her grandfather's experiences in his diary while travelling to and spending time in Israel, the West Bank and Gaza. The gap between the past and the present – and between Britain as an imperial power and as a postcolonial nation – is not only bridged through the familial bond between the two protagonists; Kosminsky also chooses a material object, the grandfather's diary, to establish a strong connection between Len and Erin, similar to what Ina Dentler does in *Zerbrochenes Deutsch* (discussed in Chapter 1) to connect Anja with her past. However, compared to Dentler's treatment, in Kosminsky's work this leads to a much more critical assessment of the relationship between Britain's past and present responsibilities in Palestine/Israel. Kosminsky's use of the diary aligns with what Andrew Jones has observed in relation to memory and material culture: 'Objects have the power to affect us as a kind of material "echo" from the past'.[14] Apart from being a 'material echo from the past', the diary functions as a narrative tool which facilitates a 'literal' echo in the series. When Erin first reads her grandfather's diary on the plane to Israel, the audience sees Len's handwriting while hearing his voiceover, which then leads into a flashback of Len's time as a British soldier. Len sits in an army tent, writing his first diary entry about the liberation of Bergen Belsen in April 1945 before the episode turns to black and white archival footage of this historical moment.

Griselda Pollock argues that through the inclusion of archival footage of the liberation of Bergen Belsen, Kosminsky, like many others, draws on the concentration camp as a metaphor for the Jewish experience of the Holocaust:

> 'the concentration camp' (fences, barbed wire, watch towers, shaven prisoners in striped uniforms, unburied and emaciated corpses) has . . . become the iconic signifier of both general Nazi atrocity and its racialized genocide despite the fact that the sites of the two are distinct.[15]

In many ways, Kosminsky uses Bergen Belsen as a familiar trope to represent the extermination of the Jewish people in British and Western European culture, where many people have already been exposed to films and pictures of the liberation of the camp. Kosminsky has explained the decision to use archival footage rather than refilming these scenes by saying that he considered the archival footage to be more 'powerful and moving'.[16] Archival footage is often associated with making an event feel more 'real', and it is interesting to briefly consider the absence of any archival footage related to the *nakba*. One could argue that by not including any archival footage related to the Palestinian experience of displacement and suffering, even though such footage was accessed as part of the research done for the TV series,[17] Kosminsky places the Holocaust in a more prominently 'factual' position within the European imaginary. However, as we will see below, Kosminsky's choice to refilm the events of the *nakba* without the addition of any archival footage works aesthetically as it means that the retelling of Len's time in Palestine is not interrupted. At the same time, it allows Kosminsky to place key characters of the series in situations directly related to the *nakba*, which facilitates the comparative narrative work between the *nakba* and the Holocaust that is at the heart of *The Promise*.

After the archival footage of Bergen Belsen, the episode returns to Len's diary, which describes Len's time in mandatory Palestine, where the British army is in charge of preventing Jewish immigration to Palestine after World War II. Len's character, who was present both at the liberation of Bergen Belsen and is now in Palestine, is used as a physical link between these two events. When they are walking past the camps where the Jewish refugees are held, another soldier, Jackie Clough (Luke Allen-Gale), makes this connection even more explicit, when he asks, 'Haven't we seen these pictures somewhere before?'[18] This layering of images and memories can be compared to Maxim Silverman's idea of palimpsestic memory. Silverman posits this type of memory as disruptive to conventional memory politics, since he suggests that it

> does not function according to a linear trajectory of a particular ethno-cultural group and lead inexorably to the distinction (and often the competition) between different groups, it functions instead according to a complex process of interconnection, interaction, substitution, and displacement of memory traces.[19]

Kosminsky's TV series exemplifies the transformative aspect of the palimpsest, when he visualises the Palestinian displacement from their villages in 1948 through long lines of people walking with suitcases, reminiscent of Jewish deportations in Europe. In addition to visually echoing this experience, Kosminsky includes accounts of the event from a Palestinian perspective. When Erin is looking for Len's Palestinian friend Abu-Hassan Mohammed (Ali Suliman), she encounters a Palestinian man in the Israeli Jewish village Ein Hod – which used to be a Palestinian village before 1948 but is now known for being an artists' colony – who tells her that, 'When the Jews came in '48, I was five years old. They rounded us up and took us to a prison camp.'[20] The experience of being rounded up and put into a camp not only echoes the experience of Jewish people during the Nazi regime but also Jewish immigration to Mandate Palestine after World War II. Kosminsky here draws on different layers of memories to create a comparative and relational framework for understanding the situation in Palestine/Israel in the late 1940s, in this case the link between the Holocaust, the establishment of Israel, and Palestinian dispossession and displacement.

Pollock observes that Kosminsky's comparison between the Holocaust, the arrival of Jewish immigrants in Palestine and the displacement of Palestinian people in 1948, 'accuse[s] the Jewish State of attempted genocide rather than of settler colonization.'[21] However, I would argue that in *The Promise*, Kosminsky does not suggest that the Jewish state attempted to exterminate the Palestinian population, nor does he compare the Jewish people in Palestine to Nazis. Instead, through his comparison, he implicitly aligns the Jewish refugees in Europe with the Palestinian refugees created by the 1948 war and the establishment of Israel. This comparison works on two levels: on one hand, it links the Holocaust to the creation of Israel, but on the other hand, and more interestingly, it foregrounds the Palestinian people as victims of a historical event, or rather of its ramifications, which they did not take part in. If we consider Silverman's proposition that palimpsestic memory is disruptive if it does not follow the accepted linearity of a specific ethno-cultural group, then Kosminsky's juxtaposition of the Holocaust, the creation of the state of Israel and the dispossession of the Palestinian people is certainly effective in demonstrating links between events that are usually not discussed together in the mainstream media.

Moreover, this juxtaposition implicitly critiques the Holocaust and the Jewish experience of displacement for eclipsing the Palestinian suffering in 1948, which is a key issue that Michael Rothberg draws attention to. Rothberg argues that using the Holocaust as a memory in a comparative context with Palestinian experiences of suffering often leads to the question of whose suffering is more 'justified'. As a solution to this, Rothberg proposes a 'radical politics of multidirectional memory' which allows us 'not only to move beyond discourses of equation or hierarchy, but equally to displace the reductive, absolutist understanding of the Holocaust as a code for "good and evil" from the center of global memory politics.'[22] Indeed, by drawing on images of Jewish deportations – rather than images of Jewish suffering in the camps, which are usually equated with quintessential Jewish suffering – Kosminsky exemplifies how the Holocaust as 'code for "good and evil"' can be displaced, even though he still draws on tropes related to Jewishness in order to illustrate the Palestinian history of displacement and suffering.

Creating links between different histories and linking the past and the present is at the heart of Kosminsky's series. In addition to the examples already discussed, Kosminsky compares the acts of the Zionist paramilitary organisation Irgun, specifically the King David Hotel bombing on 22 July 1946, with Palestinian suicide bombings in present-day Israel. The first episode of the series finishes with Erin witnessing the explosion of a bomb in a café. In episode two, this scene is repeated, before the narrative switches to Len. The audience witnesses the events leading up to the bombing, which include Len defending Mohammed, a Palestinian tea seller who will soon become his friend, and the development of his relationship with Clara Rosenbaum (Katharina Schüttler), a Jewish woman whom he met at the city hospitality club. Throughout the series, Kosminsky often uses motifs and parallel editing to connect Len's and Erin's stories; these are evident in the scene depicting the aftermath of the King David Hotel bombing. Kosminsky employs eyeline match, with Len looking at the rubble, before the camera cuts to the next shot, which shows Erin lying in the midst of rubble. This continuity between the past and the present is so effective that the viewer briefly thinks that they are watching a woman who was a victim of the King David Hotel bombing, an effect which is emphasised through the use of similar colours. In this way, Kosminsky not only implicitly links terrorism in 1940s Palestine and in twenty-first-century Israel, but he also makes this link explicit by visually aligning the two scenes. Moreover, this connection draws attention to the similarities between the reasons underlying each group's actions: the Irgun wanted to weaken the British forces in order to establish their own homeland without British interference, whereas the Palestinian people in the contemporary period are motivated by ending the Israeli occupation of the Palestinian territories and creating a Palestinian homeland. This technique can be seen as supporting solidarity with different victims and thus suggests one way of establishing an 'ethics of comparison', to use Rothberg's term. However, I would suggest that this moment is only successful because Kosminsky does not draw on tropes associated with the Holocaust, which allows him to circumvent the power imbalance that often arises when evoking the Holocaust as a conflation with Jewish victimhood, especially in relation to Palestinian suffering.

Kosminsky is keenly aware of 'supporting solidarity with different victims' and the problem of taking sides, and doing justice to each side's claims.[23] In an interview he explained that he wanted to give a balanced account of Israeli Jewish and Palestinian concerns but he insisted that, '[B]alanced does not mean that every scene is balanced but that the series as a whole offers a balanced account.'[24] Both Erin and Len act as mediators of the events in Palestine and Israel, and their points of view and their engagement with both sides guide our sympathy and solidarity with either group. In this way, both Len and Erin can be seen as allowing the audience 'to metaphorically understand political and social life through the experiences of persons and small groups', which is a common trend in popular culture, as Toine van Teeffelen has observed.[25] Whereas the character of Len offers his thoughts on the situation in a more mature and assured way, Erin appears very naive and only has limited knowledge of the situation in Israel and the Occupied Palestinian Territories, especially at the beginning of the series. She often asks questions that are obvious to viewers with some knowledge about the history of Israel and Palestine. But this technique allows the audience to go on a journey with her and to gain access to a wide range of background information about Israel, Palestine, and their political and historical relations. This perspective is strengthened by Len's depiction of the British Mandate's failure to maintain peace and support the national aspirations of both Jewish and Palestinian people, which enables the audience to situate current events in Palestine/Israel in a historical and political context.

In addition to taking a historicised approach to representing the situation in Israel and the Occupied Palestinian Territories, Kosminsky uses Erin's quest for knowledge to encourage his audience to expand their understanding of the political context in Palestine/Israel. This quest is fuelled, and its historical parallels underlined, in quite an obvious symbolic way by the trope of the key. After the attack on the café, Erin reads about a key that Len was given for safekeeping by his Palestinian friend Mohammed. When she finds the key in an envelope in Len's diary, she decides to fulfil the promise Len made to Mohammed's son and to return the key to its rightful owner. The key is an important symbol for the Palestinian dispossession and displacement in 1948 and the hope of returning to their homes and their land, as the Israeli Palestinian Omar Habash (Haaz Sleiman) explains to Erin in *The Promise*:

> We call it the *nakba*. The Catastrophe. When the British withdrew in 1948, hundreds of thousands left their homes and went into exile for fear of the Jewish army. Many people kept their front door keys because they knew that one day they would return. Of course, they never did.[26]

Omar gives Erin, and the audience, a potted history of Palestinian dispossession and displacement by stressing the Palestinian suffering during the establishment of Israel, a fact that is often overlooked in mainstream media. Moreover, the key plays an important role in the story since finding it results in Erin's decision to stay in Israel rather than returning to the UK after the attack. The quest to return the key takes her on a journey that 'unlocks' the situation in Israel and the Occupied Palestinian Territories for her as well as for the viewer, since it is this quest that leads her to Ein Hod, Hebron and Gaza, depicting sites that play an important role in Israel's occupation of Palestine but whose histories are often not known to metropolitan viewers. Through the use of British protagonists, as well as by drawing on British history, Kosminsky actively tries to bridge the distance between audiences in the UK and the situation in the Middle East, exemplifying Levy and Sznaider's argument that, 'Strong identifications are produced only when distant events have local resonance.'[27] Hence, in *The Promise*, connecting the global with the local is important for creating sympathy for distant 'others'.

Bridging the distance between British audiences and the Middle East is further strengthened through the protagonists' personal relationships with both sides, which contribute to Kosminsky's aim of offering a balanced account, representing the concerns of both (Israeli) Jews and Palestinians. However, as Tom Sutcliffe has noted in a review of *The Promise*, Kosminsky presents the viewer with an 'impeccable imbalance, tugging us emotionally from one side to the other in a way that shows you how difficult it is to achieve any facile equilibrium'.[28] In Len's case, this 'impeccable imbalance' results from being exposed to his Palestinian friend Mohammed's views on the British Mandate, as well as those of his Jewish lover Clara, and engaging and sympathising with both sides. This divided sympathy can be seen as a challenge to the prevailing sentiments among the British officials in Mandate Palestine. These sentiments were 'anti-Jewish' and 'either pro-Arab or strictly impartial in detesting both sides', as Richard Crossman noted during a visit to Jerusalem in March 1946 as part of the 'Anglo-American Committee of Enquiry', which was sent to Palestine to examine, amongst other things, the political situation.[29] Mohammed generally views the British in a benevolent light, but nevertheless criticises Britain's role in Palestine, for example when he talks about partition and refers to the proposed new Jewish homeland as 'the other part that you [the British] are allowing them to steal'.[30] Mohammed's view is contrasted with Clara's, who at the outset of her relationship with Len seems to have a neutral view on the British presence in Palestine. However, as the series progresses, she turns out to be a member of the Irgun, and has been using Len to get information about the British forces. Hence, when Len writes his final diary entry on 10 May 1948, a few days before the British leave Palestine, he is no longer torn between the Jewish and the Palestinian sides but takes a firmly pro-Palestinian stance. This change of heart could be explained by Clara's betrayal of him but it could also be attributed to the increased attacks on the British in Palestine by the Irgun, including the killing and booby-trapping of Sergeants Frank Nash (Paul Anderson) and Hugh Robbins (Iain McKee), fictionalised versions of Clifford Martin and Mervyn Paice who were killed in a similar manner in July 1947.

The competition between different memories and different political positions is further exemplified through Erin's torn loyalties between Israeli Jews and Palestinians, which manifest themselves in her relationships with both the Israeli Jew Paul Meyer (Itay Tiran), the brother of her friend Eliza, and with his Israeli Palestinian friend, Omar Habash. If we consider Erin as representing contemporary Britain, and specifically its political relationship with the Middle East, these torn loyalties could be interpreted as representing Britain's own divided stance in the contemporary period, supporting both Israel and Palestine. Contrary to her grandfather though, both of Erin's relationships are based on friendship as well as sexual desire. Nir Cohen has argued that in *The Promise*, 'Love is never the ultimate goal... but rather a mechanism through which alliances are either being established or broken.'[31] Indeed, Erin's initial turn towards Paul can be interpreted as an attempt to establish a relationship with 'Israel' – or more precisely with the Israeli Jewish Left – which she then rejects in favour of an Israeli Palestinian perspective, by sleeping with Omar. This shifting of her loyalties towards the Palestinian side becomes increasingly obvious in the final two episodes of the series when Erin defends Palestinian pupils and women against Jewish settlers in Hebron and volunteers as a human shield in Gaza to protect a Palestinian girl. Thus, similar to her grandfather, Erin takes the Palestinian rather than the Israeli Jewish side at the end of the series.

Cohen argues that by fulfilling Len's promise to Mohammed and returning the key to his family, 'Erin clears both her grandfather's and her nation's conscience regarding the fate of the Palestinians'.[32] While this act can certainly be read as a way of 'atoning' for the legacies of the British Mandate in contemporary Israel, I would argue that – read in light of Erin's other actions in Israel and the Occupied Palestinian Territories, including acting as a human shield in Gaza – Kosminsky uses the character of Erin to expose the limitations of such an atonement: it cannot 'clear' the British conscience of its involvement in Palestinian and Israeli politics, especially in the contemporary period. This is confirmed when Erin explains her reasons for being in Gaza as, 'I suppose I'm trying to help', to which Mohammed's daughter replies, 'I don't think you are succeeding.'[33] Kosminsky advocates engagement with the British past in Palestine, and nuanced engagement with both the Israeli Jewish and the Palestinian side, as exemplified by his two protagonists. This approach aligns with Bashir and Goldberg's description of a new grammar in which the Holocaust and the *nakba* 'are considered as commensurable, and their connection proves historically, politically, and ethically instructive and productive'.[34] Kosminsky's series, while certainly foregrounding a Palestinian perspective, also gives space to explaining how the Holocaust, and implicitly the Jewish experience of being discriminated against and persecuted, can be linked to the need for an independent Jewish state without eclipsing other experiences of suffering. Thus, it models productive ways of situating (Israeli) Jewish and Palestinian narratives and histories in a comparative context.

The Holocaust, the *nakba* and Britain: Relational Metaphors in Marina Lewycka's *We Are All Made of Glue*

Award-winning author Marina Lewycka, who rose to fame with her novel *A Short History of Tractors in Ukrainian* (2005), spoke to both Israeli Jewish and Palestinian people as part of the research for her third novel *We Are All Made of Glue* (2009).[35] She said that, 'It took a lot of listening and reading and travelling to find out that matters are much more complex than I thought.'[36] Similar to Kosminsky, Lewycka uses her British protagonist as a means to make the so-called conflict in Palestine/Israel more accessible to her audience. At the outset, Lewycka's novel appears to be about personal relationships rather than political issues, as it focuses on Georgie Sinclair, who has recently broken up with her husband Rip. However, the 'political' soon intrudes in the form of an old Jewish woman named Ella Wechsler, whom Georgie meets on the street. This encounter and their subsequent meetings are not only a source of comedy but also serve as a means of accessing the history of the Holocaust, the establishment of Israel, and the dispossession and displacement of the Palestinian people during the *nakba* exemplifying Georgie's role as a mediator for these narratives, similar to the characters of Len and Erin in *The Promise*.

Many of the Holocaust stories in *We Are All Made of Glue* are familiar to readers from novels, films or history lessons, as they focus on the Jewish experience in the ghettos. Lewycka – like Kosminsky – turns to images associated with Bergen Belsen. However, her approach differs in that she does not start by invoking the concentration camp. Instead, she tells the story of the Danish Jews, who were rescued from Nazi deportations by non-Jewish people in Denmark facilitating their escape to Sweden. For Georgie, the most moving moment in this story is when she finds out that the Jewish people's neighbours looked after their houses and pets. These acts of kindness are contrasted with the atrocities perpetrated in the concentration camps, and Georgie explicitly addresses the fate that would have awaited the Danish Jews if they had not been rescued, saying that: 'I've seen the pictures of stick-like walking dead of Belsen, the heaps of corpses, the terrible pile of shoes.'[37] Lewycka draws on well-known imagery linked to the Holocaust by invoking Bergen Belsen, exemplifying how the concentration camp functions as a trope to symbolise Jewish suffering during the Holocaust. This use of Bergen Belsen, which Kosminsky also avails himself of, confirms Pollock's argument that the concentration camp has been turned into a metaphor that is now linked to a specific Jewish context, even though this is not historically accurate.

Like Kosminsky's series, Lewycka's novel creates a historical linearity between the Holocaust and the establishment of Israel. This is embodied in the character of Artem, Ella's husband, who moves to Israel after World War II. Since Artem is not present as a character in the novel, the link is established by means of tangible objects: several photographs and a series of letters, which, like the diary in Kosminsky's TV series, constitute an echo from the past and a means to bring the past into the present. One of the pictures is described as being 'only a landscape in black and white of a not very appealing hillside, barren and rocky', and carries the inscription 'Kefar Daniyyel' on the back.[38]

Susan Sontag has argued that looking at pictures 'offers, in one easy, habit-forming activity, both participation and alienation in our own lives and those of others – allowing us to participate, while confirming alienation.'[39] While seemingly providing an easy means of participating in someone else's life, looking at photographs also alienates the person looking, which is confirmed by Georgie's engagement with these pictures. She is unable to fully participate in the lives, or rather the landscape, depicted since she is not familiar with the history of Zionism. As a result, her engagement with this picture illustrates above all her alienation and distance from this history, which demonstrates what Daniel Levy and Natan Sznaider have argued in relation to engaging with distant suffering: 'The current suffering of others . . . must be integrated into a cognitive structure that is connected to the "memory" of other people's suffering.'[40] Without context of her own, Georgie is unable to interpret or understand how the establishment of Israel has affected Jewish and Palestinian people, and throughout the novel she draws on other people's memories to make sense of this history. In this case, Georgie uses the memory of Artem's first wife Naomi, who in a series of letters describes her life in Kfar Daniel in the 1950s, explaining that this place is a kibbutz. Thus, these different objects form a palimpsestic memory, which allows Georgie to piece together the story of the early state-building years of Israel and to fill in the gaps in her own knowledge.

Lewycka has explained that her starting point for writing her novel was a perplexity at how 'some Jews, who had recently come through the horrors of the

Holocaust, could behave in such a cruel and arbitrary manner towards the hapless people of Palestine'.[41] Although this statement is problematic in some ways, it draws attention to how people might perceive how (Israeli) Jewish people treated the Palestinian people in the lead-up to the creation of Israel and in the state-building years, and how much background knowledge they need in order to grasp the complexities of this situation. The establishment of a Jewish state in Palestine plays a key role in Lewycka's novel to help unpack the complexity and power dynamics of Israeli–Palestinian encounters for her readers – as does the British involvement in Mandate Palestine. The character of Mr Ali, a Palestinian handyman whom Georgie meets at the hardware store B&Q, is used to introduce this history in the novel and to highlight British amnesia about their colonial presence in Palestine. When Georgie admits that she does not know anything about the British Mandate, Mr Ali explains that, after World War II, 'the cunning British say – look, we will give them this land in Palestine. Land without people, people without land. Typical British, they give away something which doesn't belong to them.'[42] This explanation situates the British Mandate in Palestine within a long history of colonisation and redistribution of land, and criticises their involvement in Palestine, where their presence did not help to maintain peace nor to cater for the national aspirations of both peoples as they were mandated to do by the League of Nations. Moreover, it creates a strong link between British colonialism and Zionism by putting the Zionist slogan, 'A land without people for a people without land', into the mouth of the British, emphasising how the British government ignored the Palestinian presence and their aspirations to self-determination during the Mandate period and how they continue to do so in the contemporary period.

In order to remedy the absence of the Palestinian narrative in the British cultural sphere, Mr Ali shares his memories of individual suffering during the *nakba* with Georgie so that she can comprehend distant and collective suffering. This suffering, as many critics, such as Nur Masalha, have argued, has ramifications into the present:

> The *Nakba* as a continuing trauma occupies a central place in the Palestinian psyche.... It changed the lives of Palestinians at both individual and national levels drastically and irreversibly; it continues to structure Palestinians' lives and inform Palestinian culture.[43]

Georgie sees a picture in Ella's house thinking that it is a church in Greece, but Mr Ali clarifies that the picture was taken in Lydda, a town near Tel Aviv Airport, which is now called Lod.[44] The picture serves as a means of introducing the Palestinian history of dispossession and displacement in 1948. Lydda, together with the neighbouring Ramle, is a town that has gained sad notoriety in historical accounts of the establishment of Israel since its inhabitants were forcefully expelled from their homes in preparation for the creation of Israel. As Honaida Ghanim explains, this was part of 'Operation Danny', 'whereby residents were systematically expelled and prevented by armed force from returning to their villages'.[45] Mr Ali recounts his personal experience of this historical moment, describing the fear of the Palestinian people, when Jewish soldiers were driving out the population of Lydda: 'Soldiers were herding everyone out into the streets, shoving them with the barrels of their guns if they were too slow, shooting them if they resisted.'[46] These images can be aligned with images of Jewish people being rounded up during the Nazi regime. However, very early on in the novel, Mr Ali adamantly refuses the connection between (Israelis) Jews and Nazis, when he tells Georgie about the *nakba*: 'No, not like the Nazis. . . . You must not exaggerate. Israelis do not plan to exterminate all Arab people, only to drive them out of the land.'[47] Despite the emphatic disconnection between the Holocaust and the dispossession and displacement of the Palestinian people, this image still constitutes a powerful link with Jewish deportations and expulsions from their homes, a trope that Kosminsky also uses in *The Promise* to represent the Palestinian experience during this time.

However, Mr Ali implicitly references the Holocaust when recounting his own experience of the *nakba*, thus drawing on the Holocaust as a cultural metaphor in the twenty-first century. When the inhabitants of Lydda flee from their village, Mr Ali's older brother sees a woman carrying two babies. She asks him to help her by taking care of one of them, which reminds the reader of William Styron's 1979 Holocaust novel *Sophie's Choice*. Styron tells the story of a Polish Catholic woman who had to choose between her two children in Auschwitz, sending one of them to death and the other one to the children's camp. In Lewycka's novel, the baby that Mr Ali's brother chooses is Mr Ali himself, who is saved by this act of kindness, but possibly at the expense of his baby brother. This story not only evokes the non-Jewish victims of the Holocaust but can equally be read as a metaphor for the creation of the Jewish state:

by providing a refuge for one persecuted ethnic group, another ethnic group was displaced, dispossessed and still suffers from the consequences today. Thus, the interaction between Palestinian and Jewish memories results in what Silverman has described as a 'complex process of interconnection, interaction . . . and displacement of memory traces',[48] which disrupts the accepted linear trajectory from the Holocaust to the establishment of Israel – especially a linearity that does not take into account the Palestinian victims of the *nakba* and the ongoing discrimination against, and occupation of, Palestinian people and lands.

In addition to positing the Holocaust as a means of accessing the Palestinian experience of 1948, Lewycka uses two general metaphors, or parallels, to explain the relationships between Israeli Jews and Palestinians to her readers. This approach exemplifies Toine van Teeffelen's argument that metaphors play a key role in understanding reality as they 'transmit common-sense reasonings, or lay theories, from concrete and familiar domains of experience and knowledge to more abstract and less familiar domains',[49] Unsurprisingly, Lewycka chooses metaphors that are easily relatable to readers, in order to illustrate the power dynamics that govern encounters between Israeli Jews and Palestinians. The first metaphor is her protagonist's broken marriage. Georgie makes several references to the impossibility of world peace if she and her husband Rip are not even able to communicate and repair their relationship: 'Peace in the world was all very well, but no way was it going to extend to Rip and me. . . . When someone hurts you like that, what you want is revenge, not peace.'[50] Comparing Israeli Jewish and Palestinian people to a married couple suggests that there used to be a sense of mutual understanding at some point in the past, for instance during their more peaceful coexistence before the establishment of the state of Israel. However, despite its reference to a shared understanding, this depiction eschews the widely circulated idea that dialogue will solve the differences between Palestinians and Israeli Jews. Instead, it represents a more complicated situation, where one party might seek revenge due to events that happened in the past. It also references the power imbalance between Israel as an occupying power and the Palestinians living under occupation, and implicitly the Palestinians living in Israel as second-class citizens.

This imbalance is further addressed towards the end of the novel, when Ella, Ella's husband's son Chaim, Mr Ali, his nephew Ismail, and Ismail's friend Nabeel all live together in Ella's house. The living situation is presented as a metaphor for, or rather a caricature of, the history of Israel and Palestine. The Israeli Jewish character Chaim immediately asks for the Palestinian characters to be housed upstairs, underlining the idea of partition and referencing the 1947 United Nations plan for partitioning historic Palestine into a Palestinian and a Jewish state. Moreover, it addresses the physical separation between Israeli Jews living in Israel and the Palestinians living in the West Bank and Gaza since 1967. Mr Ali explicitly links this idea to the increased fragmentation of the Palestinian West Bank, especially as epitomised in the building of the separation wall since the Second Intifada: 'Next you will build a wall . . . Checkpoints on the stairs. Then you will steal some more rooms for settlements.'[51] In addition to drawing attention to the ways in which this wall partitions the West Bank and impedes daily life in Palestine, Mr Ali makes a clear link between the building of the wall, which according to the Israeli government was done for security purposes, and the fact that the wall has led to the expansion of the Jewish settlements in the West Bank and taken away land from the Palestinian people.

Unfortunately, these more critical engagements with Israel's treatment of the Palestinian people in the West Bank are undermined by the second metaphor that Lewycka uses throughout her novel: the idea of glue as a bonding agent. Glue emphasises connection, rather than difference, without taking into account the power imbalance between two people or groups, as is the case with Israeli Jews and Palestinians. Despite addressing many of the injustices that Palestinians face, such as restrictions of mobility, expropriation of their land and unlawful occupation, in the end Lewycka focuses on the commonalities between Palestinians and Israeli Jews. This is summed up by Georgie in the final pages of the novel as follows: 'I understand now that everything – whales and dolphins, Palestinians and Jews, stray cats, rainforests, mansions and mining villages – they're all interconnected, held together by some mysterious force – call it glue, if you like.'[52] Apart from suggesting that dialogue might be the solution for Israel's settler-colonial occupation of the Palestinians, this conclusion takes away the specificity of the situation in Palestine/Israel and demonstrates how Palestine and Israel and the encounters between them have been transformed into a metaphor for conflict in the twenty-first century. Indeed, some readers have interpreted the ending of the novel as Lewycka's comment on the 'human condition' and praised it for exemplifying how differences can be bridged, reading the tensions between Israeli Jews and Palestinians as a metaphor for the failure of Britain as a multicultural state.[53] This transposition highlights one of the pitfalls of juxtaposing different types of memory: the transformation of the Holocaust, and the situation in Palestine/Israel, into a metaphor for other conflicts, and the resulting danger of losing the specificity of a certain historical and political situation.

Relating Jewish and Palestinian Memories

The question remains whether the Holocaust as a metaphor 'helps or hinders' Kosminsky's and Lewycka's attempts to open up a critical space for comparatively discussing Jewish and Palestinian memories of suffering. In his 2019 book *The Implicated Subject: Beyond Perpetrators and Victims*, Michael Rothberg returns to the idea of using the Holocaust in a comparative context and concludes that

> even critical invocations of the Holocaust under the sign of equation keep in place Israel's most potent legitimating symbol: a narrative genealogy of ultimate victimization coupled with absolute innocence. The displacement called for today does not entail a removal of Holocaust memory from the public sphere, but rather a decentering of its abstract and reified form.[54]

I would argue that the Holocaust certainly helps Kosminsky and Lewycka to open up a comparative framework for different histories of marginalisation and suffering, at the same time as it contributes to decentring the Holocaust in 'its abstract and reified form'. Kosminsky achieves this by only devoting a relatively small part of his narrative to the Holocaust, and not exclusively representing the Holocaust as being conflated with the concentration camp or as a signifier for Jewish victimhood. Similarly, Lewycka establishes a framework for understanding the establishment of Israel and the resulting displacement and dispossession of the Palestinians in relation to, and indeed through, the Holocaust, which allows readers to extend the situation beyond its original historical context and to apply its 'lessons' to other situations. However, she also draws attention to the non-Jewish victims of the Holocaust, offering a broader perspective on the Nazi genocide. This is further supported by Kosminsky's and Lewycka's characters' personal accounts of the history and politics of Israel and Palestine, which contribute to offering a more nuanced view of Palestinian–Israeli Jewish relations to contemporary audiences. In this sense, their works can be seen as exemplary of 'an ethics of comparison that coordinates the asymmetrical claims of . . . victims', to use Rothberg's words.

Nevertheless, the competition of suffering is not completely resolved in either Kosminsky's or Lewycka's work. Kosminsky draws primarily on tropes associated with the Jewish experience of the Holocaust, which problematises not only his representation of the Palestinian history of dispossession and displacement, but equally confirms that the situation in Palestine/Israel can rarely be discussed without also referencing the Holocaust. This makes effective decentring, in the way proposed by Rothberg, very difficult, if not impossible. Lewycka, on the other hand, chooses an almost saccharine ending that emphasises shared humanity to reconcile different histories of suffering, which takes away the specificity of the histories. But even though these moments confirm the problems of redressing the power imbalance that arise from using the Holocaust in a comparative context, Kosminsky's and Lewycka's juxtaposition of different memories and the creation of 'relational memories' is still successful. They disrupt accepted historical and causal linearities between the Holocaust and the establishment of Israel, while foregrounding the key role that the United Kingdom has played, and continues to play, in the region.

The works discussed in the third chapter, entitled 'Libidinal Relationality: Humour, the Holocaust and Palestine/Israel in German Culture', are Theresa Bäuerlein's *Das war der gute Teil des Tages* (*That Was the Good Part of the Day*, 2008) and Markus Flohr's *Wo samstags immer Sonntag ist* (*Where Saturday Is Always Sunday*, 2011). They consider the idea of a rapprochement between Germany and Israel, and reflect on Germany's 'special' relationship with Israel and the ways in which this has precluded a productive engagement with Israel's treatment of the Palestinian people. I show that the trope of the libidinal relation between German and Israeli Jewish characters, together with the use of humour, allows Bäuerlein and Flohr to create a framework for critical engagement with the connections between Germany and Israel. However, the chapter also draws attention to the limitations of these relations through the failure of the libidinal relation between a German and an Israeli Jewish character in Flohr's book, and the inability to critically engage with Israel's occupation of Palestine in Bäuerlein's novel.

Notes

1. For an overview of some of these uses, see Arlene Stein, 'Whose Memories? Whose Victimhood? Contests for the Holocaust Frame in Recent Social Movement Discourse,' *Sociological Perspectives* 41, no. 3 (1998): 519–40, https://doi.org/10.2307/1389562.
2. Claire Jean Kim, 'Moral Extensionism or Racist Exploitation? The Use of the Holocaust and Slavery Analogies in the Animal Liberation Movement,' *New Political Science* 33, no. 3 (2011): 333, https://doi.org/10.1080/07393148.2011.592021.
3. Andreas Huyssen, *Urban Palimpsests and the Politics of Memory* (Stanford: Stanford University Press, 2003), 18.
4. Nur Masalha, *The Palestine Nakba: Decolonising History, Narrating the Subaltern, Reclaiming Memory* (London: Zed Books, 2012), 89.
5. Stav, 'Nakba and Holocaust,' 89.
6. Rothberg, *Multidirectional Memory*, 9.
7. Michael Rothberg, 'From Gaza to Warsaw: Mapping Multidirectional Memory,' *Criticism* 53, no. 4 (2011): 526, https://doi.org/10.1353/crt.2011.0032.
8. Bashir Bashir and Amos Goldberg, 'Introduction: The Holocaust and the Nakba: A New Syntax of History, Memory, and Political Thought,' in *The Holocaust and the Nakba: A New Grammar of Trauma and History*, ed. Bashir Bashir and Amos Goldberg (New York: Columbia University Press, 2018), 5.
9. Shu-mei Shih, 'Comparison as Relation,' in *Comparison: Theories, Approaches, Uses*, ed. Rita Felski and Susan Stanford Friedman (Baltimore: Johns Hopkins University Press, 2013), 79.
10. Shih, 'Theory in a Relational World,' 723.
11. Marianne Behar, 'Rencontre avec Peter Kosminsky, Réalisateur Du "Serment",' *L'Humanité*, 22 March 2011, https://www.humanite.fr/rencontre-avec-peter-kosminsky-realisateur-du-serment. All translations from French are my own unless otherwise indicated.
12. Behar, 'Rencontre avec Peter Kosminsky.'
13. Gilroy, *After Empire*, 97.
14. Andrew Jones, *Memory and Material Culture* (Cambridge: Cambridge University Press, 2007), 57.
15. Griselda Pollock, 'Introduction: A Concentrationary Imaginary?,' in *Concentrationary Imaginaries: Tracing Totalitarian Violence in Popular Culture*, ed. Griselda Pollock and Maxim Silverman (London: I. B. Tauris, 2015), 11.
16. Peter Kosminsky, 'Audio Commentary,' *The Promise*, directed by Peter Kosminsky. (London: Daybreak Pictures, 2011), DVD.

17. Kosminsky has explained that in order to research the Palestinian and the British experience during the British Mandate, they interviewed over eighty veterans who had been in Palestine at the time and accessed archival material at the Imperial War Museum, the Airborne Forces Museum at Duxford and the public record office in Kew (Peter Kosminsky, 'A Film-Maker's Eye on the Middle East,' *The Guardian*, 28 January 2011, http://www.theguardian.com/world/2011/jan/28/the-promise-peter-kosminsky-middle-east).
18. *The Promise*, Part 1, directed by Peter Kosminsky, featuring Claire Foy and Christian Cooke. Aired 6 February 2011, on Channel 4 (London: Daybreak Pictures, 2011), DVD [00:23:30–00:23:33].
19. Silverman, *Palimpsestic Memory*, 28.
20. *The Promise*, Part 2, directed by Peter Kosminsky, featuring Claire Foy and Christian Cooke. Aired 13 February 2011, on Channel 4 (London: Daybreak Pictures, 2011), DVD [01:09:40–01:09:47].
21. Pollock, 'A Concentrationary Imaginary?,' 13.
22. Rothberg, 'From Gaza to Warsaw,' 540.
23. From the outset of making the series, Kosminsky was aware that Palestine/Israel was a controversial topic that needed to be researched in depth, using first-hand testimonies from British veterans that served in Mandate Palestine, archival material, and stories from people in Palestine and Israel (Kosminsky, 'A Film-Maker's Eye on the Middle East').
24. Behar, 'Rencontre avec Peter Kosminsky.' In general, Kosminsky's series was quite well-received, although it was criticised for its depiction of Jewish characters and Israel, including by the Board of Deputies of British Jews, whose letter to Channel 4 (which aired *The Promise* in the UK) can be seen as part of this article published on the Australia/Israel & Jewish Affairs Council website (Tzvi Fleischer, 'The Promise,' *Australia/Israel & Jewish Affairs Council*, 29 November 2011, https://aijac.org.au/update/the-promise). The letter used to be available on the website of the Board of Deputies of British Jews but has been removed since it was first published on 3 March 2011.
25. Toine van Teeffelen, 'Racism and Metaphor: The Palestinian-Israeli Conflict in Popular Culture,' *Discourse and Society* 5, no. 38 (1994): 390, www.jstor.org/stable/42887929.
26. *The Promise*, Part 4. Directed by Peter Kosminsky, featuring Claire Foy and Christian Cooke. Aired 27 February 2011, on Channel 4 (London: Daybreak Pictures, 2011), DVD [00:37:12–00:37:33].
27. Levy and Sznaider, *The Holocaust and Memory in the Global Age*, 38.

28. Tom Sutcliffe, 'The Weekend's TV: *The Promise*, Sun, Channel 4 Faulks on Fiction, Sat, BBC 2,' *The Independent*, 7 February 2011, http://www.independent.co.uk/arts-entertainment/tv/reviews/the-weekends-tv-the-promise-sun-channel-4brfaulks-on-fiction-sat-bbc2-2206220.html.
29. Richard Crossman, *Palestine Mission: A Personal Record* (New York: Harper & Brothers Publishing, 1947), 141.
30. *The Promise*, Part 4 [00:23:20–00:23:25].
31. Nir Cohen, 'Love and Surveillance: Politicized Romance in Peter Kosminsky's *The Promise*,' *Jewish Film & New Media* 1, no. 1 (2013): 47, https://www.jstor.org/stable/10.13110/jewifilmnewmedi.1.1.0044.
32. Cohen, 'Love and Surveillance,' 47.
33. *The Promise*, Part 4 [01:21:25–01:21:33].
34. Bashir and Goldberg, 'Holocaust and the Nakba,' 3.
35. Nicky Pellegrino, 'The Best of Both Worlds,' *The New Zealand Herald*, 2 August 2009, http://www.nzherald.co.nz/entertainment/news/article.cfm?c_id=1501119&objectid=10587866. Lewycka met Palestinian writer Raja Shehadeh at the 2008 Orwell Prize ceremony in London, for which her second novel *Two Caravans* and Shehadeh's travelogue *Palestinian Walks* were both shortlisted. Their initial meeting led to an enduring friendship and two walks, one near Ramallah in July 2008 and one on Kinder Scout in the Peak District in September 2008 (Marina Lewycka, Raja Shehadeh and Jean Seaton, 'Two Walks: Palestine and the Peak District. A Conversation between Raja Shehadeh and Marina Lewycka, September 2008,' *The Political Quarterly* 80, no. 1 (2009): 4–16, https://doi.org/10.1111/j.1467-923X.2009.01966.x).
36. Lewycka, Shehadeh and Seaton, 'Two Walks,' 9.
37. Marina Lewycka, *We Are All Made of Glue* (London: Penguin, 2010), 415.
38. Lewycka, *We Are All Made of Glue*, 216. In this chapter, I will follow the more common English spelling of 'Kfar Daniel'.
39. Susan Sontag, *On Photography* (London: Penguin, 1979), 167.
40. Levy and Sznaider, *The Holocaust and Memory in the Global Age*, 28–9.
41. Lewycka, Shehadeh and Seaton, 'Two Walks,' 9.
42. Lewycka, *We Are all Made of Glue*, 256.
43. Masalha, *The Palestine Nakba*, 12. See also Lila Abu-Lughod and Ahmad H. Sa'di, 'Introduction: The Claims of Memory,' in *Nakba: Palestine, 1948, and the Claims of Memory*, ed. Ahmad H. Sa'di and Abu-Lughod Lila (New York: Columbia University Press, 2007), 1–24.
44. It is worth noting that the locations Lewycka chooses for Naomi's kibbutz, Kfar Daniel, and Mr Ali's hometown, Lydda, are only four kilometres apart.

45. Honaida Ghanim, 'When Yaffa Met (J)Yaffa: Intersections Between the Holocaust and the Nakba in the Shadow of Zionism,' in Bashir and Goldberg, *New Grammar of Trauma and History*, 107.
46. Lewycka, *We Are All Made of Glue*, 355.
47. Lewycka, *We Are All Made of Glue*, 257.
48. Silverman, *Palimpsestic Memory*, 28.
49. Van Teeffelen, 'Racism and Metaphor,' 384.
50. Lewycka, *We Are All Made of Glue*, 345.
51. Lewycka, *We Are All Made of Glue*, 354.
52. Lewycka, *We Are All Made of Glue*, 416.
53. See, for example, the following reviews on Amazon UK: Alexical, 'A superb, warm, touching, clever novel,' Amazon UK, 12 September 2012, https://www.amazon.co.uk/gp/customer-reviews/RO5T25JCB9Q7D; Ms Sally Kirkman, 'We Are All Made of Glue,' Amazon UK, 11 May 2012, https://www.amazon.co.uk/gp/customer-reviews/R2QGQ505H2S8BU; and Veronica Guy, 'The Glue that bonds Human Relationships,' Amazon UK, 31 July 2010, https://www.amazon.co.uk/gp/customer-reviews/R25G4QCCPWRNB1.
54. Michael Rothberg, *The Implicated Subject: Beyond Victims and Perpetrators* (Stanford: Stanford University Press, 2019), 139.

3

LIBIDINAL RELATIONALITY: HUMOUR, THE HOLOCAUST AND PALESTINE/ISRAEL IN GERMAN CULTURE

Dark humour permeates Israeli Jewish author Etgar Keret's writing. Israeli Palestinian Sayed Kashua's sitcom *'Avodah 'Aravit* (*Arab Labour*) humorously engages with the life of Palestinians in Israel. Palestinian writer Suad Amiry sardonically and ironically tells of her dog getting a coveted Jerusalem passport, a privilege that she herself is being denied in *Sharon and My Mother-in-Law: Ramallah Diaries*. As these examples show, humour is becoming an increasingly important tool in contemporary Palestinian and Israeli culture. However, one of the crucial issues in relation to using humour is how it delineates 'insiders' and 'outsiders', and as Chrisoula Lionis argues, '[t]his line demarcates a point of difference contingent on the appreciation of cultural references and signifiers that are employed to elicit laughter.'[1] While Lionis is referring to the position of the audience, and its potential exclusion on the basis of not understanding Palestinian cultural signifiers, in this chapter I examine how the idea of a delineation between outsiders and insiders, others and selves, is reflected in the use of humour by outsiders travelling to Israel and Palestine.

The works discussed in this chapter, both by German journalists and writers – Theresa Bäuerlein's *Das war der gute Teil des Tages* (*That Was the Good Part of the Day*, 2008) and Markus Flohr's *Wo samstags immer Sonntag ist* (*Where Saturday Is Always Sunday*, 2011) – use humour to encounter the other, both as characters and in the form of the political situation, which contributes to making this other more accessible to audiences at home. Arthur Asa Berger has noted that using humour in relation to political figures 'brings [them] close' and 'familiarizes [them] and, in doing so, enables people to judge them more realistically'.[2] While Bäuerlein's and Flohr's books do not necessarily deal with political figures, they do engage with a very politicised issue: Israel's occupation of the Palestinian Territories and, in Flohr's case, also Israel's treatment of Mizrahi Jews – Jews from Arab-speaking countries. Moreover, as Lawrence E. Mintz observes, '[h]umor is a way of processing and appreciating fundamental incongruities and conflicts, often ones with the gravest implications, dressing them in such a way that they seem less threatening, more acceptable.'[3] While Mintz and Berger emphasise the importance of humour in creating a sense of closeness that is linked to creating familiarity, John Morreall suggests that humour provides us with 'distance and perspective', and that this 'distance from the practical side of any situation' enables us to be 'free from being dominated by that situation'.[4] At first glance, these positions might seem contradictory but bringing the unfamiliar close is often necessary for achieving a critical distance from it. The same applies to political situations and, thus, bringing Israel and Palestine into the realm of the familiar not only makes it more relatable for distant audiences but equally opens up a space for critical judgement – a function that has often been associated with humour but interestingly also with travel writing as a mode for engaging with others.[5] Hence, humour becomes a self-reflexive tool for Bäuerlein and Flohr to examine Germany's 'special' relationship with Israel and the ways in which this has precluded productive engagement with Israel's treatment of the Palestinian people.

While humour as a tool for engaging with Israel and Palestine is not unusual, and indeed there are other examples of travelogues that use this mode,[6] Bäuerlein's and Flohr's works were chosen as case studies for this chapter because they combine the use of humour with the trope of the romance across the divide, to establish a critical framework for examining the relations between Germany and Israel. In discussing the romance-across-the-divide trope in the context of Northern Ireland, Joe Cleary has argued that it allows authors and their audiences 'to imagine some kind of reconciliation between two conflicting communities'.[7] In Bäuerlein's and Flohr's works, libidinal relationships are used to metonymically comment on the relationship between Germany and Israel, including by pre-empting Fabian Wolff's idea of Germany's 'unconditional love' for Israel as a way to overcome Germany's guilt for the Holocaust, which I discussed in the introduction to this book and in Chapter 1. Olaf Glöckner and

Julius H. Schoeps have examined the relationship between Germany and Israel in a similar light, albeit arguing that, '[I]t is not a "love relationship", rather something like love from a distance, to follow Max Brod, who decades ago coined the term "distanced love" to describe the German-Jewish relationship.'[8]

This idea of love from a distance, or even 'distanced love', suggests that there cannot be a rapprochement between the two countries. In Bäuerlein's case, the relationship between her German protagonist Lena and the Israeli Jewish character Tom is successful, thus confirming that a rapprochement is possible, while Flohr's account gives a less optimistic outlook on this possibility through the failure of his main character Markus's relationship with Noa, an Israeli Jewish woman.[9] These relationships can also be read in light of how desire and libidinal relationships function in Orientalist discourse, where the desire for the Orient is contrasted with the Orientalist's desire for knowledge and mastery, which 'produces the effects of splitting and slippage and prompts a latent practice of decentering both', as Ali Behdad has argued.[10] Hence, by depicting a libidinal relationship between Israel and Germany, Bäuerlein's and Flohr's works decentre both, enabling them to critically engage with how Germany's Nazi past, and particularly its sense of guilt and responsibility, shapes and constrains German engagement with both Israel and Palestine in the twenty-first century and especially after the Second Intifada.

Of course, each writer's political viewpoint significantly shapes their encounters with these highly politicised spaces and concomitantly influences both how they mediate events in the Middle East to their audiences and the type of humour they employ. Both writers' political positions can be situated on the left. Bäuerlein does not express her political position overtly in her text, partly due to the fact that she has fictionalised her own experience of living in Israel. However, based on her interviews and her non-fictional writing, she can be situated on the left, but not on what would typically be considered the pro-Palestinian side of the German Left. Flohr writes for left-wing newspapers and magazines such as *Der Spiegel* and *Die Zeit*. In an interview, he has explained that he distances himself from the Far Left in Germany, which is very critical of Israel:

> Most people on the left . . . are against Israel, but I don't feel this way. One should at least get an idea of one's own position in relation to this country. Going there [Israel] was certainly one of the best decisions of my life![11]

Flohr is intent on taking a balanced approach, reflecting what Peter Ullrich has identified as a common trend among the contemporary Left in Germany, as people do not identify clearly with either Palestinians or Israeli Jews.[12]

As such, the writers discussed in this chapter can be seen as exemplifying what Carl Thompson has observed in relation to travel writing, which is that it not only reflects the author's background but that it 'reveals something of the culture from which that writer emerged, and/or the culture for which their text is intended.'[13] I consider to what extent humour reveals 'something of the culture' from which the authors emerge, including how Germany's Holocaust memory has shaped its engagement with Palestine and Israel on a political and cultural level in the lead-up to and after the Second Intifada. But I also suggest that the use of humour facilitates critical engagement with German culture, including its engagement with the Holocaust, and how the Holocaust prevents Germany from criticising the ways in which Israel treats Palestinians in Israel and the Occupied Palestinian Territories. In this context, it is important to consider what Michael Mulkay has defined as the 'paradox of humour':

> [A]lthough humour appears to be a radical alternative to serious discourse in the sense that it is socially separated from the serious mode and is organized in terms of contrary discursive practices, it seems in practice overwhelmingly to support and reaffirm the established patterns of orderly, serious conduct.[14]

While humour is often seen as offering 'radical alternatives' to serious – and, I would add, mainstream – discourses, it can nevertheless support conservative values. This is also a characteristic of travel writing as a genre, a genre that, as Debbie Lisle convincingly argues, is typically perceived as 'encourag[ing] a particularly conservative political outlook that extends to its vision of global politics'.[15] This chapter asks to what extent libidinal relationality and humour create a framework for critical engagement with the connections between Germany and Israel in the twenty-first century, but also, especially in Flohr's work, how this can lead to self-reflexive engagement with the Holocaust and a German sense of guilt that leaves space for depicting and discussing Palestinian perspectives and narratives.

Humour and the Holocaust in Germany and Israel: Theresa Bäuerlein's *Das war der gute Teil des Tages*

Theresa Bäuerlein, a German journalist and author known for her writing on sex and ethics, was inspired to write her first novel *Das war der gute Teil des Tages (That Was the Good Part of the Day*, 2008) during her travels to Israel in 2000. Bäuerlein was born in 1980 and, like her protagonist Lena, she worked as a volunteer in a home for autistic people in Israel. In 2008 she moved to Tel Aviv, after meeting her Israeli Jewish boyfriend Tom in Guatemala in 2006. By this time she had already started writing her novel, and she had named her protagonist's main love interest Tom. Her semi-autobiographical work, which has been adapted into a film entitled *Hannas Reise* (*Hanna's Journey*, 2013), follows her protagonist Lena who falls in love with Tom, who works at the Home for Autistic Children that she volunteers at, and they move to Munich together at the end of the novel. A key aspect of Bäuerlein's novel is examining how Lena comes to terms with the 'guilt complex' that Bäuerlein experienced while living in Israel.[16] As such, Lena not only stands in for Bäuerlein herself but also for the German reader, and explains and mediates life in Israel for German audiences.

Bäuerlein's novel takes place in the final months before the start of the Second Intifada, a period which was seen by many Israeli Jews as leading towards peace, especially in the wake of the 1993 Oslo Peace Accords. Palestinians, on the other hand, were increasingly experiencing discontent and frustration during this time as the promises made as part of these accords were not upheld, and their everyday lives, especially in the Occupied Territories, became more and more restricted. Bäuerlein's protagonist Lena lives in Tel Aviv, which even today is commonly seen as being removed from Israel's occupation of the Palestinian Territories. As Bäuerlein notes, Tel Aviv is a 'cheerful bubble', which makes it easy to forget about larger issues in Israel and Palestine.[17] This idea of Lena living in a 'cheerful bubble' is emphasised early on in the book, when Tom tells her that, 'You only see one half because you happen to be a tourist, who deals with privileged, liberal people from Tel Aviv.'[18] Lena is categorised as the much-despised 'tourist', who is considered to be diametrically opposed to the traveller and often wrongly accused as one who does not want in-depth engagement with the place they are visiting and the people living there. This approach is contradicted, or at least complicated, by John Urry and Jonas Larsen's concept of the tourist gaze. Although in many ways they are critical of the position of the tourist, Urry and Larsen see the tourist gaze as enabling active engagement with the tourist's environment: '[G]azing is not merely seeing, but involves cognitive work of interpreting, evaluating, drawing comparisons and making mental connections between signs and their referents.'[19] Bäuerlein's protagonist is an interesting case in relation to the distinction between seeing and gazing, and ways of engaging with the unfamiliar. Lena can certainly be considered as a visitor and a tourist, but she also lives in Tel Aviv, approximating on a small scale some of the experiences of everyday life in Israel. She combines her own outsider point of view with that of the 'native informant' through her relationship with an Israeli Jewish character.[20] In addition, she often moves between seeing and gazing, or rather from seeing to gazing, asking questions to clarify or subvert preconceptions that a German reader might have in relation to the situation in Israel, and thus modelling the cognitive work that Urry and Larsen identify.

This cognitive work is supported by humour, which is significant in Bäuerlein's book as a formal strategy, including as a relief mechanism and as a social corrective, as well as constituting a thematic concern as Bäuerlein focuses on the relationship between humour and the Holocaust in both Germany and Israel. For example, humour is used to address prevalent stereotypes about life in Israel, such as the issue of terrorism. Early on in the novel, Lena describes her feelings of unease while walking through Tel Aviv: 'It is one thing to know that Israel is dangerous, and another, to stand at a crossroads, where people have actually blown themselves up.'[21] She then uses humour as a relief mechanism, and as a social corrective, when she observes: 'There are certainly studies that show that statistically, it is more dangerous to use a revolving door in Stockholm than to stand around on the market in Tel Aviv.'[22]

Debbie Lisle notes that the travel writer's use of humour supports a shift in the subject position, which is opened up as a result of writers 'laugh[ing] at themselves as they laugh at others'.[23] This opening up of the subject position results in an opening up of the position of the reader. While the reader is laughing at Lena and her fear of terrorists, they are able to critically engage with their own beliefs, thus aligning with Edward Said's observation that the Orient and the Occident are constantly transformed through encounters with each other.²⁴ This effect of humour also emerges in Flohr's text, as we will see below. In addition, the use of Stockholm – a location that is not only geographically but, in many ways, culturally closer to Germany than Tel Aviv – as a point of comparison exemplifies how the subject of humour needs to be brought close in order to allow us to 'see our customs, which we often take for granted as a natural way to do things, as just one possible way of doing things'.²⁵

However, humour not only functions as a critical mode but is equally used on a thematic level to consider the relationship of the third generation of Germans with the Holocaust, a generation which – as previously discussed – continues to be preoccupied with how it should position itself in relation to the legacy of the Holocaust and which asks to what extent the Holocaust can be situated in a comparative context. This concern similarly shapes Germany's engagement with Israel, exemplifying Thompson's idea that the travelogue not only reflects the culture and country the traveller visits but also their own. One of the key questions that Bäuerlein's book addresses is whether one can laugh at the Holocaust and, if yes, who is entitled to do so. Laughing at the Holocaust is closely linked to the idea of a 'normal' – or rather normalised – engagement with the Holocaust. The late Israeli Jewish writer Amos Oz was adamant that 'normal relations between Germany and Israel are not possible and not appropriate' as such relations have been ambivalent for more than 200 years.²⁶ While Oz conceded that contemporary Germans cannot be blamed for the crimes of the Nazis, he emphasised that they still have to take responsibility: 'responsibility towards themselves, responsibility towards its collective memory or its collective forgetting, which is possibly not less than the responsibility towards the victims of Nazi Germany.'²⁷ Although this outlook on German–Israeli Jewish relationships is quite pessimistic, Oz addresses a key problem that Germany has had to grapple with in the post–World War II period, and which I started to unpack in Chapter 1, in relation to second-generation German authors and directors: how to define a twenty-first-century German identity in relation to the Holocaust.

As discussed in the introduction to this book, Caroline Pearce suggests that in the contemporary period, German engagement with the Nazi past has been shaped by 'a dialectic of normality', encompassing the tension between a need for remembering the Holocaust and a desire to become a 'normal' nation.²⁸ In Bäuerlein's novel, this 'dialectic of normality' manifests itself in Tom's and Lena's respective positions on the use of humour to engage with the Holocaust but equally in the relationship between their respective countries. When Lena takes the morning after pill because they had unprotected sex, Tom jokes: 'You are German and you take these pills . . . maybe you are exterminating Jewish genes.'[29] This crass comparison between contraception and the Nazi murder of the Jewish people during the Holocaust is an example of what Nicolas Holm calls 'provocative humour', which 'does not shy away from confrontation' but instead 'actively seeks it and foregrounds its own lack of respect'.[30] Tom's humour is obviously intended to provoke Lena and to confront her with her Holocaust guilt, while encouraging her to overcome cultural taboos and to take a more critical stance towards her country's engagement with the Holocaust. Nevertheless, Lena condemns this humour as 'abnormal' and potentially disgusting, confirming that she does not think that the Holocaust should be joked about and that she is weary of her identity being conflated with Nazism.[31]

This exchange demonstrates Rod Martin's argument that humour is able to 'convey critical or disparaging messages that might not be well received if communicated in a more serious manner'.[32] Although Tom's message is certainly not well received, I want to suggest that his discussion with Lena, and particularly her reaction to his joke about the Holocaust, is symptomatic of a wider issue in German culture, which is emphasised through its comparison with the Israeli context. In Israel, jokes about the Holocaust are more common, and since the 1990s, TV shows have started to engage with this topic through the use of humour and, specifically, satire.[33] Liat Steir-Livny argues that these humorous engagements 'do not diminish the Holocaust but rather critique the politicization of Holocaust memory in Israel', thus highlighting the subversive potential of humour.[34] However, in Germany, as Bäuerlein notes, 'this type of joke is impossible. If anyone made a funny remark about the Holocaust, people would be appalled, irritated or dutifully shocked – no one would laugh.'[35] This idea that the Holocaust should not be joked about shows that the Nazi past has not been normalised yet, confirming Pearce's observation that the need to remember the Holocaust complicates the desire for normality.

There has been a recent surge in humorous engagements with this period of German history, as evidenced by the number of satirical depictions of the figure of Hitler[36] – but, of course, laughing at Hitler is not the same as laughing at the Holocaust. Joking about the Nazis is certainly not a new phenomenon in Germany, but the rise in satire shows the emergence of a potential avenue for critical engagement with the German past through humour. Gavriel D. Rosenfeld notes that this trend, which emerged in the 1990s, 'reveals that Germans have begun to abandon their previous moralistic attitudes in favor of a more normalized perspective typical of their Anglo-American neighbors',[37] positing humour as a key mode for achieving a more 'normalised' engagement with the past and potentially as a way to address the 'dialectics of normality'.

Lena, however, exemplifies the fact that even the third generation of Germans is still experiencing Holocaust guilt and that the Nazi past has not been fully 'normalised' yet. Her relationship with Tom, whom she is dating after he asked her to marry him to obtain a visa to go to Germany, mirrors on a micro level what is happening on a macro level between Germany and Israel in the contemporary period. This aligns with what Doris Sommer has argued in the context of nineteenth-century Latin American novels, which is that these texts use the 'romance-across-the-divide' trope to reflect a desire between different nations for 'reconciliations and amalgamations of national constituencies'.[38] However, while on Lena's part there is certainly a desire for reconciliation, Tom tells Lena more than once that she has only agreed to marry him due to her Holocaust guilt:

> You thought you would marry a Jewish guy . . . and as a reward, all the people that you gassed and transformed into soap will blow kisses at you from heaven. Then only everyone else is evil but you are no longer evil.[39]

Again, this is quite a crass engagement with the Holocaust, but it brings up important concerns regarding reparation and redemption and the extent to which Germany can atone for what happened to the Jewish people during the Nazi regime. Moreover, it constitutes a challenge to the possibility of transcending Holocaust guilt through unconditional love for Israel. This joke is meant to provoke Lena and thus can be read as Tom's attempt to encourage her to engage critically with her Holocaust guilt and the role of the Holocaust for third-generation Germans more generally – an engagement which is closer to the self-reflexiveness that Eyal Zandberg has attributed to the third generation in Israel. Zandberg defines this generation culturally and emphasises that 'their works are a reaction to the products and concepts of the two generations preceding them'.[40]

While Bäuerlein herself says that she lost her guilt complex while she lived in Israel, as she understood that it was not about feeling responsible for what happened but about preventing it from happening again, by the end of the novel her protagonist Lena has not overcome her feelings of guilt in the same way.[41] Interestingly though, Bäuerlein chooses to end the novel with Lena and Tom living in Munich and Lena revealing that she is expecting their child, literally confirming the desire for 'amalgamation' identified by Sommer, but also suggesting that there is a possibility for reconciliation between Germany and Israel, albeit at the expense of the Palestinian people.

Throughout the novel, Lena's focus on the Holocaust, and Germany's responsibility for it, makes it hard to offer a critical account of Israel's treatment of the Palestinian people. Bäuerlein's narrator does not encounter nor engage with any Palestinians, apart from seeing a group of Palestinian schoolchildren in the distance. If Palestinians are referred to, either by Lena or by Tom, it is often in more than questionable terms, including as 'terrorists', 'lunatics' and implicitly in descriptions about suicide bombings.[42] These descriptions confirm one of the two types of Palestinians that emerged in the Israeli Jewish mind after 1967. This stereotype, as Edward Said has noted, is the 'intransigent, rebellious type of fellow, the so-called terrorist, the wicked enemy of Israel', who is opposed to the 'good Arab, the reasonable man'.[43] Bäuerlein's depiction of Palestinians foreshadows Israeli Jewish perceptions of Palestinians during the Second Intifada, when, as Tanya Reinhart has noted, 'Israel . . . describes its handling of the Palestinian uprising as a war of defense: The Palestinians are terrorists – they are violent, non-compromising, fanatical people who reject Israel's generous peace offers.'[44] This depiction of Palestinians as terrorists denigrates their claims for liberation and statehood at the same time as it contributes to justifying Israel's security discourse and its occupation of the Palestinian Territories.

These stereotypical depictions, alongside the absence of any Palestinian voices in Bäuerlein's novel, can be situated within a longer history of representing otherness, especially in colonial travel writing. David Spurr has identified this as the 'rhetorical strategy of negation', 'by which Western writing conceives of the Other as absence, emptiness, nothingness, or death', which in many ways echoes early Zionist discourse and its depiction of the Palestinians.[45] Spurr goes on to explain that this 'negation serves to reject the ambiguous object for which language and experience provide no framework of interpretation', which suggests that Palestine and the Palestinians are an 'ambiguous' object which is outside of language.[46] This absence of the Palestinians, and what could almost be construed as an inability to bring them into the narrative through language, can be linked to a West German tradition of writing about Israel, especially in the 1950s and 1960s, where 'Palestinians were only noted as a backdrop', aligning their representation with depictions of the Orient as backward and unchanging.[47] However, in Bäuerlein's case, her inability to engage with Palestinians is strongly linked to the presence of the Holocaust in Germany. In her novel, she is mainly preoccupied with how the third generation of Germans should engage with the Holocaust and whether the Holocaust can be encountered with humour, which she concludes is possible in Israel but not in Germany. This in turn suggests that in Bäuerlein's view the Nazi past has not been normalised yet, preventing a normalised engagement with Israel. Such normalised engagement includes a critical assessment of Israel's treatment of the Palestinians, whose absence can be read in light of the idea of Palestine being a 'thorn' in Germany's memory politics – an idea discussed in the introduction to this book – as Palestine complicates Germany's unconditional support for Israel as a way to atone for the Nazi past.

Jokes and German Responsibility in Markus Flohr's *Wo samstags immer Sonntag ist*

Markus Flohr's travelogue *Wo samstags immer Sonntag ist* (*Where Saturday Is Always Sunday*, 2011) addresses similar concerns to Bäuerlein's text, including how to remember the Holocaust in the contemporary period and the ways in which the protagonist's German identity shapes his encounters with Israeli Jews and Palestinians. Flohr, who like Bäuerlein was born in 1980, studied history in Jerusalem in 2008–2009 and now works as a journalist and author. He first published his reflections on his time in Israel and the Occupied Palestinian Territories as a series of diary entries for the German left-wing magazine *Der Spiegel*'s online portal between January and October 2009. The diary entries – like the travelogue that they were adapted for, which won the Swiss

Hirzen Book Prize for first books in 2011 – describe Flohr's daily life in Jerusalem and his travels around Israel and the Occupied Palestinian Territories after the Second Intifada. In general, Flohr offers light-hearted accounts of life in Israel and humorous appraisals of customs and people, an approach which is already implied in the title of his book, 'Where Saturday Is Always Sunday'. This strategy can be aligned with humour's function of revealing shared cultural values and overcoming differences, a function attributed to travel writing by Debbie Lisle,[48] thus bringing both Israel and Palestine into the realm of the familiar for German audiences. Flohr himself has said that, '[H]umour is the best and the most humane way to deal with reality and problems',[49] which aligns with theories about humour as a relief mechanism.

In Flohr's text, Markus – like Bäuerlein's narrator Lena – not only uses humour as a relief mechanism but equally as a social corrective to engage with stereotypes about Israel and Palestine, including the dangers of travelling in both countries. While waiting for someone to give him a lift back to Jerusalem from the Negev, where Markus attended a music festival, he goes behind a tree to pee but sees a scorpion and jumps out into the street in front of a car. He muses that, 'I narrowly escaped being hit by a Hamas rocket, having sex with Lior, having a sun stroke and being bitten by a scorpion. But now I'm being run over by a grey Peugeot.'[50] His dry summary of the events of the music festival suggests that it is more likely for him to get hit by a car than by a rocket, which allows Markus to laugh at himself and to rationalise his fear of the latter. This is another example of how narrators open up their subject position in order to encourage their audiences to critically engage with their own perceptions.

This technique is recurring throughout Flohr's account, especially in relation to the likelihood of Palestinian attacks. When Markus is on his way to the Oktoberfest in Taybeh, a village in the West Bank famous for its beer, the bus suddenly drives off-road. Markus is worried and resigns himself to the fact that: 'That was it. What a shame! Kidnapped in the West Bank on the way to the Oktoberfest. A shot in the head instead of a Taybeh beer.'[51] Juxtaposing potentially life-threatening situations – being kidnapped and shot in the head – with mundane events – drinking beer – is so over the top that it enhances the humour of the situation. On the other hand, however, it draws attention to the daily experiences of many Palestinians in the West Bank and Gaza, who might be doing a very ordinary task one moment and then being confronted with the Israeli military and a potentially dangerous situation the next – illustrating to Flohr's audience the absurdity of everyday life in the Occupied Palestinian Territories.

Interestingly, Flohr has observed that especially young Israeli Jews use humour to try to 'master the absurdity of the country they live in',[52] but in his book, he shows that Palestinians do the same. Unlike Bäuerlein, Flohr gives Palestinians a voice in his travelogue. One of the Palestinians that Markus talks to is Nassim, who lives close to the Israeli Jewish settlement of Neve Daniel, and who has not left the West Bank since 2002. He tells Markus and his German friend Friedrich about a meeting with a woman that a friend had arranged for him at the Bethlehem checkpoint. In spite of the odds, they find an Israeli soldier who allows them to meet in an interrogation room. While this sets up the expectation of a happy ending, the episode culminates in Nassim running away when he sees the woman. He explains his action through the fact that the woman had blue eyes and 'whoever is missing colour in their eyes is also missing it in their soul'.[53] This is quite a funny moment. but equally one of empowerment as it subverts the checkpoint as a place of fear and humiliation – at least for Nassim – and shows how Palestinians take charge of their own representation and defy stereotypes about themselves as abject victims. It aligns with the idea of humour as having an 'emancipatory capacity', as noted by Lionis in the context of Palestinian culture, where 'through laughter, the marginality faced by oppressed groups is given a new passage for expression'.[54]

The humour in this scene is developed further later on in the book when Friedrich says to Markus, after they do a tour of Hebron with a rabbi, 'Nassim would say that the rabbi has pretty blue eyes',[55] using Nassim's joke as a shorthand for expressing his opinion about the tour. These examples align with what Lionis has argued in relation to the use of humour in Palestinian art and film, which is that it 'creates a shared social world that encourages the international community to understand the scale of political absurdity, violence and trauma that reigns in Palestine/Israel.'[56] While Flohr's audience is certainly not able to grasp the full extent of the absurdity of everyday Palestinian life under occupation, sharing this joke encourages them to rethink their perceptions of the situation in the Middle East, including the representation of Palestinians and Palestinian agency.

However, there is also a different type of humour at work in Flohr's book, which takes the form of jokes, and especially jokes about Markus's Germanness. These jokes fulfil two critical functions. On one hand, they allow the Israeli Jews that Markus encounters to critically engage with the Holocaust and Germany's role in this historical event, in the way that Bäuerlein's character Tom does. But on the other hand, they enable Markus, and his German audiences, to reassess their own relationship with the Holocaust and Israel. In his encounters with Israeli Jews and Palestinians, Markus's German identity and Germany's Nazi past play a key role. For the Palestinian people that he meets, his Germanness has positive connotations, but Israeli Jewish perceptions are quite different. Markus's friend Friedrich sums these up as follows: 'Every German passport reminds the person at the immigration desk of Auschwitz',[57] which conflates contemporary German identity with the crimes of Nazi Germany. This association crystallises when Markus and his Israeli Jewish flatmate Simson have an accident with Simson's scooter because Markus put his arms abruptly around Simson. Simson gets very angry and starts shouting: '*Ma se? Ma atah osseh? Atah meschuggah? Eise Germani! Eise Nazi*! You want to kill me? You want to finish the Holocaust?'[58] While Simson asks in Hebrew, 'What is this? What are you doing? Are you crazy?' he immediately links this action to Markus's Germanness and Germany's Nazi past, and then he asks Markus in English whether he wants to finish the Holocaust. Like in Bäuerlein's text, there is a sense that Germans cannot be trusted and that they are still intent on killing Jewish people and finishing what Hitler started.

But Israeli Jews also make jokes about the Holocaust and its aftermath, which Markus, like Lena, finds disconcerting as it would not be possible in Germany, at least not for someone who is not Jewish. Throughout the book, Markus does not make any jokes about the Holocaust, but he is often the subject of jokes related to his identity. A running joke is that Markus is taken for a Jew because he has a 'Jewish' nose. This happens again when Markus meets an Orthodox Jew in Mea Shearim. Markus immediately says, 'Please don't say anything about my nose.'[59] In an interview, Flohr has argued that, '[S]tereotypes often lose some of their power if people whom they are used against make a joke about them.'[60] On one hand, making jokes about Markus's 'Jewish' nose is a way for Israeli Jews to reclaim and subvert this stereotype about themselves. But in this scene, Markus is trying to reclaim the joke – albeit unsuccessfully, as the unnamed Orthodox

Jew replies: 'Ah. No, honestly. Your face . . . maybe your grandma was raped by a Jew.'[61] This response inverts not only the running joke about Markus's nose by substituting it for 'face', but equally addresses the Holocaust and the image of the Jew as threatening the purity of the German race.[62] In addition, the joke challenges the power relationship between German and Jewish people, as Markus's grandmother is represented as the victim, whereas the Jewish man in this story is given agency, even though certainly not a noble form of agency. This joke exemplifies Simon Critchley's argument that 'jokes tear holes in our usual predictions about the empirical world', but equally that they 'let us see the familiar defamiliarized, the ordinary made extraordinary and the real rendered surreal'.[63] In many ways, the joke offers a new perspective on how the Holocaust is usually represented in Germany, which equally encourages the object of the joke to critically reassess their own position in relation to the representation of the Holocaust, even though Markus clearly does not find the joke funny. But similar to Tom's jokes about the Holocaust in Bäuerlein's text, in Flohr's book these jokes are meant to encourage self-reflexive engagement with the Nazi past and accepted representations of this past in Germany. This aligns with what Eyal Zandberg has noted in an Israeli Jewish context: 'Third-generation commemoration looks at the Holocaust from a different point of view, one that encompasses both thoughts about the event and its memory, raising questions about history and its representation'[64] – which is also what Flohr's book is doing.

This becomes evident in jokes about Markus's Germanness and Germany's relationship with Israel. When Markus signs the lease for the flat, Simson tells him, 'Now you have committed yourself and your family to hundreds of years of paying reparations.'[65] This references the reparations that (West) Germany has been paying to Israel since 1952 and implicitly addresses the guilt that contemporary Germans are still experiencing about the Holocaust, as well as the ways in which they are trying to atone for their guilt. The issue of reparations and atonement is less prominent in Flohr's text than in Bäuerlein's, but once again it emerges most strongly through the trope of the libidinal relationship between Markus and a Mizrahi Jewish woman called Noa. For Noa, and especially for her family, Markus's German identity is doubly problematic: 'You epitomize what my parents have been suffering from for decades. The Europeans.'[66] Markus is here identified as European and as the oppressor of the Middle Eastern Jews, but Noa takes this a step further when she says, 'You're not even

Jewish. And on top of that you're German,' emphasising that the main problem for her parents is Markus's German identity, which is inseparable from the history of Nazism.[67] Noa confirms that this distinction is becoming increasingly difficult for her, which crystallises in the following exchange between her and Markus after his visit to Yad Vashem, Israel's Holocaust museum:

> [Noa] 'Did you find your grandfather?'
> [Markus] 'What do you mean? In the directory?'
> [Noa] 'No. In the Nazi pictures.'[68]

Noa's comment only allows Markus to experience this history from the perspective of the Nazi, not the German. It leads to a discussion of what Markus's grandfather did during World War II and Noa's accusation that Markus is only in Israel to ask for forgiveness. However, as they keep discussing the issue, Noa admits that the Holocaust 'is nothing personal for me. I don't want it to become that, either. When I make jokes about the Germans and your nose and that kind of stuff, I'm playing with it [Holocaust consciousness and commemoration]'.[69] This comment shows that Noa, like Tom in Bäuerlein's book, does not shy away from making jokes about the Holocaust, confirming what Zandberg has noted above in relation to the third generation of Israeli Jews using jokes as a critical tool to encounter the Holocaust. However, Noa's emphasis on not having a personal connection with the Holocaust demonstrates how ideas related to Germanness and German guilt have become entrenched within Israeli Jewish society, which confirms, as Bernd Faulenbach and Helmuth Schütte have noted, that in Israel Germany is still strongly linked to the memory of the Holocaust, as 'Germans as perpetrators and bystanders are part of the Jewish memory of the Holocaust, which to this day shapes the idea of Germany in Israel'.[70] This manifests itself in Noa's family's inability to separate Markus's Germanness from the crimes committed against the Jews by the Nazis.

Noa's opinion of Markus stands in stark contrast to Markus's own experience of his visit to Yad Vashem:

> I was never more aware, who the Nazis were and who perpetrated the Holocaust, who tried to kill Jews from across the world, than on that day, when I stood in Yad Vashem among the soldiers with their chewing gums and I was ashamed to speak my own language.[71]

Markus feels both shame and a sense of responsibility, confirming Gudrun Brockhaus's idea that in the 1980s, with the emergence of a discourse advocating the normalisation of the past in West Germany, the 'morally charged concept of collective guilt' was replaced with the idea of 'responsibility'.[72] This process encouraged a transition from guilt to responsibility, from feeling personally accountable for the crimes of the Nazis to taking responsibility on a collective level for what had been done in the name of the German nation, a transition that was heavily debated during the *Historikerstreit* of the 1980s. However, the idea that the past has, and indeed can, be worked through is certainly arguable. Caroline Pearce, for instance, observes that

> [t]he Nazi past, including the Holocaust in particular, remains difficult to 'process' as it is so alien to the democratic, tolerant, and anti-extremist profile of the country today and it continues to both repel and fascinate as a period of history that defies rational explanation.[73]

This tension between a desire for normality and the problem of representing an event that is beyond 'rational explanation' is a pressing concern in German culture and politics and constitutes an integral part of working through the past. It is reflected in Flohr's book as ultimately, his relationship with Noa fails, suggesting that the macro-interdependencies between Germany and Israel are too complicated and the divide cannot easily be bridged or 'normalised'. Joe Cleary argues that the failure of relationships across divides

> is ultimately symptomatic of a corresponding faltering of political will: one that refuses to confront the fact that resolution to the sectarian conflict would require not just a modification of attitude on the part of the communities involved but substantive transformation of the existing structures of state power in the region as well.[74]

Applied to the German context, the failure of the relationship above all emphasises that the necessary 'transformation of existing structures of state power' has not been successfully completed yet. As a result, the shadow of the Holocaust makes it impossible, or at least very hard, to imagine a reconciliation between Germany and Israel – or if a reconciliation can be imagined, it comes at the expense of engaging with Palestinian experiences of suffering and Palestinian aspirations to statehood, as we have already seen in Chapter 1.

Nevertheless, Flohr's account exemplifies that the relationship between the two countries is slowly changing, as he exhibits a dialectic of normality in his approach to Holocaust memory. On one hand, he shows a desire to remember the Holocaust, but on the other hand, he wants to be part of a normal nation. His attempts at 'normalisation' are at least partly achieved through his engagement with Palestine and the Palestinian people. Flohr's account contributes to rethinking the relationship between Germany and the Holocaust, and Germany and Israel, at the same time as it puts Palestine as a key issue on the German political map. Markus himself describes the responsibility he feels while being in Israel as a 'backpack' filled with 'boulders': 'one for religion, one for the Holocaust, one for the war in Gaza, one for the language, one for the heat.'[75] He uses the image of the boulder to illustrate the different pressures he is exposed to, but interestingly, he includes Gaza in this list, thus gesturing towards Germany's responsibility for both Israel and Palestine in the present day. Flohr exemplifies on a narrative level the political argument of German leftist politicians Wolfgang Gehrcke, Jutta von Freyberg and Harri Grünberg:

> If Germany is fundamentally, indissolubly linked to Israel, then logic forces us to recognise that Germany is also linked to the fate of the Palestinians: with Israel through the German crime against humanity, with the Palestinians through the consequences of that crime.[76]

This is arguably not a widespread or popular perspective, but it is certainly an important one as it takes into account the ramifications of the Holocaust and contemporary German and European politics in the Middle East for Palestinians. This mirrors the relational memory work that Kosminsky and Lewycka are doing, as discussed in Chapter 2. Thus, Flohr's account challenges contemporary ideas about how Germany's engagement with Israel precludes solidarity with the Palestinian people. Instead, by including and engaging with both Israeli Jewish and Palestinian perspectives and narratives, Flohr suggests a way in which Germany can remember the Holocaust while acknowledging the impact of Israel's actions on the Palestinians living in Israel and in the Occupied Palestinian Territories.

The Limits of Normalising German–Israeli Jewish–Palestinian Relations

Both Bäuerlein and Flohr use humour to challenge received ideas about Israel and, in the case of Flohr, Israel's treatment of Palestinians in the Occupied

Territories. In their texts, humour contributes to encouraging a more critical and self-reflexive approach to the memory of the Holocaust in contemporary Germany, and the role this should play in people's engagement with Israel, Israel's occupation of the Palestinian people and territories, and Israel's treatment of Mizrahi Jewish citizens. Humour allows Bäuerlein to subvert some of the preconceptions about Israel, for example the likelihood of dying in an attack – at least before the Second Intifada – but her criticism of the Israeli government and its treatment of the Palestinians is quite limited due to the 'guilt complex' of her protagonist, which extends to the author. Flohr's book demonstrates a more progressive account of the relationship between his German identity and a critical engagement with Israel's occupation of the Palestinian territories. Although his protagonist Markus feels ashamed about his country's past, he nevertheless self-reflexively draws attention to his own stereotypical perceptions of Palestinians, and he emphasises the power imbalances that govern encounters between Israeli Jews and Palestinians as occupiers and occupied. This confirms that his desire for normalisation is linked to the construction of a new German identity, which not only positions itself in relation to the Holocaust and Israel but also takes into account Palestinian suffering. Flohr's text thus models productive ways of using relations between Israel, Palestine and Germany to show that support for Israel and Palestine does not need to be a zero-sum game. There can be an acknowledgment of both people's narratives of suffering and their national aspirations that is relational rather than exclusive.

Using the concept of 'disrupted familial relationality', defined as disrupting traditional kinship models as metaphors for the nation, the works examined in the fourth chapter – Claire Hajaj's novel *Ishmael's Oranges* (2014) and Hugo Blick's miniseries *The Honourable Woman* (2014) – depict Jewish-Palestinian marriage and friendship as well as Jewish-Palestinian children to challenge perceptions of Jewish and Palestinian suffering as separate and to imagine alternative alliances. By focusing on disrupted families – including disrupted relations between parents and children but also (disrupted) relations across divides – I argue that Hajaj and Blick consider how families and the ideologies that they transmit contribute to the exclusion of those that are seen as outside the collective national or ethnic community. Instead, both works foreground Palestinians and their narratives of suffering, and their displacement and dispossession at the hands of Israel, as well as Palestinian aspirations to statehood. In this way, the artists encourage their audiences to reflect on the power differentials that govern these contexts, including those between Israel, Palestine and international powers. These imbalances are often occluded in discussions that emphasise a kinship approach on a national and international level, including those that use being part of the 'family of nations' as a justification for Israel's treatment of the Palestinian people and to obscure Israel's role as a settler-colonial and occupation power, alongside the UK's involvement as a mandatory power in Palestine at the start of the twentieth century.

Notes

1. Chrisoula Lionis, *Laughter in Occupied Palestine: Comedy and Identity in Art and Film* (London: I. B. Tauris, 2016), 4.
2. Arthur Asa Berger, 'The Politics of Laughter,' in *The Social Faces of Humour: Practices and Issues*, ed. George E. C. Paton, Chris Powell and Stephen Wagg (Aldershot: Ashgate Publishing, 1996), 16.
3. Lawrence E. Mintz, 'American Humor as Unifying and Divisive,' *Humor – International Journal of Humor Research* 12, no. 3 (1999): 237, ttps://doi.org/10.1515/humr.1999.12.3.237.
4. John Morreall, *Taking Laughter Seriously* (Albany: State University of New York, 1983), 104. Humour has been identified as a key mechanism for engaging with the unfamiliar and to provide relief. For a general discussion of this see, for example, Rod A. Martin, *The Psychology of Humour: An Integrative Approach* (Burlington: Elsevier Academic Press, 2007). For an exploration of humour as a relief mechanism in travel writing, see Piers Michael Smith, 'Culture of the Turnip: Humour in the Travel Writing of Alexander Kinglake (1844) and Wilfred Gifford Palgrave (1865),' *Arab Journal for the Humanities* 25, no. 97 (2007): 205–22.
5. See, for example, Michael Billig, *Laughter and Ridicule: Towards a Social Critique of Humour* (London: Sage, 2005); Martin, *Psychology of Humour*; and Morreall, *Taking Laughter Seriously*. For a discussion of how travel writing facilitates and mediates encounters with others, see Patrick Holland and Graham Huggan, *Tourists with Typewriters: Critical Reflections on Contemporary Travel Writing* (Ann Arbor: University of Michigan Press, 2000). Theresa Bäuerlein and Markus Flohr are not what one would typically consider professional travel writers, but their accounts can be classified as travel writing in the way that Tim Youngs has defined it, as 'predominantly factual, first-person prose accounts of travels that have been undertaken by the author-narrator' (Tim Youngs, *The Cambridge Introduction to Travel Writing* (Cambridge: Cambridge University Press, 2013), 3).

6. See, for example, the following travelogues: British comedian Mark Thomas's *Extreme Rambling: Walking Israel's Separation Barrier. For Fun* (2011), German journalist and author Andreas Altmann's *Verdammtes Land: Eine Reise durch Palästina (Damned Country: A Journey through Palestine,* 2014) and journalist and novelist Martin Schäuble's *Zwischen den Grenzen: Zu Fuss durch Israel und Palästina (Between the Borders: On Foot Through Israel and Palestine,* 2013).
7. Cleary, *Literature, Partition and Nation-State*, 112.
8. Olaf Glöckner and Julius H. Schoeps. 'Vorwort,' in *Deutschland, die Juden und der Staat Israel: Eine politische Bestandsaufnahme*, ed. Olaf Glöckner and Julius H. Schoeps (Hildesheim: Georg Olms Verlag, 2016), 10.
9. To distinguish between the narrator and the author, I will refer to the narrator as 'Markus' and use the last name or the full name to refer to the author.
10. Ali Behdad, *Belated Travelers: Orientalism in the Age of Colonial Dissolution* (Durham, NC: Duke University Press, 1994), 15.
11. Charlotte Steenken, 'Als würde Bassum Raketen auf Syke schießen,' *Kreiszeitung*, 18 January 2011, https://www.kreiszeitung.de/laeuft/als-wuerde-bassum-raketen-syke-schiessen-1086696.html.
12. Ullrich, 'Antisemitismus, Antizionismus und Kritik an Israel in Deutschland,' 111.
13. Carl Thompson, *Travel Writing* (New York: Routledge, 2011), 10.
14. Michael Mulkay, *On Humour: Its Nature and its Place in Modern Society* (Cambridge: Polity Press, 1988), 211–12.
15. Debbie Lisle, *The Global Politics of Contemporary Travel Writing* (Cambridge: Cambridge University Press, 2006), xi. Some critics have drawn attention to how humour can function as a critical tool in travel writing, such as Catherine Stevenson, 'Mary Kingsley's Travel Writings: Humor and the Politics of Style,' *Exploration* 8 (1980): 1–13.
16. Ofer Aderet, 'I Was Afraid I'd Be Treated Like a Murderer,' *Haaretz*, 2 June 2008, http://www.haaretz.com/news/i-was-afraid-i-d-be-treated-like-a-murderer-1.247033.
17. Theresa Bäuerlein quoted in Evelyn Runge, 'Roman-Debütantin Bäuerlein: Wo die Liebe stolpert,' *Spiegel Online*, 8 October 2008, http://www.spiegel.de/kultur/literatur/roman-debuetantin-baeuerlein-wo-die-liebe-stolpert-a-582833.html.
18. Theresa Bäuerlein, *Das war der gute Teil des Tages* (Frankfurt: Fischer, 2008), 33.
19. John Urry and Jonas Larsen, *The Tourist Gaze 3.0*, 3rd ed. (Los Angeles: SAGE, 2011), 13.
20. Gayatri Spivak uses this anthropological term to delineate an insider's view, who is, however, 'denied autobiography' (Gayatri Chakravorty Spivak, *A Critique of Postcolonial Reason: Toward a History of the Vanishing Past* (Cambridge, MA: Harvard University Press, 1999), 6). This term can be applied to a certain extent

to the character of Tom in Bäuerlein's book as he does fulfil the role of a native informant, but he is also given some background and presented as a fully rounded character.

21. Bäuerlein, *Das war der gute Teil des Tages*, 24.
22. Bäuerlein, *Das war der gute Teil des Tages*, 24.
23. Lisle, *Global Politics of Contemporary Travel Writing*, 101.
24. Said, *Orientalism*, xvii.
25. Morreall, *Taking Laughter Seriously*, 102–3.
26. Amos Oz, *Israel und Deutschland: Vierzig Jahre nach Aufnahme diplomatischer Beziehungen*, trans. Lydia Böhmer (Frankfurt: Suhrkamp, 2005), 7.
27. Oz, *Israel und Deutschland*, 7.
28. Pearce, *Contemporary Germany and the Nazi Legacy*, 2.
29. Bäuerlein, *Das war der gute Teil des Tages*, 99.
30. Nicolas Holm, *Humour as Politics: The Political Aesthetics of Contemporary Comedy* (Cham: Palgrave Macmillan, 2017), 146.
31. Bäuerlein, *Das war der gute Teil des Tages*, 108. When Bäuerlein lived in Israel with her boyfriend, she was worried about her identity being conflated with the crimes committed by the Nazis but when she met her boyfriend's grandmother, a Holocaust survivor, the latter said that 'she understood that [Theresa] was not responsible for what happened to her' (Aderet, 'I Was Afraid I'd Be Treated Like a Murderer').
32. Martin, *Psychology of Humour*, 17.
33. For an overview of the use of Holocaust humour in Israeli culture, see Eyal Zandberg, 'Critical Laughter: Humour, Popular Culture and Israeli Commemoration,' *Media, Culture & Society* 25, no. 4 (2006): 561–79, https://doi.org/10.1177/0163443706065029 and Liat Steir-Livny, *Is it OK to Laugh About it?: Holocaust Humour, Satire and Parody in Israeli Culture* (Elstree: Vallentine Mitchell, 2017).
34. Liat Steir-Livny, 'Holocaust Humour, Satire and Parody on Israeli Television,' *Jewish Film & New Media* 3, no. 2 (2015): 194, https://doi.org/10.13110/jewifilmnewmedi.3.2.0193.
35. Theresa Bäuerlein, 'Mein Freund, der Jude: Lieben in Tel Aviv,' *Jetzt.de*, 13 May 2007, http://www.jetzt.de/jetztgedruckt/mein-freund-der-jude-lieben-in-tel-aviv-381130. Exceptions include German Jewish people using humour to discuss the Holocaust, such as comedian Oliver Polak, who regularly makes jokes about the Holocaust and contemporary Germany's engagement with the Nazi past in his stand-up comedy work and in his book *Ich darf das, ich bin Jude* (*I'm Allowed to Do This, I'm Jewish*, 2012).

36. These include Timur Vermes's novel *Er ist wieder da* (*Look Who's Back*; 2012, now also a major motion picture) and Daniel Levy's *Mein Führer: Die wirklich wahrste Wahrheit über Adolf Hitler* (*My Führer: the Actual Truest Truth About Adolf Hitler*, 2007).
37. Gavriel D. Rosenfeld, *Hi Hitler!: How the Nazi Past is Being Normalized in Contemporary* Culture (Cambridge: Cambridge University Press, 2015), 223.
38. Doris Sommer, *Foundational Fictions: The National Romances of Latin America* (Berkeley: University of California Press, 1991), 24.
39. Bäuerlein, *Das war der gute Teil des Tages*, 166.
40. Zandberg, 'Critical Laughter,' 569, 576. Asher Ben-Natan, who was the first Israeli ambassador in West Germany from 1965 to 1970, notes that in Israel, they use the word '*Shilumim*', which means 'payment', rather than the term for 'reparation' as they do not believe that this relationship can be repaired (Asher Ben-Natan, 'Ansprache,' in *Israel und die Bundesrepublik Deutschland: Dreißig Jahre diplomatische Beziehungen*, ed. Renate Schlief-Ehrismann (Berlin: Argon, 1995), 19). George Lavy emphasises that

    > Israel . . . considered that the Germans owed to the Jewish people and, by extension to the Israeli Jews, a moral debt of which material compensation was only one factor, to be followed by aid to Israel in the diplomatic, economic and military fields. (Lavy, *Germany and Israel*, xi)

41. Bäuerlein, 'Mein Freund, der Jude.'
42. Bäuerlein, *Das war der gute Teil des Tages*, 12, 33, 34. Lena has an unpleasant encounter with Asad, an Arab man she meets while visiting Jordan. He tries to have sex with her without her consent and only desists when she shouts, 'Stop! . . . I am engaged' (Bäuerlein, *Das war der gute Teil des Tages*, 176). This scene heavily draws on the Orientalist trope of the Arab man as a danger to the Occidental woman, who is only defined by his desire for said woman.
43. Edward Said, 'Arabs and Jews,' *Journal of Palestine Studies* 3, no. 2 (1974): 6, https://doi.org/10.2307/2535796.
44. Tanya Reinhart, *Israel/Palestine: How to End the War of 1948*, 2nd ed. (Crow's Nest: Allen & Unwin, 2003), 13.
45. David Spurr, *The Rhetoric of Empire: Colonial Discourse in Journalism, Travel Writing, and Imperial Administration* (Durham, NC: Duke University Press, 1993), 92. For a critical engagement with the Zionist idea of the land as empty, see, for example, Gabriel Piterberg, *The Returns of Zionism: Myths, Politics and Scholarship in Israel* (London: Verso, 2008).

46. Spurr, *The Rhetoric of Empire*, 92.
47. Braach-Maksvytis, 'Germany, Palestine, Israel, and the (Post)Colonial Imagination,' 304.
48. Lisle, *Global Politics of Contemporary Travel Writing*, 101.
49. Steenken, 'Als würde Bassum Raketen auf Syke schießen.'
50. Markus Flohr, *Wo samstags immer Sonntag ist: Ein deutscher Student in Israel* (Hamburg: Rowohlt, 2011), 48.
51. Flohr, *Wo samstags immer Sonntag ist*, 82.
52. Steenken, 'Als würde Bassum Raketen auf Syke schießen.' Many Palestinian authors have used the 'absurd' as a strategy to engage with a situation that defies logic, such as Suad Amiry in *Sharon and my Mother-in-Law: Ramallah Diaries* (London: Granta, 2005). For an academic overview of these discussions see, for example, Lionis, *Laughter in Occupied Palestine*; Nadine Adel Sinno, 'Family Sagas and Checkpoint Dramas: Tragedy, Humor, and Family Dynamics in Suad Amiry's *Sharon and My Mother-in-Law: Ramallah Diaries*,' *Journal of Middle East Women's Studies* 9, no. 1 (2013): 30–53, https://www.muse.jhu.edu/article/493764; and Mairi Neeves, 'The Pursuit of Selfhood: Writing the Absurd in Palestinian Life Narratives,' in *Life Writing: The Spirit of the Age and the State of the Art*, ed. Meg Jensen and Jane Jordan (Newcastle-upon-Tyne: Cambridge Scholars Publishing, 2009), 52–61.
53. Flohr, *Wo samstags immer Sonntag ist*, 228.
54. Lionis, *Laughter in Occupied Palestine*, 94.
55. Flohr, *Wo samstags immer Sonntag ist*, 234.
56. Lionis, *Laughter in Occupied Palestine*, 19.
57. Flohr, *Wo samstags immer Sonntag ist*, 7.
58. Flohr, *Wo samstags immer Sonntag ist*, 26.
59. Flohr, *Wo samstags immer Sonntag ist*, 120.
60. Steenken, 'Als würde Bassum Raketen auf Syke schießen.'
61. Flohr, *Wo samstags immer Sonntag ist*, 120.
62. For a discussion of racism in Nazi Germany, see, for example, Michael Burleigh and Wolfgang Wippermann, *The Racial State: Germany 1933–1945* (Cambridge: Cambridge University Press, 1991).
63. Simon Critchley, *On Humour* (London: Routledge, 2002), 1, 10.
64. Zandberg, 'Critical Laughter,' 575.
65. Flohr, *Wo samstags immer Sonntag ist*, 21.
66. Flohr, *Wo samstags immer Sonntag ist*, 102.
67. Flohr, *Wo samstags immer Sonntag ist*, 192.
68. Flohr, *Wo samstags immer Sonntag ist*, 164.
69. Flohr, *Wo samstags immer Sonntag ist*, 165.

70. Bernd Faulenbach and Helmuth Schütte, 'Zur Einführung,' in *Deutschland, Israel und der Holocaust: Zur Gegenwartsdeutung der Vergangenheit*, ed. Bernd Faulenbach and Helmuth Schütte (Essen: Klartext, 1998), 8.
71. Flohr, *Wo samstags immer Sonntag ist*, 160.
72. Gudrun Brockhaus, 'The Emotional Legacy of the National Socialist Past in Post-War Germany,' in *Memory and Political Change*, ed. Aleida Assmann and Linda Shortt (Basingstoke: Palgrave Macmillan, 2012), 40.
73. Pearce, *Contemporary Germany and the Nazi Legacy*, 2.
74. Cleary, *Literature, Partition and Nation-State*, 115.
75. Markus Flohr, 'Warum bist du bloß so deutsch?' *Der Spiegel,* 19 October 2009, http://www.spiegel.de/spiegel/unispiegel/d-67414810.html.
76. Wolfgang Gehrcke, Jutta von Freyberg and Harri Grünberg, *Die deutsche Linke, der Zionismus, und der Nahost-Konflikt*: *Eine notwendige Debatte* (Köln: Papyrossa, 2009), 264.

4

DISRUPTED FAMILIAL RELATIONALITY: ETHNICITY, ALTERNATIVE ALLIANCES AND HYBRIDITY IN CONTEMPORARY BRITISH CULTURE

> Far from being 'narrow', 'apolitical' or merely 'domestic', the family is, in fact, deeply political and intricately connected to society . . . [T]hrough a glimpse of the most private experiences, it reveals the entrenched fractures of public life.[1]
> – Shreya Chatterjee

> The idea, the essence of a family of nations – not always united, but a family of nations conducting a dialogue and trying to do good in sustainable development, solving problems, poverty, and human rights – that's really amazing.[2]
> – Ron Prosor, Israel's Permanent Representative to the United Nations, 2011–2015

As the epigraphs to this chapter show, families are deeply embedded in politics. They also play a key role in creating and maintaining relations between individuals and collectives, both on a literal and a metaphorical level. Indeed, in the context of nation formation, as Anne McClintock has argued, '[n]ations are frequently figured through the iconography of familial and domestic space' and hence they become 'domestic genealogies'.[3] Moreover, families are often used to present a unified position to the outside and to confirm existing hierarchies and divisions. Sarah Harwood, for example, suggests that in times of conflict, conservative ideologies are usually reified as the family offers refuge through an 'unassailable moral position' that lies outside of history and culture.[4] As such, the use of the family as a means to depict relations between Israel and Palestine is not surprising. Toine van Teeffelen, in discussing how Israel and Palestine are represented in popular fiction from outside the region, has argued that 'gender and family relations' often 'make it easy to understand political life', emphasising how the family is a convenient way to access what is often perceived as a political situation that is too complex to understand.[5] But on the other hand, and as we will see in further detail below, the family also functions as an important unit for making visible the tensions and fissures of society at large. This emphasis can be read as part of a wider trend whereby, as Shreya Chatterjee argues in the first epigraph of this chapter, families 'reveal the entrenched fractures of public life'. What we see in the two works discussed in this chapter – Claire Hajaj's novel *Ishmael's Oranges* (2014) and Hugo Blick's TV series *The Honourable Woman* (2014) – is a focus on the disrupted family, and on families that do not neatly represent a unified, ethnically homogenous unit. This approach challenges existing discourses about exclusion and inclusion that are central to nationalism. It also interrogates representations of narratives and histories of Israel and Palestine as exclusive and non-relational in British and German culture and, of course, in European and Anglophone contexts more widely.

Similar ideas emerge when discussing the use of kinship in international relations. Ronnie Hjorth, for example, has noted that the idea of the 'family of nations' is exclusionary through its emphasis on 'familiarity among the political communities that count as equals, and indicating something that is not shared by all communities'.[6] This is particularly salient in the case of Palestine, which is usually not included in these discussions as it is not recognised as an independent nation state. This is what the second epigraph to this chapter reveals, where the 'family of nations' is used as a concept to theorise the relationships between different countries in terms of politics and international relations. Ron Prosor, who was Israel's Permanent Representative to the United Nations between 2011 and 2015, emphasises that a sense of kinship between nations facilitates dialogue, even if it is at times antagonistic, but that equally it adds a sense of cohesion in terms of working together to address common issues, such as development and human rights.

Interestingly, Prosor then adds the following sentence: 'I feel proud that Israel is part and parcel of the family of nations',[7] which praises Israel for being included in the family of nations as a country that champions human rights. This emphasis on human rights and upholding democratic values is a common tendency, especially when trying to deflect attention from how Israel violates the human rights of the Palestinians living in the Occupied Territories and from how Israel treats Palestinians in Israel as second-class citizens. As Ariella Azoulay and Adi Ophir have argued, '[w]hen especially blatant assaults on human rights . . . are subject to public and legal debate, they enjoy much more support among the Israeli Jewish public than the government does in other matters' because they are 'presented in terms of national security, overruling legal and moral considerations'.[8] Hence, using the idea of a national community that needs to be protected creates a sense of inclusion for Israeli Jewish people at the same time as it excludes Palestinians as the other or the enemy.

In order to unpack these ideas of exclusion and inclusion, and the relations between Israeli Jewish and Palestinian narratives and histories outside of the region, in this chapter I examine how Hajaj's and Blick's works consider how families, and the ideologies that they transmit, contribute to the exclusion of those that are seen as outside the collective national or ethnic community. They foreground Palestinians and their narratives of suffering, and their displacement and dispossession at the hands of Israel, which in turn allows both artists to question the absence of Palestine from the 'family of nations'. If we read their disruption of the family in light of social contract theory, which considers family as a metonym for the nation and purports that '[a]t the basis of a democracy, a social contract presupposes that its parties come to it with rights that are theirs already. The contract itself is specifically designed to respect, defend, and even enhance these prior rights',[9] then Hajaj's and Blick's works can also be read as criticising the idea of Israel as a democratic state if it emphasises its Jewish ethnography, a definition that only extends the rights conveyed by the social contract to its Jewish citizens.[10]

In Hajaj's novel, this challenge manifests itself through an emphasis on the conjugal bond between a Jewish woman and a Palestinian man, which brings together Jewish and Palestinian narratives of suffering and emphasises the ways in which these narratives can be read as relational. Ruth Perry has noted that '[t]he obligations of spouses to each other are stressed above and against their ties of filiation'.[11] Hence, depicting a union between a Jewish and a Palestinian character in Hajaj's novel challenges the separatist imaginary and refutes the idea of the family as a neat microcosm for the nation. Instead, it draws attention to the blind spots of ethnocentric conceptions of the nation as a family. The romance-across-the-divide trope plays a key role in this context, as it can be used, as Ilan Pappé has argued, 'to prepare the Jewish-Israeli palate for new kinds of critiques and viewpoints'[12] – an argument that can also be made in relation to the British or Anglophone audiences that Hajaj is addressing in her novel. Examining the continuation of this trend into the twenty-first century, Hella Bloom Cohen notes that 'imagined and lived mixed intimacies radicalize the political trajectory for Israel-Palestine by portending a mixed public sphere'.[13] A key aspect of using this trope is not only to draw attention to the importance of a 'mixed public sphere' and the similarity and relationality between Jewish and Palestinian narratives of suffering, but equally to highlight the fact that, as Edward Said already noted in 1974,

> [n]o Arab today has an identity that can be unconscious of the Jew, that can rule out the Jew as a psychic factor in the Arab identity; conversely, I think, no Jew can ignore the Arab in general, nor can he immerse himself in his ancient tradition and so lose the Palestinian Arab in particular and what Zionism has done to him.[14]

Through her use of a Jewish-Palestinian relationship, Hajaj's novel challenges the separatist imaginary that often shapes perceptions of the relations between (Israeli) Jews and Palestinians, including in British culture. Moreover, by using fictionalised narratives of family and kinship Hajaj draws attention to the ways in which Jewish and Palestinian identities are connected on an individual and a collective level, and how British colonialism and Zionism have historically impacted on the circulation of Israeli Jewish and Palestinian narratives as separate, and continue to do so until today. This, in turn, foregrounds not only the ways in which (Israeli) Jewish and Palestinian histories are entangled but also how global powers such as the UK have shaped the depiction and circulation of these histories since the turn of the twentieth century.

In Blick's TV drama, the family as a microcosm for the nation is challenged through the main character, British Jewish businesswoman Nessa Stein (Maggie Gyllenhaal), who throughout the series is depicted as a lone and lonely figure and not firmly embedded in a family unit. This emerges most prominently in contrast to the family unit that her brother belongs to, which includes a wife and children. Instead, what we see in Blick's work is an attempt to create alternative alliances that are based on affiliation rather than filiation through Nessa's attempts to connect with Atika Halabi (Lubna Azabal), who is her Palestinian translator and later becomes her confidante and her brother's nanny and lover. Edward Said famously defined 'filiation' as 'the culture to which one is bound by birth, nationality, profession', and 'affiliation' as the 'system acquired . . . by social and political conviction, economic and historical circumstances'.[15] The tension between filiation and affiliation that *The Honourable Woman* sets up contributes to challenging the family as representative for tribalism and clear-cut ethnic distinctions, and demonstrates how a sense of loyalty that is based on an imagined ethnic community can be challenged through relations that transcend ethnic ideas of belonging. Hence, the family, and especially the disrupted family, becomes a testing ground for thinking through relations between (Israeli) Jews and Palestinians, especially those that are defined as antagonistic based on considerations of ethnicity.

By focusing on disrupted families – including disrupted relations between parents and children but also (disrupted) relations across divides – Hajaj and Blick challenge traditional models of kinship based on shared ethnicity. They show how ideas of kinship are used to depict the political relations between Israel and Palestine, and between both countries and the wider world. These include how being part of the 'family of nations' is used to justify Israel's treatment of the Palestinian people and to obscure Israel's role as a settler-colonial and occupation power, alongside the UK's involvement as a mandatory power in Palestine at the start of the twentieth century. In both cases, this challenge is linked to the presence of children that have both Palestinian and Jewish heritage. Hella Bloom Cohen, drawing on the work of miscegenation theorist Gilberto Freyre, has argued that the 'miscegenated child' can 'embod[y] a third vision for a statist future that is not dependent upon a Western, Anglo-centric public sphere for its political trajectory'.[16] However, as we will see below, it is significant that in neither case is the mixed heritage of children considered a way of resolving the competition between Palestinian and Jewish narratives. This is the case even though in Blick's work, the hybrid child becomes a way of imagining reconciliation between (Israeli) Jews and Palestinians, albeit without addressing how these relations have been and continue to be shaped by Zionism, colonialism and occupation.

Jewish–Palestinian Relations in Claire Hajaj's *Ishmael's Oranges*: Comparative, Competitive, Hybrid

Claire Hajaj's novel *Ishmael's Oranges* (2014), which was shortlisted for the Jewish Quarterly-Wingate Prize in 2016 and was a finalist for the Authors' Club Best First Novel Award in 2015, was inspired by Hajaj's own experience of growing up with a Jewish mother and a Palestinian father. Hajaj decided to use her unique perspective to write about both Jewish and Palestinian narratives, which, as she says herself, are 'in many ways . . . incredibly similar'.[17] In order to address the similarities between the Jewish and the Palestinian narratives, in her novel Hajaj uses the idea of kinship, specifically the libidinal and later conjugal relationship between a British Jewish woman, Jude,[18] and a Palestinian man, Salim, and the fact that they have two children together, to situate Jewish and Palestinian histories in a comparative context. These ideas will be explored in more detail below but first I want to examine how Hajaj sets up a comparative and relational context for Jewish and Palestinian histories in her novel.

The first part of *Ishmael's Oranges*, entitled 'Journeys', is set in 1948. It opens with an epigraph by Hungarian writer Stephen Vizinczey: 'Each man's life involves the life of all men, each tale is but the fragment of a tale.'[19] This part, which is crucial to setting up the comparative (and later on competing) narratives of Salim and Jude, establishes a clear sense of relationality by emphasising how different lives are implicated in each other – similar to Edward Said's argument discussed in the introduction to this chapter. At the same time, the first part's epigraph draws attention to the fact that the narratives that people present are often fragments, thus offering only a partial view of tensions between different groups. This idea of a fragmented perspective is mirrored in the structure of this section, which keeps moving between Salim's and Jude's narratives. It opens with Salim's story, which is set in Jaffa during the final days of the British Mandate and ends with Salim and his family leaving Jaffa as a result of the increasing violence perpetrated on Palestinians and the Irgun, a paramilitary Zionist organisation, advancing on Jaffa. This section introduces the key themes of displacement and dispossession that recur throughout the novel. When Salim and his family move to Nazareth, they are described as 'lucky', since they ran 'ahead of the *Nakba* – the great Catastrophe',[20] even though they later find out that their house was taken by the State of Israel under the Absentee Property Law.[21] Hence, although Salim and his family did not experience the physical violence of the *nakba* first-hand, they are still affected by the trauma of losing their home. This aligns with what critics such as Nur Masalha have emphasised, namely the importance of considering the *nakba* not only as a past but also as a present and future trauma.[22] In Hajaj's novel, Salim is the character through which this trauma becomes most tangible, especially later in the novel.

When Salim leaves Israel in 1959 to study in the UK, he is excited about starting a new life in London, where he calls himself 'Sal' and he is not immediately identified with Palestine or with the so-called Israeli–Palestinian conflict. Meeting Jude at a party in 1967, Salim reflects that she is 'white as a canvas . . . white as a new page, a place to make a fresh start',[23] indicating Salim's expectation that this relationship will contribute to him becoming a different person. Interestingly though, what first attracts Salim to Jude is her Star of David necklace, which 'for one confused moment reminded him of home'.[24] This is exemplary of the complicated relationship that Salim has with his past in Palestine and, as a result, with Jude. The Star of David as a symbol of Israel connects Salim with Palestine as a lost homeland, specifically a homeland that was lost with the creation of Israel. Moreover, he sees Jude as a refuge or haven for him when he admits that he 'longed to be cherished in the same way' as the necklace.[25] The Star of David thus becomes both a symbol of hope and loss, mirroring the way in which Salim wants to move on and start a new life, while at the same time he is unable to forget about his past, a past that is made palpable through a photograph of his family in front of their house in Jaffa. Susan Sontag has observed that 'to photograph is to appropriate the thing photographed', and that 'photographs give people an imaginary possession of a past that is unreal'.[26] For Salim, this picture of their former house functions as a substitute for the possibility of recovering ownership of this house, while drawing attention to the fact that the past depicted in the photograph is irrevocably lost.

Salim's story of his and his family's dispossession and displacement in 1948 is followed by Jude's story, which is set in Sunderland, in northern England, in 1956. Salim's and Jude's narratives are initially not connected, apart from the fact that Jude was born on the same day that the State of Israel was established, as her grandmother Rebecca explains: '[A] tiny, limp girl born struggling for oxygen just as the new State of Israel was drawing its first breath.'[27] However, Hajaj does not posit Jude as an allegory for Israel, as not much is made of this parallel in the novel. Instead, the parallel mainly seems to serve the narrative purpose of establishing a link between Jude and Israel (which throughout her life is rather tenuous) and thus with Salim and his fate, as Jude's birth is implicitly linked to the dispossession and displacement that Salim's family experiences as part of the establishment of the state of Israel. Jude's childhood is similarly marked by displacement and persecution through the story of her grandmother, who had to leave Russia at the turn of the twentieth century because of the pogroms, as well as Jude's adopted sister Gertie, who arrived on the *Kindertransport* and is a haunting presence of the Holocaust throughout the novel. As an eleven-year-old, Jude herself experiences anti-Semitism as part of a cruel incident where she is invited to another girl's party only to find a sign saying 'NO JEWDES ALLOWED' at the entrance to the porch.[28] While Hajaj does not set up any direct links between the discrimination that Jude experiences and Salim's displacement, by moving back and forth between Salim's and Jude's narratives, she encourages her readers to think about these experiences as similar and connected.

In spite of Salim's strong attachment to the past and the loss of his family's house during the *nakba*, initially, there is no competition between Jewish and Palestinian memories for Jude and Salim:

> She told him about the grandmother who fled the Russians and he had talked about the siege of Nazareth and the Jewish commander who'd refused to sack the city. They'd agreed that religion didn't matter, that they had a lot in common and some nonsense about peace that reminded Salim of the flower songs.[29]

For Jude and Salim, the differences between (Israeli) Jews and Palestinians are linked to religion, which aligns with the commonly held view of an age-old antagonism between 'Jews' and 'Arabs' due to religious differences, which is how the 'tensions' between Israeli Jews and Palestinians are commonly represented in the media, as Ella Shohat, amongst others, has argued.[30] This view conveniently occludes the fact that the situation in Palestine/Israel is not driven by age-old religious opposition but by Palestinians living under Israeli occupation and being dispossessed and displaced. However, it soon emerges that for other people, Jude's and Salim's ethnicities are a problem. When Salim tells his brother Hassan about their relationship, emphasising that Jude is 'not a Zionist. She understands us. She understands *me*', Hassan responds that, 'No matter what you think, they can't understand an Arab. It's not in their nature.'[31] While Salim makes an important distinction between Zionist and non-Zionist Jews, for Hassan all Jews have unbridgeable differences with Palestinians. Indeed, this view is prominent on both sides, since a lack of differentiation between individuals and groups also emerges in Jude's family. When Jude tells her uncle Tony that she is dating a Palestinian, his reaction is similar to Salim's brother's, as Tony emphasises that, '[H]e'll never forgive you.'[32] Again, this statement does not consider people as individuals but as representatives of an ethnic group, which can be read in light of McClintock's argument cautioning against the dangers of the family as 'legitimizing exclusion and hierarchy within non-familial (affiliate) social formations'.[33] This stance posits Jude and Salim as unable to move beyond the division that is set up between Jewish and Palestinian collectives due to the histories of the Holocaust and the *nakba*, which, as discussed throughout this book, are seen as exclusive narratives.

While Jude and Salim are mostly able to avoid this view in their relationship, the pressures from outside increasingly grow and their relationship starts to become a typical post-Zionist romance, modelled on the Romeo-and-Juliet plot type, which as Ilan Pappé explains, involves 'a Jewish woman fall[ing] in love with a Palestinian man against the wishes of their respective families and societies'.[34] But as Jude notes, 'the birth of their perfect twins [had] reconcil[ed] doubters on both sides. Marc and Sophie had been wondrous, glorious affirmation of their courage.'[35] The children are supposed to embody the ideal of a balanced Jewish-Palestinian identity, one that is not torn between the two sides but able to reconcile the heritage and history of both parents. This aligns with 'a desire to reconstitute the public sphere through the trope of miscegenation', as Hella Cohen Bloom observes.[36] However, in Hajaj's novel, this interethnic relationship and its offspring only seem to work in the space of the United Kingdom, which – while not neutral – at least does not have an identity that is defined closely in relation to either Jewish or Arab people.

As Jude and Salim move to Kuwait with their twins, reconciling their contrasting identities and histories becomes increasingly difficult, not least because of Salim's frustration with not being promoted at work, which he blames on the Jewish people. He tells Jude: 'You know, if it wasn't for your people, for the Jews, I would already be somebody.'[37] In Salim's mind, his personal failure becomes tied up with the collective failure of the Palestinian people to reclaim their land and get closer to the goal of self-determination. As Jude astutely observes: 'Over the years Salim had turned his "betrayal" at work into something more destructive – a reliving of all betrayals of his past, a fear that he himself was a traitor – to his own heritage.'[38] When their son Marc says that he wants to go back to England, Salim tells him that Kuwait is their home and that he is 'an Arab too. [He] belong[s] here, not there.'[39] Making sure that his children are Palestinian and remember their history becomes Salim's obsession, to make up for both his professional failure and for his personal inability to become the person he would have been if it had not been for the *nakba*.

This is an interesting development of the 'power dynamics of [interethnic] unions' where, as Hella Cohen Bloom points out, 'the marriage discourse is concentrated on the Jewish woman', who is seen as key to continuing the Jewish lineage and often comes to symbolise the ability to 'control a Zionist or post-Zionist future for Israel, dependent on whether she produces a racially/diasporically stable or unstable national citizen'.[40] While Jude can certainly be read as destabilising the idea of a 'stable national citizen' through the twins' hybrid identity, it is Salim who is more worried about how his children are becoming 'racially unstable', which is tied to a fear of Palestinian history being forgotten. This forgetting would not only entail the loss of Salim's personal memories and his family's history; as Lila Abu-Lughod and Ahmad H. Sa'di argue, from a Palestinian perspective, remembering 1948 is also paramount since these memories 'must serve as evidence of what happened in the mounting of political claims about injustice'.[41] Marc's desire to move back to England is thus doubly vexing for Salim as it not only removes him from the Middle East and a sense of 'Arabness' that Salim had hoped Kuwait would instil in him, but it also situates him closer to his mother's identity as a British Jewish woman through his decision to move back to the 'West'.

Marc is the one who draws attention to how his parents' 'tribalism' constitutes a problem for his identity as a Jewish Palestinian person. *Ishmael's Oranges* opens with a letter from Marc to his twin sister Sophie, dated December 1988, one year into the First Intifada. From the start, this letter sets up encounters between (Israeli) Jews and Palestinians as a never-ending recurrence of violence and a repetition of histories, which haunts Marc's generation as one that has inherited conflicting narratives from his Jewish mother and his Palestinian father. Through Marc, Hajaj emphasises how divisive this approach is on a personal level, which translates to the collective level when Marc talks about '[t]he two tribes, hers and his'.[42] The reference to tribalism already suggests that this gulf cannot be bridged, either by Jude and Salim or by their children, who similar to Hajaj herself have a hyphenated identity that is seen as incompatible by many, if not most. As Hajaj has explained in an interview, 'Belonging to a tribe gives you all sorts of certainties . . . It gives you a pre-inherited set of qualities – who is my friend, who is my enemy, what kind of life shall I live, which values shall I hold.'[43] This sets up a key tension between ethnicities or 'tribes' in the novel, reflecting the idea of a clash of civilisations as an unbridgeable gap, which will be discussed further in Chapter 5. The reference to tribalism can also be linked to the significant role family is seen as playing in corroborating wider ideas related to exclusion, as discussed in the introduction to this chapter. While tribalism is important for 'identity-formation, self-knowledge and communal belonging', as Sameena Karim has argued, 'the emphasis on the "tribal" should not be so great that it ignores the value of other cultures, and seeks to normatize its own to a point where no other culture is considered acceptable.'[44] Indeed, as is obvious in the case of Israeli Jews and Palestinians, and as Dan Bar-On and Saliba Sarsar confirm, '[t]he conflict has resulted in a total separation between them [Palestinians and Israeli Jews], and this is expressed through their respective narratives, rituals and myths, which compress the present into the past and mobilize the future.'[45] Against this separatist imaginary that draws on a past that emphasises differences rather than connections, Hajaj has explained in an interview that, in her novel, she 'wanted to answer the question – "what happens when a Jew or a Palestinian chooses to take a different course, to shape a life that doesn't conform to the traditions of those tribes?"'[46]

In the novel, we can see this resistance to conforming to tribalism when Jude reminds Salim that, 'We promised not to do this . . . We promised not to make it our fight.'[47] However, it becomes increasingly apparent, especially in light of political events such as the 1982 massacre in the Sabra and Shatila camps, that it is impossible for Jude and Salim to separate their individual identities from their collective histories, and hence to combine their Jewish and Palestinian heritages and histories. This manifests itself once again through their son Marc, who tells his father that

> I don't want to be a Palestinian or a Jew . . . Sophie and me, we're not like that. We don't want to get involved in all that fighting. You never ask us what *we* want, who *we* want to be.[48]

This aligns with Hajaj's own experience, when she says, 'How on Earth is a person supposed to choose between these stories?'[49] When Salim asks Marc what he wants to be, he responds 'a dancer', emphasising that he wants to define himself outside of prescribed categories that are usually seen as oppositional: Palestinian and Jew.[50]

Jude and Salim similarly confirm that it is impossible to combine these categories as, eventually, their relationship fails. This aligns with the 'tragic endings' that Anna Bernard has identified in the genre of the 'partition romance', where 'unification' is 'unrealizable in the present' and 'the desired union of the lovers often has the effect of intensifying the divide rather than undermining it'.[51] Indeed, the divide between Salim and his family becomes unbridgeable, mainly due to Salim's inability to find a sense of belonging with his family in the present as he continues to look back to the past and tries to recover a pre-*nakba* self that no longer exists. At the end of the novel, this is corroborated by Marc, who sets off three Molotov cocktails inside Salim's family's former house in Jaffa, which destroys the house but also kills Marc. This attack can be read as a clear attempt to get his father to move on from his past and to make space in his life for the present – his children and his wife – an objective which Marc voices when he tells Salim before the attack that the house 'was always more your child than I was'.[52] While it is not clear whether Marc intended to commit suicide or whether his death was an accident, through her decision to have him die at the end, Hajaj questions how successful the identity of a 'hybrid child' like Marc can be – especially given the difficulty of reconciling Jewish and Palestinian identities, as expressed through Marc's character throughout the novel.

The failure of Jude and Salim's marriage challenges a common trope whereby, as Ruth Perry has argued in relation to eighteenth-century popular fiction, an emphasis on the 'loyalty of blood relations' is often seen as an 'antidote' to personal issues.[53] Hajaj does not use the 'loyalty of blood relations' as a remedy for the competing histories and narratives of Jewish and Palestinian people. Through the very act of failing, Jude and Salim's relationship interrogates the idea that relationships between Jewish and Palestinian people, as Ilan Pappé suggests, are 'a way to avoid and evade rational recognition of the arguments and feelings of the other side'.[54] Instead, through the character of Salim and his inability to move on, Hajaj's novel makes clear how the suffering inflicted on the Palestinian people during the *nakba* continues to impact Palestinian lives into the present, and draws attention to the ways in which competing narratives shape both Jewish and Palestinian people across the generations.

Hajaj's focus on the ways in which the competition between Jewish and Palestinian narratives disrupts one specific family can thus be read as a model for reconsidering how Jewish and Palestinian narratives of suffering and displacement are represented in the UK more widely. This model foregrounds the benefits of situating Jewish and Palestinian narratives alongside each other and of drawing attention to their connections. It also emphasises the ways in which critical dialogue between them allows us to identify hidden power relations, such as the relative silence surrounding the British Mandate in Palestine in British culture and politics, and the impact this has had on contemporary Israel and Palestine, including the absence of sustained engagement with the Palestinian *nakba* and its aftermath.

Hugo Blick's *The Honourable Woman:* Israel, Palestine and the United Kingdom

An emphasis on competing narratives similarly shapes British director Hugo Blick's TV drama *The Honourable Woman* (2014), an eight-part miniseries produced for and shown on the BBC and Sundance TV. The series won a Peabody Award in 2014, and Maggie Gyllenhaal received a Golden Globe Award for Best Actress in 2015 for her role as Nessa Stein. *The Honourable Woman*, like some of Blick's earlier work, uses the political thriller format in order to unpack the relationships between Israel, Palestine and international actors such as the United Kingdom. At its centre is British Jewish businesswoman Nessa Stein, who tries to improve conditions in the Occupied Palestinian Territories through her family's foundation and her company, which lays fibre optic cables in the West Bank. Blick uses different relationships, including those between children and parents, and Jewish and Palestinian people, to consider the ways in which Jewish and Palestinian narratives are related to each other and how they are entangled with the United Kingdom and its politics in the region.

Blick's series could be seen as commodifying a real-life situation with important consequences for individual lives, especially Palestinian lives. He has explained in an interview that in his TV drama, 'it was very interesting to take a world issue, distil it into a single family and then to explore how this tested them.'[55] Toine van Teeffelen has argued that in Anglophone popular literature about Palestine/Israel the family often functions as a metaphor to exacerbate difference between Jewish and Palestinian people, typically aligning the former with the 'West' and the latter with 'the Orient'.[56] Blick, however, challenges the separation between Jewish and Palestinian narratives and histories and foregrounds Palestinian aspirations to statehood, linking them to both (Israeli) Jewish and British decisions and actions. This is partly achieved through the inclusion of the character of Atika Halabi, which defies the conventions of political thriller genre. As British Palestinian writer Mischa Hiller has noted, in this genre, 'Arabs are badly represented or stereotyped'.[57] Blick's TV series, his first about the Middle East, subverts some of these conventions and stereotypes in interesting ways: through Atika, he not only represents a fully rounded Palestinian character with a backstory, challenging ideas of Palestinians as either terrorists or victims without agency, but equally he questions ideas about victimhood through Nessa and Atika's relationship, as we will see below. Moreover, on a metaphorical level, this alliance asks the audience to reconsider the relations between Israel and Palestine as well as between the UK and Palestine.

In this context it is important that Blick's political thriller, following the conventions of the genre, emphasises that there is not always a clear-cut distinction between good and evil, indicating from the start of the series that the audience's perceptions might get subverted. This approach challenges the 'sharp division between good and evil' and the 'need for the setting of strict standards of behavior' that George Lakoff sees as central to the model of the Strict Father morality, a model that applies quite neatly to Nessa's father, Eli Stein (Aidan Stephenson).[58] For Nessa, resisting this type of morality and defining herself in opposition to her father is at the heart of the series. Eli Stein, who arrived in the UK as part of the *Kindertransport*, supported Israel's military efforts by producing rifles, mortar shells and tanks and selling them to Israel. He can be seen as typical for the first generation of Holocaust survivors, who often had strong feelings of loyalty for Israel. This is emblematic for the wider British Jewish community up to the 1970s, where 'solidarity with Israel became a vehicle for communal pride and ethnicity', which was also linked to providing financial and public support for Israel.[59] Nessa, however, can be seen as exemplifying the split between British Jewry and unconditional support for Israel that became apparent after the 1982 Lebanon War and the First Intifada.[60] Hence, Nessa – in contrast to her father – wants to help Israel in a different way: she tells her audience that, 'We believe that the strongest wall that we can help Israel to maintain is the one through which equality of opportunity can pass.'[61] It becomes clear that Blick's protagonist does not fit the typical mould of individuals who seek refuge in their families at times of conflict, which as Sarah Harwood argued above, is done in order to 'search for absolute values, unassailable moral positions, which are apparently outside ideology, outside history'.[62]

While the relationships with her family, including with her father and her brother, serve as a foil to highlight the ways in which Nessa runs the company differently and adopts a more critical stance vis-à-vis events in the Middle East, the relationship between Nessa and Atika is the one that anchors Nessa and provides an alternative family to her, at least from Nessa's own perspective. A key event in Nessa's life, and one that is at the heart of her personal conflict and which cements her friendship with Atika, occurs when Nessa goes to the Gaza Strip to resolve an issue related to corruption within the foundation set up by her family. Through a series of flashbacks, the audience finds out that Nessa and Atika were kidnapped and that Nessa was raped by one of their Palestinian captors. It is important to briefly discuss this scene to examine the motives for this rape. Saleh Al-Zahid (Philip Arditti), Nessa's rapist, enters the room where Nessa and Atika are held captive. He is represented as very emotional but also exhausted, breathing heavily. Al-Zahid pins Nessa to the wall and shows her pictures of his wife and daughter while telling her: 'When you take away my wife, when you take away my child, my life and all you've got is nothing, you will fight with whatever you have left.'[63] This statement is followed by him ordering her to lie down, clearly linking his intention to rape her to a sense of revenge and making her – as a British Jewish woman – stand in for

Israel, who is being blamed for the death of his family. After the rape, Al-Zahid repeats 'with whatever we have left',[64] showing Nessa two pictures of bloodied body parts among rubble, suggesting that his wife and child were killed during an Israeli military operation in the Gaza Strip.[65]

If we read Nessa's rape in light of colonial fantasies about women, this moment constitutes an example of what Anne McClintock has called a 'compensatory gesture', making up for a loss of power.[66] In this case, the loss of power is associated with grief and a desire to get revenge on Israel by inflicting pain on a Jewish woman as a substitute for Israel. This aligns with Ann J. Cahill's argument that

> [t]he meaning of rape is never individualistic. Rapists do not rape individuals, but members of a class; the act of rape, then, becomes a reminder to both assailant and victim that membership in one of these classes is the defining element of identity.'[67]

Following Cahill, we can conclude that Nessa is not raped in her capacity as an individual but as a representative of the Jewish people, and that one of the intentions is to degrade her status as an 'untainted' woman within her society and national community, one who can produce a 'stable national citizen', to use Hella Cohen Bloom's idea discussed in relation to Hajaj's novel.

While still in captivity, Nessa finds out that she is pregnant, but she is unable to get an abortion since under Sharia law all life is sacred, as Atika tells her. After the birth of her son Kasim, Nessa and Atika are able to leave Gaza, and it is agreed that Atika will look after Kasim as her own. While the rape seems to be motivated by the rapist's personal circumstances and tragedy, Zahid Al-Zahid (Nasser Memarzia), the rapist's father, later discloses that he ordered his son to rape Nessa to take revenge on the late Eli Stein. Zahid Al-Zahid reflects: 'The grandson of Eli Stein. With my blood in its veins. First, I ordered his death, now I take his heritage.'[68] This situates Nessa's rape within a wider framework of using rape in the context of war, where rape becomes a 'brutally enforced hybridity'.[69] In the twisted logic of Zahid Al-Zahid, the child, who is of mixed Jewish-Palestinian heritage, is seen as a way to dilute the Jewishness of the Stein family – even though in light of matrilineal descent, Kasim's identity would still be considered Jewish. However, Kasim's hybridity is hidden, as he grows up as part of Nessa's brother's household; meanwhile, his mixed heritage is not discussed as he is presented as Atika's son for most of the series.

One of the events that leads to Nessa revealing that she is Kasim's mother is Kasim's kidnapping at the end of the first episode. Finding Kasim is one of the driving forces of the series, culminating in the final episode, and is also important for fully understanding both Nessa's and Atika's identities and their relationship with each other. Nessa is kidnapped again after a bomb is set off at an event that she held in Hebron for her company's Phase 3 broadband roll-out. During their renewed captivity, Atika confesses that she knew that they would kidnap Nessa when they went to the Gaza Strip but that she 'didn't know what that man would do to [her]'.[70] When Nessa asks her why, Atika explains that when she was twelve, she lost all of her family. She then shows Nessa a piece of shrapnel from a bomb that has the name Stein on it, indicating that her family was killed by a weapon manufactured by Nessa's father. In this way, Atika draws attention to the relations between their families, including the invisible relations between actions in the West – such as providing weapons to Israel – and the deaths of Palestinians. Nessa explains that she tried to help but Atika emphasises that the Palestinian people need a nation, and that 'what [Nessa] tried doesn't change anything for [her] people, [they] need so much more'.[71] While Nessa's efforts to improve communication are admirable but naive, they do not translate into any specific progress in terms of Palestinian liberation and self-determination. Nessa asks Atika whether she needs her to die, to which Atika responds, 'Me, no. But if it's the price for a nation, I'm sorry to tell you, yes.'[72]

However, in spite of this nationalistic fervour, after a disagreement Atika has with Zahid Al-Zahid during which Al-Zahid attacks her with a knife, Atika fittingly stabs him with the piece of shrapnel of the Stein bomb that killed her family, thus implicitly defending Nessa and emphasising her loyalties towards her. Atika is also the one who saves Kasim and brings him to Nessa, after Nessa asked Al-Zahid to release him and Al-Zahid refused to do so. This is an interesting moment in the series as it is the first time that Nessa publicly acknowledges Kasim as her son, even though there were other instances where her feelings towards Kasim were hinted at either verbally or through camera movements, including by indirectly voicing her regrets for not raising him as her own. Nevertheless, in the final episode, it is Atika who is cast in the role of the 'honourable' woman of the title, defying stereotypes about Arabs and Palestinians. This is confirmed when she sacrifices herself by authorising MI5 to carry out an airstrike against Robert Hardy (Christian Contreras) who has been sent to kill them, so that Nessa and Kasim can escape, even though she knows that this airstrike will kill her too. Her final words are, 'Get off my land.'[73] These words are addressed to Robert Hardy as an intruder on her land, but equally to a British audience and the United Kingdom, drawing attention to how the British Mandate in Palestine has contributed to Atika's land being taken from her.

Interestingly, Blick's drama is the only work discussed in *Reimagining Israel and Palestine in Contemporary British and German Culture* that imagines a solution for Palestinian aspirations to their own homeland, and by extension Israel's role as an occupation power. After the bombing in Hebron, when Nessa is believed to be dead, the US Secretary of State describes Nessa as an 'unending campaigner for reconciliation in the Middle East' and announces that if the Palestinian Authority were to resubmit their application to the United Nations for the recognition of Palestine as a state, the United States 'will not stand in the way of Palestine's quest for statehood'.[74] This ironically echoes Atika's statement about the 'price for a nation', as it establishes a direct, but in reality very unlikely, link between Nessa's death and the United States's support for Palestine. In spite of the improbability of the scenario, this is an important moment as the quest for Palestinian statehood is one of the crucial driving forces in Blick's TV drama. However, as soon as it transpires that Nessa is still alive, the United States withdraw their support, emphasising the short-lived nature of this solution as well as its unlikelihood.

Hugo Blick has noted that his TV drama is 'certainly not offering any actual, specific answers to such a complex and emotionally provocative issue'.[75] However, read in light of Michael Denning's observation that 'spy thrillers have been "cover stories" for our culture, collective fantasies … paralleling reality, expressing what they wish to conceal' as well as having close links with histories in the contemporary world,[76] the very act of imagining what a solution to the situation in Palestine/Israel, however simplified, might look like is significant. It showcases a desire, at least on an imaginary level, to transcend the impasse that discussions about a just solution for both Israel and Palestine currently find themselves in, which is also something that we will see in Chapter 5 in relation to a German desire to imagine coexistence between Israelis and Palestinians. Blick's imaginative quest for resolution can be applied to a British sense of wanting to be absolved of their responsibility for Israel and Palestine that started with the British Mandate. This is confirmed when analysing the final scene of the series.

In this final scene, Nessa and Kasim visit Nessa's brother's wife Rachel in hospital to meet her newborn child. Nessa stands apart from Rachel and Kasim, suggesting that she is still unable to fully belong anywhere. Blick has described Nessa as 'constantly battling a consuming internal conflict – this internal struggle for reconciliation with her past and her search for personal equilibrium' which is evident 'in her political activities – to try to reconcile a conflict that has equally haunted a region of the world, countless lives, and political agendas for many years'.[77] The series presents contributing to a reconciliation between Israeli Jews and Palestinians as a way to further Nessa's personal reconciliation, since the absence of the former is at the heart of why she feels conflicted. However, this connection also already indicates that personal reconciliation will be an impossible goal to achieve, since reconciliation between Israelis and Palestinians seems increasingly out of reach in the contemporary period, especially if such a reconciliation is attempted – as exemplified by Nessa on a personal level – without achieving Palestinian liberation and self-determination first.

Unlike Nessa, Kasim is depicted as easily fitting in with the Stein family, in spite of his hybridity. This is visualised when Rachel puts Kasim's hand on her baby's arm, establishing a physical and familial relation between them that is not based on blood ties. Ironically, it is Kasim as the hybrid child who finds belonging through affiliation. To a certain extent, he can be read as a 'symbol of a utopian reconciliatory future' between Jewish and Palestinian narratives within the context of the UK, thus emphasising the importance of creating a framework, or in this case a figure, that brings these two narratives together. Hence, this final scene emphasises the idea of a British desire for dialogue and reconciliation, which was also expressed through imagining a 'solution' earlier in the series. It suggests that envisioning an end to the occupation of Palestine would constitute a means to be absolved of the guilt related to the British Mandate. While ending the occupation and creating an independent Palestinian state might be impossible – and the series is certainly ambivalent about this, contrasting the failed Palestinian quest for statehood with the success of Kasim as a hybrid child – this is nevertheless an important imaginative and rhetorical move as it does not give precedence to Jewish suffering. Instead, it acknowledges the importance of considering both Jewish and Palestinian stories of dispossession, displacement and suffering, while emphasising the need to think comparatively about Israel and Palestine and their histories.

Alternative Kinship as Metaphor

What we see in the two cultural works discussed in this chapter is a deliberate refusal to legitimise exclusion through the use of the family. Instead, both Hajaj and Blick disrupt the family as a model for the nation, especially for a nation or national community defined by ethnicity. Both artists use alternative alliances – including libidinal and amicable relations across divides, and the presence of Jewish Palestinian children – to bring together Jewish and Palestinian narratives and to uncover the at times hidden relations between them. In her novel, Hajaj shows both Jewish and Palestinian perspectives on their respective histories of suffering by bringing together Jewish and Palestinian narratives and presenting them as interrelated, from the *nakba* to the First Intifada. Implicit in her novel is the sense that the recognition of the Palestinian narrative of suffering as related to Jewish narratives of suffering is a key aspect of working towards Palestinian liberation and independence in Palestine, Israel and beyond. Blick's work draws a more complex picture of the Palestinian resistance and its motivations through the character of Atika Halabi. He also engages more explicitly with the future of Israel and Palestine, envisioning a short-lived solution that clearly foregrounds the ways in which Palestinian self-determination is not only dependent on Israel but equally on the support of its powerful allies, such as the United States and the United Kingdom. While both works have their limitations, through their emphasis on relationality and an alternative approach to kinship, both artists encourage their audiences to reflect on the power differentials that govern these contexts, including those between Israel, Palestine and international powers, which are often occluded in discussions that emphasise a kinship approach on a national and international level.

The fifth chapter, 'Relational Coexistence: Donations Across Divides and Imagined Kinship in Palestine/Israel', extends the idea of kinship by considering how German authors and directors establish a 'relational coexistence' – a coexistence between (Israeli) Jewish and Palestinian characters that models relations between Israel and Palestine, taking into account each community's history of suffering and displacement and emphasising the relations between these histories. Werner Sonne's novel *Wenn ich dich vergesse, Jerusalem* (*If I Forget You, Jerusalem*, 2008; translated into English as *Where the Desert Meets the Sea*, 2019) and Leon Geller and Marcus Vetter's documentary *Das Herz von Jenin* (*The Heart of Jenin*, 2008) do this by using blood and organ donations across divides as a way to interrogate ideas of kinship and universal humanity, and the possibilities of coexistence between Israeli Jews and Palestinians in a shared state. This chapter develops the concept of 'relational coexistence' to challenge ideas in the European imaginary of Israeli Jews and Palestinians as antagonists. Meanwhile, it draws attention to a German desire to imagine a solution to Israel's occupation of the Palestinian Territories, and Palestinian aspirations for statehood. This emphasis on relationality and coexistence is linked to a desire to be absolved of Holocaust guilt.

Notes

1. Sreya Chatterjee, *Family Fictions and World Making: Irish and Indian Women's Writing in the Contemporary Era* (New York: Routledge, 2021), 1.
2. Ron Prosor quoted in Maya Shwayder, 'JPost Conference Preview: Ron Prosor on Israel and the United Nations,' *The Jerusalem Post*, 2 March 2014, https://www.jpost.com/features/in-thespotlight/jpost-conference-preview-ron-prosor-on-israel-and-the-united-nations-344030.
3. Anne McClintock, *Imperial Leather: Race, Gender and Sexuality in the Colonial Conquest* (New York: Routledge, 1995), 357.
4. Sarah Harwood, *Family Fictions: Representations of the Family in 1980s Hollywood Cinema* (New York: St. Martin's Press, 1997), 3.
5. Van Teeffelen, 'Racism and Metaphor,' 390.
6. Ronnie Hjorth, *Equality in International Society: A Reappraisal* (London: Palgrave Macmillan, 2014), 70.
7. Shwayder, 'Jpost conference preview.'
8. Ariella Azoulay and Adi Ophir, *The One-State Condition: Occupation and Democracy in Israel/Palestine* (Palo Alto: Stanford University Press, 2012), 247.
9. David Novak, *The Jewish Social Contract: An Essay in Political Theology* (Princeton: Princeton University Press, 2005), 2.
10. See, for example, Oren Yiftachel, *Ethnocracy: Land and Identity Politics in Israel/Palestine* (Philadelphia: University of Pennsylvania Press, 2006) and Yerach Gover,

Zionism: The Limits of Moral Discourse in Israeli Hebrew Fiction (Minneapolis; London: The University of Minnesota Press, 1994).

11. Ruth Perry, *Novel Relations: The Transformation of Kinship in English Literature and Culture, 1748–1818* (Cambridge: Cambridge University Press, 2004), 2.
12. Ilan Pappé, 'Post-Zionism and its Popular Cultures,' in *Palestine, Israel, and the Politics of Popular Culture*, ed. Rebecca L. Stein and Ted Swedenburg (Durham, NC: Duke University Press, 2005), 87.
13. Hella Bloom Cohen, *The Literary Imagination in Israel-Palestine: Orientalism, Poetry, and Biopolitics* (New York: Palgrave Macmillan, 2016), 4.
14. Said, 'Arabs And Jews,' 3.
15. Said, *World, the Text, and the Critic*, 25.
16. Cohen, *Literary Imagination*, 33.
17. T. J. Raphael, and Mythili Rao, 'Her Mom is Jewish. Her Dad is Palestinian. She Sees Both Sides,' *The Takeaway*, 31 July 2014, https://www.pri.org/stories/2014-07-31/her-mom-jewish-her-dad-palestinian-she-sees-both-sides.
18. Jude's full name is Judith but, as a teenager, she decides to adopt the name 'Jude' – even though her family is horrified as this is the German word for 'Jew' and reminds them of the persecution of the Jewish people in Nazi Germany.
19. Claire Hajaj, *Ishmael's Oranges* (London: Oneworld, 2014), xi.
20. Hajaj, *Ishmael's Oranges*, 50.
21. For an overview of this law, see Hillel Cohen, 'The Internal Refugees in the State of Israel; Israeli Citizens, Palestinian Refugees,' *Palestine – Israel Journal of Politics, Economics and Culture* 9, no. 2 (2002): 43–51, https://pij.org/articles/159/the-internal-refugees-in-the-state-of-israel---israeli-citizens-palestinian-refugees.
22. Masalha, *The Palestine Nakba*, 12. See also Abu-Lughod and Sa'di, 'Claims of Memory,' 1–24.
23. Hajaj, *Ishmael's Oranges*, 124.
24. Hajaj, *Ishmael's Oranges*, 113.
25. Hajaj, *Ishmael's Oranges*, 117.
26. Sontag, *On Photography*, 4; 9.
27. Hajaj, *Ishmael's Oranges*, 24.
28. Hajaj, *Ishmael's Oranges*, 84.
29. Hajaj, *Ishmael's Oranges*, 123.
30. Ella Shohat, 'On Orientalist Genealogies: The Split Arab/Jew Figure Revisited,' in Bashir and Farsakh, *Arab and Jewish Questions*, 89. As Shohat emphasises, this idea is a recent invention as there were many alliances between Jewish and Arab people before the twentieth century. An interesting example of this tendency is evident in Mark D. Charney's article about the First Intifada, where the 'rivalry' between

Israeli Jews and Palestinians is described as being 'as old as the contest between Moslem and Jew for the legacy of their common father, Abraham' (Marc D. Charney, 'Arab and Israeli – The Roots of the Conflict,' *The New York Times*, 28 February 1998, https://www.nytimes.com/1988/02/28/weekinreview/world-arab-israeli-roots-conflict-battleground-jordan-sea.html). Interestingly, Charney also uses the term 'fratricidal agony', suggesting that Israeli Jews and Palestinians are two siblings locked in an eternal fight, aligning with the biblical story of Ishmael who was banished with his mother after the arrival of his brother Isaac. By naming Salim's father Ishmael, Hajaj draws attention to how the Jewish people displaced or 'banished' the Palestinian people after the creation of the state of Israel.

31. Hajaj, *Ishmael's Oranges*, 133; original emphasis.
32. Hajaj, *Ishmael's Oranges*, 145.
33. Anne McClintock, 'Family Feuds: Gender, Nationalism and the Family,' *Feminist Review* 44 (1993): 64, https://doi.org/10.2307/1395196.
34. Pappé, 'Post-Zionism and its Popular Cultures,' 87.
35. Hajaj, *Ishmael's Oranges*, 183.
36. Cohen, *Literary Imagination*, 23.
37. Hajaj, *Ishmael's Oranges*, 224.
38. Hajaj, *Ishmael's Oranges*, 234.
39. Hajaj, *Ishmael's Oranges*, 190.
40. Cohen, *Literary Imagination*, 30–1.
41. Abu-Lughod and Sa'di, 'Claims of Memory,' 17.
42. Hajaj, *Ishmael's Oranges*, viii.
43. Ben East, 'Claire Hajaj's novel Ishmael's Oranges is a love story set against unrest in the Middle East,' *The National*, 19 July 2014, https://www.thenational.ae/arts-culture/books/claire-hajaj-s-novel-ishmael-s-oranges-is-a-love-story-set-against-unrest-in-the-middle-east-1.307044.
44. Sameena Karim, 'The Co-Existence of Globalism and Tribalism: A Review of the Literature,' *Journal of Research in International Education* 11, no. 2 (2012): 140, https://doi.org/10.1177/1475240912452465.
45. Dan Bar-On and Saliba Sarsar, 'Bridging the Unbridgeable: The Holocaust and Al-Nakba,' *Palestine-Israel Journal of Politics, Economics and Culture* 11, no. 1 (2004): 63, https://www.pij.org/articles/17.
46. Deborah Kalb, 'Q&A with author Claire Hajaj,' *Book Q&As with Deborah Kalb*, 31 July 2014, https://deborahkalbbooks.blogspot.com/2014/07/q-with-author-claire-hajaj.html.
47. Hajaj, *Ishmael's Oranges*, 196.
48. Hajaj, *Ishmael's Oranges*, 250, original emphasis.

49. Raphael and Rao, 'Her Mom is Jewish.'
50. Hajaj, *Ishmael's Oranges*, 272.
51. Bernard, 'Forms of Memory,' 16.
52. Hajaj, *Ishmael's Oranges*, 307.
53. Perry, *Novel Relations*, 373.
54. Ilan Pappé quoted in Yosefa Loshitzky, *Identity Politics on the Israeli Screen* (Austin: University of Texas Press, 2001), 112–13.
55. Hugo Blick, 'Q&A with Hugo Blick, Writer, Producer and Director of *The Honourable Woman*,' BBC Writers Room, 3 July 2014, https://www.bbc.co.uk/blogs/writersroom/entries/cc86b976-3937-3b4e-accb-dce2e7f2e77b.
56. Van Teeffelen, 'Racism and Metaphor,' 390, 384.
57. Emanuelle Degli Esposti, 'Conspiracy in the Holy Land,' Review of *Shake Off*, by Michel Hiller, *The Arab Review*, http://www.thearabreview.org/shake-off-mischa-hiller-review. As the late Jack Sheehan has convincingly shown in his overview of the depiction of Arab characters in Hollywood films released between 1896 and 2001, this is not an isolated case: 'the celluloid Arab ... is what he has always been – the cultural "other"' (Jack G. Sheehan, *Reel Bad Arabs: How Hollywood Vilifies a People* (New York: Olive Branch Press, 2001), 2, 13).
58. George Lakoff, *Moral Politics: What Conservatives Know That Liberals Don't* (Chicago: University of Chicago Press, 1996), 84.
59. Toby Greene and Yossi Shain, 'The Israelization of British Jewry: Balancing Between Home and Homeland,' *The British Journal of Politics and International Relations* 18, no. 4 (2016): 853, https://doi.org/10.1177/1369148116669061.
60. Greene and Shain, 'The Israelization of British Jewry,' 853. For an overview of the British Jewish community's relationship with Israel, see also Colin Shindler, 'The Reflection of Israel Within British Jewry,' in *Israel, the Diaspora and Jewish Identity*, ed. Danny Ben-Moshe and Zohar Segev (Brighton; Portland: Sussex Academic Press, 2007).
61. *The Honourable Woman*, Episode 1, 'The Empty Chair,' directed by Hugo Blick, featuring Maggie Gyllenhal, Lubna Azabal and Andrew Buchan. Aired 3 July 2014, on BBC Two. Streamed via Stan, https://play.stan.com.au/programs/1333466/play [00:14:52–00:15:01].
62. Harwood, *Family Fictions*, 3.
63. *The Honourable Woman*, Episode 4, 'The Ribbon Cutter,' directed by Hugo Blick, featuring Maggie Gyllenhal, Lubna Azabal and Stephen Rea. Aired 24 July 2014, on BBC Two. Streamed via Stan, https://play.stan.com.au/programs/1333469/play [00:47:30–00:48:51].
64. *The Honourable Woman*, Episode 4 [00:51:44–00:51:46].

65. The series does not indicate as part of which military operation Saleh's wife and child were killed but given that it is set after the United Nations rejected the Palestinian bid for statehood in 2011, it could either have been Operation Cast Lead (2008/2009) or one of Israel's more recent military operations, such as Operation Pillar of Defense (2012).
66. McClintock, *Imperial Leather*, 24.
67. Ann J. Cahill, *Rethinking Rape* (Ithaca: Cornell University Press, 2001), 19.
68. *The Honourable Woman*, Episode 4 [00:56:55–00:57:04].
69. McClintock, *Imperial Leather*, 67.
70. *The Honourable Woman*, Episode 8, 'The Paring Knife,' directed by Hugo Blick, featuring Maggie Gyllenhal, Lubna Azabal and Eve Best. Aired 21 August 2014, on BBC Two. Streamed via Stan, https://play.stan.com.au/programs/1333473/play [00:21:00–00:21:30].
71. *The Honourable Woman*, Episode 8 [00:23:12–00:26:10].
72. *The Honourable Woman*, Episode 8 [00:23:12–00:26:10].
73. *The Honourable Woman*, Episode 8 [00:48:00–00:48:02].
74. *The Honourable Woman*. Episode 8 [00:05:43–00:06:00]. This references Palestine's failed 2011 application to become a full member of the United Nations and its successful 2012 application to become a 'non-member observer state' of the United Nations.
75. Blick, 'Q&A with Hugo Blick.'
76. Michael Denning, *Cover Stories: Narrative and Ideology in the British Spy Thriller* (London: Routledge & Kegan Paul, 1987), 1.
77. Blick, 'Q&A with Hugo Blick.'

5

RELATIONAL COEXISTENCE: DONATIONS ACROSS DIVIDES AND IMAGINED KINSHIP IN PALESTINE/ISRAEL

Yoni Jesner, a Scottish Jewish young adult, died in a bus bombing carried out by a Palestinian in Tel Aviv in 2002. Ahmed Khatib, a Palestinian boy, was killed by an Israeli soldier in Jenin in November 2005. What unites Yoni and Ahmed is that both of their families decided to donate their son's organs, knowing that they might go to someone 'across the divide', as in Israel, you cannot decide which 'religion' the recipient of your organ donation should have.[1] As Chris McGreal notes in a *Guardian* article about the Khatib family's decision, 'the move [to donate Ahmed's organs] was hailed by stunned Israeli leaders as a "remarkable gesture for peace"' and 'a bridge between warring communities' and the family was 'praised' 'for its "remarkable humanity"' by then–deputy prime minister Ehud Olmert.[2]

These organ donations are seen as a model for crossing and bridging divides, which might seem distant from reality but, as Emily Russell convincingly argues in the context of South Africa, organ donations can function 'as a powerful metaphor in the critique of racist policies' by emphasising a 'universal humanity, imagined as an essential sameness "under the skin"'.[3] Organ, and blood, donations can thus be read as challenges to the boundaries between two national communities, especially boundaries defined by ethnicity. As William Hughes notes, '[t]he nation, the race, the family are all structured metaphorically and/or metonymically in terms of blood relations, the individual functioning as a blood-bearing synecdoche of the greater unity in which he – and his blood – circulate.'[4] This chapter extends the discussions in Chapter 4 about the disrupted family as a critical mode for engaging with exclusionary ethnic communities, by asking what it means for the idea of the nation, especially one defined by ethnicity, if an Israeli Jewish individual receives an organ donation from a Palestinian boy, or a Palestinian woman receives blood from a Jewish woman. In discussing the 'sharing of substances', Kath Weston perceptively asks '[i]f kinship can ideologically entail shared substance, can transfers of bodily substance create – or threaten to create – kinship?'[5] I am particularly interested in how donations across divides result in fictive kinships that question the separatist imaginary that posits Palestinians and Israeli Jews as oppositional and precludes any coexistence between the two communities on an individual and a collective level. I also consider to what extent donations across divides contribute to imagining a different way of coexisting in Palestine/Israel – what I term for the purpose of this chapter 'relational coexistence' – which takes into account the power imbalances between Palestinians and (Israeli) Jews before 1948 and after the Second Intifada.

The literature and film discussed in this chapter – German author and former foreign correspondent Werner Sonne's novel *Wenn ich dich vergesse, Jerusalem* (*If I Forget You, Jerusalem*, 2008; republished under the title *Jerusalem, Jerusalem* in 2018 and translated into English as *Where the Desert Meets the Sea* in 2019) and German director Marcus Vetter and Israeli Jewish American director Leon Geller's documentary entitled *Das Herz von Jenin* (*The Heart of Jenin*, 2008) – were chosen as case studies because they imagine coexistence between Israeli Jews and Palestinians through consanguineal ties as expressed through blood or organ donations. *Wenn ich dich vergesse, Jerusalem* uses a blood transfusion between a Jewish and a Palestinian character before the establishment of the state of Israel to challenge common perceptions of Jews and Palestinians as 'polarized identities',[6] which are often expressed in terms of a clash between civilisations. This is a framework that Samuel Huntington has employed to think about the post–Cold War world, arguing that, '[T]he fundamental source of conflict in this new world will not be primarily ideological or primarily economic. The great divisions among humankind and the dominant source of conflict will be cultural.'[7] Sonne demonstrates that the 'clash' between (Israeli) Jews and Palestinians is not cultural or based on religion or ethnicity, which in Europe as elsewhere is often encapsulated in the misconceived phrase of 'an age-old conflict', or as Ella Shohat puts it, in the idea of 'perennial enemies locked in perpetual conflict'.[8] Instead,

Sonne returns to a specific historical period – between 15 February 1947 and 11 June 1948. This period includes key events such as the Deir Yassin massacre and the attack on a Hadassah hospital convoy, which both happened in April 1948, to foreground one of the roots of the 'clash' between Palestinians and Israeli Jews that shapes their engagement until today: the dispossession and displacement of around 750,000 Palestinians in the lead up to, and aftermath of, the establishment of the state of Israel.

Contrary to Sonne, Marcus Vetter and Leon Geller's documentary *Das Herz von Jenin* offers more critical engagement with the possibility of coexistence. The documentary, set in 2007, uses organ donation as a practice and an idea to reflect on the relationships between Israeli Jews and Palestinians in the contemporary period. It focuses on the story of Ismael Khatib, Ahmed's father, and his visits to three of the children who received his son's organs. Vetter and Geller's work offers a critical outlook on the future of Palestine/Israel, drawing attention to one of the major problems that Israeli Jews and Palestinians are faced with if they want to implement a one-state solution: making 'the initial acknowledgment of the Other as an equal', as Edward Said has noted.[9] While in a Palestinian context this means acknowledging the necessity of a Jewish state, in the Israeli Jewish case, this means offering reparations to Palestinians who have been displaced and dispossessed since the *nakba*, including, but not limited to, by providing Palestinians with the option to live in a Palestinian state. Acknowledging the other has become particularly important in the wake of the Second Intifada, when it became clear that the two-state solution, which was celebrated in the wake of the 1993 Oslo Accords, was not a feasible idea any more – especially given Israel's continued fragmentation of the West Bank through building new settlements, which makes the creation of a coherent Palestinian geopolitical entity impossible. Hence, since the turn of the twenty-first century, a shared state seems the most likely solution to Israel's settler-colonial occupation of Palestine, and to Israeli Palestinian and Palestinian national aspirations. As Ghada Karmi summarises, there are several models for a one-state solution, the two main ones being the binational or parallel-state model, where Israelis and Palestinians share the land but retain separate religious/ethnic communities, and the secular model, which would give everyone individual citizenship and equal rights.[10]

However, as Edward Said has rightly argued, the prerequisite for achieving any type of solution, including a one-state solution, is 'coexistence and sharing in ways that require an innovative, daring, and theoretical willingness to get beyond the arid stalemate of assertion, exclusivism, and rejection'.[11] This statement takes on further poignancy with Israelis and Palestinians becoming increasingly distant and separate from each other on a physical level. At the same time, the need to imagine and envision models of coexistence has become more and more pressing, after more than seven decades of Palestinian dispossession and displacement and over five decades of living under occupation for Palestinians in the West Bank, Gaza and East Jerusalem. This has not only affected Palestinian people living under occupation and Palestinians living in Israel as second-class citizens, but also Israeli Jews who have had to reconcile their identity with what Hagar Kotef has astutely called 'the colonizing self', an identity that has been created and shaped by the establishment of Israel on another population's homeland and exacerbated by Israel's occupation of the West Bank, Gaza and East Jerusalem since 1967.[12]

While depicting the act of donating organs across divides is in and of itself a critique of the divisions between (Israeli) Jews and Palestinians, this chapter reads the donations as a means to challenge ideas of kinship and universal humanity and the possibilities of coexistence between Israeli Jews and Palestinians in a shared state. Both works' critique is achieved by uncovering some of the limitations of creating familial links through the means of donations, especially on the level of an ideology which necessitates the strict separation of Palestinians and (Israeli) Jews, and of their respective narratives of suffering. This is a key aspect of the 'relational coexistence' that this chapter focuses on: a coexistence between (Israeli) Jewish and Palestinian characters that models relations between Israel and Palestine in a way that takes into account each community's history of suffering and displacement, and emphasises the relations between these histories. However, as I discuss in the conclusion to this chapter, this concept also foregrounds a German desire to imagine an end to the 'tensions' between Israeli Jews and Palestinians, which is linked to a desire to be absolved of Holocaust guilt and a desire to '(co)exist' as a normal nation with a normalised approach to engaging with Israel and Palestine.

Shared Blood and Shared Histories in Werner Sonne's *Wenn ich dich vergesse, Jerusalem*

Werner Sonne, who has published a range of novels, including political thrillers, used to be a foreign correspondent for the *ARD*, one of Germany's publicly funded TV channels, and he covered amongst other things the 1973 Yom Kippur War in Israel. His novel *Wenn ich dich vergesse, Jerusalem* reflects this interest in the Middle East but equally the ways in which the stories of Israel and Palestine interweave with German history. Sonne tells the story of Judith Wertheimer, a German Jewish Holocaust survivor who was interned at Dachau. After arriving in Palestine on board the fictional ship *Morning Cloud*, Judith feels alienated and lonely, especially when she learns of the death of her uncle – her only living relative in Palestine. After a suicide attempt, she moves to a kibbutz and becomes part of the Jewish underground resistance. Judith's perspective is situated alongside those of other characters, such as Uri Rabinowitsch, a Jewish underground fighter and later her lover, and Hana Khalidy, a Palestinian nurse from Deir Yassin who works at the Hadassah Hospital on Mount Scopus in Jerusalem.

In the afterword to his novel, Sonne explains that, '[I]t is difficult to understand why two people simply cannot find common ground, even though solutions seemed to be within reach, at least in the nineties ... instead they are reverting to old patterns of hostility.'[13] This perception of the 1990s as a turning point in Palestinian–Israeli Jewish relations is one that is commonly held outside of Israel and Palestine and especially in the West, where the handshake between Yasser Arafat and Yitzhak Rabin on 13 September 1993 on the lawn of the White House in Washington, after the signing of the Oslo Accords, was celebrated as an iconic moment in the peace process. As Cherine Hussein argues, this handshake was '[p]erceived to have inaugurated a new era of hope in the search for peace and justice in Palestine/Israel'.[14] Sonne sees his novel as a contribution to returning to this moment where peace seemed possible, using the Palestinian and Jewish employees of the Hadassah hospital as an example.[15] Hadassah hospital, which now has campuses on Mount Scopus and Ein Kerem in West Jerusalem, has gained international renown for employing staff without taking into account their ethnicities and religions and for fostering an environment where patients feel treated well irrespective of their ethnicity or faith.[16] Palestinian Kamel Husseini, drawing on his own experience of taking his mother to Hadassah hospital for cancer treatments, has described this approach as the 'Hadassah model' in an article published in the Hebrew daily newspaper *Yedioth Ahronoth*. Husseini praised Hadassah staff for 'ris[ing] above the conflict and the hate and becom[ing] simply human'.[17] This article, which was translated and reprinted in numerous media outlets, was taken up enthusiastically by several people, including by Ehud Kokia, director-general of the Hadassah Medical Organisation from 2011–2013, who used the story to publicise Hadassah's work. Kokia quotes outpatient head nurse Fatma Hussein, who said that, 'If the whole world got along as well as our department, the whole world would be a better place.'[18]

This is exactly the rhetoric that appeals to Sonne and serves as the starting point for his novel. But rather than simply considering the possibilities of coexistence in the present, *Wenn ich dich vergesse, Jerusalem* returns to a key moment of coexistence in the past, focusing on the final days of the British Mandate and the establishment of Israel, in order to understand the roots of the so-called conflict. His novel examines one of these roots, namely the establishment of a Jewish state on land already inhabited by another population. Sonne shows both Jewish and Palestinian perspectives on the period between 15 February 1947 and 11 June 1948, and depicts key events for both communities, such as the Deir Yassin massacre and the attack on a Hadassah convoy in April 1948. As already implied by including both Jewish and Palestinian characters, the novel returns to a period of history where there was coexistence between Jewish and Palestinian people. This history of coexistence has often been occluded, especially by a Zionist discourse which portrayed the land as empty. As Gabriel Piterberg argues, this approach did not simply negate 'the presence of Arabs in Palestine, but rather the fact that their presence and resistance were consequential to the institutional dynamics and collective identity of the settler community and later nation-state'.[19]

However, as relational histories that have started to emerge since the 1980s, such as Zachary Lockman's book *Comrades and Enemies: Arab and Jewish Workers in Palestine, 1906–1948* (1996), demonstrate, there were 'mutually formative interactions' between Jewish and Palestinian communities before 1948.[20] In many ways, Sonne's novel adds to these academic studies about coexistence between Jewish and Palestinian people before the establishment of Israel by returning to this period and imagining the relationship between Judith and Hana. An important aspect of Sonne's novel is that Judith's and Hana's narratives are represented as connected and relational. This is unusual, since in Germany, as elsewhere, the Holocaust and the establishment of Israel are often seen as linked and the latter almost as a logical outcome of the former, while the Palestinian narrative of suffering is often marginalised or occluded in this context. As German academic

Wolfgang Benz has noted in a personal interview with Pól Ó Dochartaigh, '[t]he official foreign policy of the Federal Republic of Germany does not have room to manoeuvre. It cannot decide for the Arabs and against Israel. This contravenes the basic principles of German politics.'[21] Support for Palestinians is represented as being incompatible with supporting Israel, often due to fears of comparing the *nakba* to the Holocaust, which would diminish the memory of the Holocaust and challenge its status as a unique event in Germany, as discussed throughout this book. By drawing attention to the Palestinian experiences of displacement and dispossession leading up to and during the *nakba*, giving a prominent role to a Palestinian voice in his novel, and by situating these narratives alongside discussions of Judith's experience of Dachau, Sonne's work contributes implicitly to opening up a comparative framework between Jewish and other types of suffering in German culture.

Judith's and Hana's narratives intersect early on when Judith is brought to Hadassah hospital, after trying to commit suicide as a result of her experience during the Holocaust and her sense of loneliness and alienation in Palestine. She has lost a lot of blood, and since they have the same blood group – AB, which the novel depicts as rare – Hana is asked to donate blood to Judith.[22] Later, when Hana is stabbed by her ex-fiancé Youssef, Judith donates blood to her, mirroring Hana's earlier act of kindness while reinforcing the idea of a shared kinship between the two women as well as their dependence on each other. Sharing blood creates a sense of kinship between them that transcends the animosity of their respective collectives, at the same time as it challenges membership in these collectives as defined by blood and ethnicity. This is particularly salient in the case of the Jewish community since Israel increasingly defined itself as an ethnically Jewish state after 1948.[23] Judith and Hana's shared blood also leads them to consider how the actions of the ethnic group that they are part of impact on their 'enemy' friend. This emphasis on caring for someone outside of their ethnic community can be read in light of Timothy Wright's suggestion that 'blood cannot be reduced to a product separate from the lived human relations that created it', and that 'it retains an indelible trace of the other'.[24] By sharing blood Judith and Hana share a sense of kinship and belonging beyond their national community, which is defined along ethnic lines. Hence, this sharing of bodily substances emphasises a physical and imaginary leap across identarian boundaries.

Their friendship and blood relation challenges separatist narratives about Palestinians and Jews, specifically in the Mandate period, an idea that is voiced in the novel by the character Abraham Horowitz, a Jewish underground fighter, who says that, 'Peaceful coexistence is impossible. It's either them or us.'[25] This statement posits the tensions between Jews and Palestinians in the lead-up to the establishment of Israel as a zero-sum game, mirroring later German perceptions of support for Israel and support for Palestine as exclusive. It also foreshadows how the histories of the Holocaust and the *nakba* will be seen as exclusive after the establishment of Israel. As Bashir Bashir and Amos Goldberg have explained, this emphasis on exclusive narratives can be explained through the fact that the Holocaust and the *nakba* are considered as defining aspects of how Israeli Jews and Palestinians interact and that 'each relies . . . on the simultaneous and forceful negation (explicit or implicit) of the catastrophe of the other'.[26] As we will see in the discussion of Vetter and Geller's documentary *Das Herz von Jenin* below, this unwillingness or even inability to acknowledge the suffering of the other side is certainly still one of the major problems of 'acknowledg[ing] the other as equal', to return to Edward Said's quotation.

However, as Sonne's novel demonstrates, before the establishment of Israel there was mutual interest in the other's history of suffering, at least on an individual level. Gil Z. Hochberg has argued that 'repression and active forgetting' are rooted in creating and maintaining the 'radical separation' between Israeli Jews and Palestinians.[27] Moreover, as Bashir and Goldberg have shown, the Holocaust and the *nakba* are defining aspects of how Israeli Jews and Palestinians interact, since both are considered as 'foundational pasts', and thus they are 'often used to demonize the other side and establish a complete self-justification. Hence, they further widen the gap between the two peoples and disable the possibilities of conducive Jewish-Arab discussion of the question of Israel/Palestine.'[28] Thus, showing an interest in the other's history constitutes a challenge to this separation and an attempt to cross the gap that exists between Palestinian and Jewish narratives of suffering.

While Judith is recovering in hospital, Hana asks her about her concentration camp number, and Judith reflects that, 'Hana was the first person who had asked about her time in the camp since she arrived in Palestine.'[29] This comment confirms how initially there was no space in the new Jewish national community for stories of the Holocaust and Jewish suffering, since this contradicted the idea of the new Jew, the *sabra*, as a strong, pioneering identity. More importantly, this scene challenges the idea that Palestinians cannot accept the Jewish experience of the Holocaust, at least not if it 'means accepting the moral ground for the creation of the State of Israel'.[30] It is significant that this acknowledgment of the Jewish experience of suffering during the Holocaust and, as we will see below, the acknowledgment of the Palestinian experience of suffering during the *nakba,* happens before the official establishment of Israel, since, as many critics have shown, after 1948 there was 'an underlying fear that the acknowledgment of the tragedy of the "other" [would] justify their moral superiority and imply acceptance of their collective rationale'.[31] Part of this 'collective rationale' is linked to the need for a sovereign state, which is why it became harder to accept the other's tragedy after 1948, when the Jewish people had established Israel and the Palestinian people aspired to the right of self-determination, two demands that continue to be seen as exclusive and at odds with one other.

Judith, who moves to a kibbutz after recovering from her suicide attempt, increasingly questions the radical separation between the two peoples and their national aspirations, but also the means used by the Jewish people to achieve statehood. This criticism is often linked to her own experience, and that of Jewish people more generally, during the Holocaust. For example, Judith has a nightmare about a train with two thousand dead people on it, which is a reference to the infamous 'death train' of April 1945. This train, images of whose carriages have been widely circulated, brought concentration camp inmates from Buchenwald to Dachau, many of whom did not survive the journey. In the wake of this nightmare, Judith asks '[w]e Jews have just experienced the meaning of violence in Europe. We were turned into victims. Are we about to become perpetrators? . . . Are we not obliged to find a peaceful solution?'[32] She raises the common question of how people who were previously victimised are able to victimise someone else, but as many critics have shown, victims of violence and abuse are not less likely to commit violence against other people. As Mahmood Mamdani puts it 'victims of yesterday . . . may yet be victims again'.[33]

Moreover, as Hanna Yablonka has deduced, about a third of the soldiers fighting in the 1948 war were Holocaust survivors.[34] While this is understandable, since at the time many people considered the existence of the state of Israel to be paramount to preventing another Holocaust from happening, the involvement of Holocaust survivors in this war raises important questions about the ethics of violence. As Diane Enns has pointed out, 'if any act of violence can be excused by the perpetrator as a response to an earlier violation, then violence ceases to be a moral issue at all.'[35] In Sonne's novel, Judith continues to reflect on this issue, asking, 'Was there such a thing as a just war? A just war and she was on the right side?'[36] This questioning of the actions of the Jewish people and the ways in which the Holocaust is used as a justification for the suffering inflicted on the Palestinian people, draws attention to the potential for 'social responsibility' through the act of sharing substances, as Kath Weston has suggested.[37] The fact that the blood donations across divides have changed the ways in which Judith thinks about the 1948 war is confirmed after she joins the Jewish resistance. After reminding the reader that Hana's blood runs in her veins, she asks: 'Was [Hana] now an enemy, because she is an Arab?'[38] This question interrogates the separation between self and other that the act of sharing blood already challenged, but equally interrogates the categories of friend and foe based on ethnicity that the 1948 war necessitated and cemented.

This idea of a division along ethnic lines, and especially one that is corroborated in the lead-up to the establishment of Israel, which effectively pits one community's gaining of statehood against the loss of another community's home, recurs throughout the novel. An example is Hana's libidinal relationship with David Cohen, a Jewish doctor whom she works with at Hadassah hospital. As discussed in Chapters 1 and 3 in relation to German–Israeli Jewish libidinal relations, this romance-across-the-divide trope is common in order 'to imagine some kind of reconciliation between two conflicting communities'.[39] Here, the relationship between a Palestinian woman and a Jewish man is used to further highlight the growing national conflict between Palestinians and Jews, throwing into relief the implications of key events in the final days of the British Mandate for each collective and their aspirations to nationhood. When Hana hears about the results of the United Nations vote on the partition of Palestine on 29 November 1947 she is described as 'paralysed. Her face was pale.'[40] Hana's shock is contrasted with David's reaction, who while understanding her feelings, is still pleased with the result: 'It would be, he realised in this moment, his state as well. He was Jewish and wanted to be Jewish . . . But he sat next to an Arab woman – next to the woman he loved.'[41] Sonne foregrounds Hana's and David's ethnicities as an unbridgeable gap, which reflects common perceptions of the so-called conflict between Israeli Jews and Palestinians as a clash of cultures, as discussed in the introduction to this chapter.

However, this conception occludes the settler-colonial aspect of Palestinian–Israeli relations and the fact that, as part of the establishment of Israel, Palestinians were displaced and dispossessed, often deliberately, as detailed in Plan Dalet. Walid Khalidi has noted that this plan described a series of attacks in April and May 1948, which 'entailed the destruction of the Palestinian Arab community and the expulsion and pauperization of the bulk of the Palestine Arabs', and that these attacks 'were calculated to achieve the military *fait accompli* upon which the state of Israel was to be based'.[42] Sonne's novel quotes from the plan and depicts how it was put into practice, for example in the Palestinian village of Deir Yassin. Hana witnesses how the Haganah – the main Zionist paramilitary organisation, which was seen as more moderate than the Irgun – drives trucks with refugees from Deir Yassin through the streets of Jerusalem. Hana unsuccessfully tries to reach her father, who is held on one of the trucks. Judith, who witnesses this scene, asks Uri, a fellow underground fighter and her lover, to release Hana's father; in order to convince him, she holds out her lower arms and says, 'Look at the veins in my arms in which her blood flows. Without her, I wouldn't be here today.'[43] Judith not only emphasises the idea that Hana saved her life but also that Hana's blood is in her veins, challenging the idea of the Palestinians as the enemy, as well as the division between Palestinians and Jews based on ethnicity.

This links back to the idea that blood is inextricably linked to the 'lived human relations that created it',[44] suggesting an alliance between Judith and Hana that allows Judith to not exclusively see her as the enemy. Instead, Judith is depicted as being able to assume social responsibility for what the Jewish people are inflicting on the Palestinian people, and to try to understand the suffering that Hana is going through and link Hana's suffering to her own. Even though this is not spelled out in the book, it is very likely that Judith is not only showing Uri the veins in her lower arms, which contain Hana's blood, but also the concentration camp number that Sonne mentioned previously, which the author describes as being tattooed onto her wrist. Setting aside the historical inaccuracy of this tattoo if we assume that Judith shows Uri her concentration camp number, I want to suggest that rather than using her experience of the

Holocaust to justify inflicting suffering on the Palestinian people, Judith here emphasises that her suffering in Dachau should not be used as a reason to inflict suffering on others. Instead, it should serve as the basis for a shared understanding of displacement and dispossession.

In spite of Judith's affirmation of their shared blood, the idea of an unbridgeable conflict between Palestinians and Jews re-emerges when Hana's husband David is killed as part of the Palestinian attacks on a Hadassah convoy. This attack, carried out four days after the Deir Yassin massacre, has often been seen as revenge for Deir Yassin. In Sonne's novel, this is emphasised through the character of Youssef, Hana's ex-fiancé, who repeatedly shouts 'For Deir Yassin' while attacking the convoy and stabbing Hana.[45] After losing David, Hana realises that she is no longer able to cross over into what she calls 'the world of the Jews', since David 'had been her bridge into the other world, into their world'.[46] She continues by saying that, 'She had involved herself in the world of the Jews, she had loved one of them, she would have a child that was half Jewish. But still there was a rift, a deep gulf that could not be bridged.'[47] The loss of David drives home the fact that she no longer feels connected to the other side, neither through her shared blood with Judith nor through her child. This rift also emerges when Judith visits Hana at home on 28 April 1948, a few weeks after the Deir Yassin massacre and the attack on the Hadassah convey, and a few weeks before the official establishment of the state of Israel. Judith offers to help Hana and her father but Hana responds: 'Help? Me? Your people are killing us, expelling us, from wherever they can, and you – you help them. . . . Do you really think, I can forget everything? Do you really think there will be peaceful coexistence?'[48] Hana emphasises that one of the obstacles to coexistence is the fact that Jewish people are dispossessing, displacing and killing Palestinian people. She is unable to forgive Judith for the suffering that her people have inflicted on the Palestinians, demonstrating that the historical events in Palestine make it impossible for her to connect with Judith on an individual level, in spite of their shared blood.

Similarly complicating the idea of connections between people whose memories and narratives are often seen as exclusive, Lebanese writer Elias Khoury discusses the relationship between the Holocaust and the *nakba*, and argues that these events 'are not mirror images, but the Jew and the Palestinian are able to become mirror images of human suffering if they disabuse themselves of the delusion of exclusionist, nationalist ideologies'.[49] Sonne does position Judith and Hana to a certain extent as 'mirror images of human suffering'. But one of the dangers of this approach, as Shira Stav has argued in discussing Israeli works that engage with both the Holocaust and the *nakba*, consists in 'the political meaning that this mirroring constructs by placing the narrative of the other – the Palestinian catastrophe – within a Holocaust-based representation of the Nakba'.[50] Stav cautions against the Palestinian narrative only ever being mentioned in relation to the Holocaust, rather than being represented and engaged with on its own terms. Sonne's refusal of an easy comparison, and his emphasis on not only considering the *nakba* in relation to the Holocaust, is reflected in the resistance to reconciliation and resolution that becomes obvious in the endings that he chooses for Hana and Judith respectively. Hana leaves her home, heavily pregnant with David's child, and her story ends as she is about to cross into Jordan, leaving her in limbo. Judith, on the other hand, marries Uri and takes up her rightful place within the new national body, cementing the ties between Jewish people. This use of marriage and conjugal ties can be linked to Timothy Wright's discussion of how, 'in imaginings of bloodlines, of lineage, of race, blood becomes a way of recalibrating and normalizing the intrusion into a social body of an alien being: blood ties leap across boundaries of individual selves to bond communal units'.[51] In some ways, the novel uses marriage and an emphasis on conjugal ties between two people from the same ethnic group to 'recalibrat[e] and normaliz[e] the intrusion' of an 'alien being' – in this case the Palestinian – into the national community, and to re-emphasise the strengthening of bonds within rather than beyond this national community in order to safeguard it against intrusion.

It is significant that Sonne decided to create a comparative framework for understanding both Jewish and Palestinian suffering, thus reflecting Bashir and Goldberg's proposition for a 'new grammar' in which the Holocaust and the *nakba* 'are considered as commensurable, and their connection proves historically, politically, and ethically instructive and productive'.[52] While Sonne introduces the Holocaust first, possibly due to considerations for historical chronology, he does give space to the *nakba* and the suffering it engenders, and discusses it independently of the Holocaust. Moreover, he questions whether a Jewish state in Israel could have been established by other means through Judith's moral qualms about the methods of Jewish paramilitary organisations in the lead up to the creation of the state of Israel. However, Sonne's book neglects to fully take into account the significant power imbalances that continue to govern encounters between Israeli Jews and Palestinians today – especially since 1967 when Israel occupied the West Bank, the Gaza Strip and East Jerusalem, which make a solution based on an independent Palestinian state alongside an independent Israeli state very unlikely. Nevertheless, *Wenn ich dich vergesse, Jerusalem* is certainly an important work in its emphasis on the relational coexistence of the late 1940s as a potential model to be adapted for the future, and in its foregrounding of the benefits of acknowledging the other and their suffering as 'equal', which – as noted by Edward Said in the introduction to this chapter – is both an important step towards the one-state solution, and an approach that we rarely encounter in German media and culture.

Organ Transplants, Universal Humanity and the Limits of Coexistence in *Das Herz von Jenin*

Similar to Werner Sonne, Marcus Vetter and Leon Geller focus on donations across divides. However, instead of fictionalising these donations and situating them in the pre-state period, they have made a documentary about Ismael Khatib – the father of Ahmed Khatib, the Palestinian boy mentioned in the opening to this chapter, who was shot by an Israeli Jewish sniper who mistook his toy gun for a real gun. Israeli Jewish–American director Leon Geller filmed scenes in the hospital immediately following Ahmed's death in 2005, documenting both the Khatib family's reactions and their decision to donate Ahmed's organs to six Israelis,[53] but also filming the families whose children received the organs. In 2007, EIKON Berlin, a German production company, asked German director Marcus Vetter, who has extensively travelled in the Middle East, if he wanted to be involved in the project.[54] As Vetter notes on his website, he 'quickly agreed' since 'the subject matter appealed to [him]' and he wanted to work with an Israeli director.[55] The resulting documentary, entitled *Das Herz von Jenin* and whose tagline is 'The story of a unique gesture of peace', won many awards, including the 2009 Cinema for Peace Award for 'Most Valuable Documentary of the Year' and the 2008 Audience Award/People's Choice Award at the Dubai International Film Festival. The documentary reconstructs the events in the aftermath of Ahmed's death that led to his organs being donated, as well as following Ahmed's family in their daily lives after his death, thus providing important insights into the role of the organ donations themselves alongside the many challenges that Palestinians face on a daily basis.

Said's emphasis on coexistence necessitating an 'initial acknowledgment of the Other as an equal' plays a prominent role in *Das Herz von Jenin*. Unlike Sonne's novel, and due to the circumstances that accompany the organ donations, this acknowledgment does not take place between donor and recipient but instead between Ahmed's father Ismael, and some of the Israeli organ recipients and their families that he visits. The transplants emphasise the similarities between Palestinians and Israelis and, on a narrative level, serve as a way to get to know and 'acknowledge the other' through Ismael's visits to three of the children that received Ahmed's organs.[56] These visits, and the act of physically crossing the structural borders between the Palestinian West Bank and Israel, show how organ donation not only works as a means to resist official narratives about separation, but equally as a metaphor to consider the relationships between Palestinians and Israelis, occupied and occupier.

The way in which these relations impact on life in the Occupied Territories is reflected in Ismael's concerns about donating his son's organs. A lot of screen time is devoted to depicting how Ismael reaches this decision, and the decision is clearly linked to acknowledging the Jewish other as worthy of receiving Ahmed's organs. When approached by Raymond Shehadeh, an Israeli Palestinian nurse who works in the children's ward at Haifa hospital where Ahmed was treated after being shot, it takes Ismael some time to agree to his son's organs being donated.[57] While listening to Shehadeh recount how he convinced Ismael to donate his son's organs, the audience sees Ismael looking at the urban landscape of Haifa, before the camera zooms out and uses a panning shot that offers a 360-degree view of what Ismael sees before ending with a shot that only shows the blue sky. The movement of the camera not only supports the process of reflection that Ismael goes through and the time it takes him to reach his decision, but also imitates a circular motion, or a cycle of life. This sets the scene for the statement that finally convinces Ismael to donate his son's organs, which is Shehadeh saying that this will be 'giving them back life'.[58] This is common rhetoric in organ donation, where it is called the 'gift of life'[59] and aligned with altruism. A study about organ donations in Israel has identified it as the most common reason for families deciding to donate organs of dead family members.[60]

However, in Ismael's case the idea of the 'gift of life' is complicated by the fact that Ahmed died at the hands of an Israeli soldier. When Ismael finds out that one of the organs will go to a Jewish child, he calls Zakaria Zubeidi, who at the time was the local leader of the Al-Aqsa Martyrs' Brigades – a coalition of Palestinian armed groups in the West Bank – and an important political figure in Jenin, to ask for advice. This shows how, as Donna McCormack has argued, the organ donation, and even the prospect of it, serves as a way to illustrate 'cultural anxieties' about 'divisions between self and other'.[61] In Ismael's case, the idea of 'giving the gift of life' to a Jewish person is linked to the fear that they might grow up and kill Palestinians. But Zubeidi emphasises that Ismael 'is donating [the organs] not to Jews but to human beings',[62] foregrounding the idea of a universal humanity and that everyone is the same – which, as Russell outlined in the introduction to this chapter, is one of the ways in which organ donations across divides can function as a critical tool to challenge ideas of separation.

While this rhetoric is certainly appealing, in the documentary, Ismael makes clear that donating his son's organs is also an act of resistance:

> My act of humanity confused the Israelis. That's much greater than killing a soldier. Do you think the Israelis liked what I did? I don't think so. Some people would have preferred me to become a suicide bomber. They would have much preferred it. They would have preferred it if a Palestinian had killed a child rather than saving one.[63]

By acting humanely, Ismael challenges the stereotype of the Palestinian as terrorist and above all the idea that all Palestinians want to kill Israeli Jews, which are often circulated in Israel and Europe in order to dismiss Palestinians as partners for peace.[64] This type of resistance is contrasted with Ismael's earlier mode of resistance, which he relates to the audience while he is on his way to visit the recipients of Ahmed's organs. His narrative about violently resisting the occupation during the First Intifada is overlaid with archival footage of Palestinians throwing stones at Israeli armoured vehicles. These images set up a clear visual rhetoric that focuses on the power imbalances between Palestinians and Israeli Jews, for example by pitting a young man throwing stones against a bulldozer. In this way, they contest the idea of Israel as a beleaguered nation, an image that the First Intifada challenged, especially in Europe and North America. However, this image is followed by footage of Palestinians firing machine guns at Israeli soldiers, which presents a more complicated portrayal of Palestinian resistance that is not reduced to stone-throwing youths. Even though Ismael does not make the link explicit, read together with the images of Ismael's everyday life under occupation, including his experience of checkpoints between the West Bank and Ismael, this series of images draws attention to the clear power dynamics that govern not only Ismael's everyday life but also his encounters with Israeli Jews after the First Intifada. They serve to indicate why Palestinians are resisting the occupation and why at times they resort to violence in order to do so.

This depiction of Ismael's previous resistance to the occupation gives further clout to his later decision to resist by showing his humanity, and challenging stereotypes about Palestinians as terrorists. This resistance is especially pertinent in relation to Jenin. Jenin is seen by Israel as one of the major hotspots where Palestinian 'terrorists' come from, and during the Second Intifada, it was subject to major attacks from Israel, including a twelve-day siege in April 2002. Moreover, Ishmael's act of donating Palestinian organs to Jewish people questions the exclusive identity propagated by the Israeli state that is based on Jewish ethnicity. Hence, these donations can be read in light of Russell's argument that 'organ exchange challenges our foundational split between self and other'.[65] This idea has been taken up by other critics and, as Wright argues in the context of blood transfusions, the blurring of the boundaries between self and other often results in a paranoia that is linked to 'the subliminal intimacy between human bodies that it is imagined to engender'.[66] This intimacy and the resulting erasure of bodily borders between selves and others will be discussed by examining Ismael's visit to Samah Gadban, an Israeli Druze girl who received Ahmed's heart.

Samah, the first child that Ismael visits, lives in Peki'in in Northern Israel, a town where three quarters of the population are Druze.[67] The Gadbans happily receive him and treat him like a family member, exemplifying how 'a new valence of "blood relation" emerges as donor families and recipients imagine themselves as a new kind of family'.[68] This is particularly interesting as the Druze, even though they are ethnically Arab, have strong affinities with the Jewish people in Israel, and they also serve in the Israeli Defense Force.[69]

Contrary to this official narrative, Samah considers the children at the Cuneo Centre of Peace in Jenin, of which Ismael is the director, to be her siblings. The documentary shows how attached Ismael is to Samah, embracing and kissing her. Their relationship exemplifies how organ transplants are often seen as a 'form of continuation of life in which something of the donor lives on in the recipient',[70] suggesting that she, as the recipient of Ahmed's heart, which Ismael was initially reluctant to donate, is now like his own daughter. This demonstrates Lesley A. Sharp's argument that donating a heart can be interpreted as a 'social act that generates new biographies or extends and enhances existing ones'.[71] There is a strong sense of kinship between Ismael and Samah and her family, showing how the act of donating Ahmed's heart and saving Samah's life has allowed them to cross the boundaries that usually separate Palestinians and Israelis. Moreover, in the case of the Gadbans and the Khatibs, we can see how 'donor and recipient bodies' can function 'as the sites through which social justice and violence can be visualised and a more just society can be imagined',[72] as Donna McCormack has argued in relation to organ donations. Ismael's interactions with the Gadban family can be read as a space where coexistence between Israelis and Palestinians is indeed possible and where both sides' struggles and suffering are acknowledged without competition.

However, Ismael's visit to the Levinsons, an ultra-Orthodox Jewish family whose daughter Menuha received one of Ahmed's kidneys, stands in stark contrast with his visit to Samah and her family. From the start, Menuha's parents seem uneasy when they find out that their daughter has received an organ from a Palestinian child, exemplifying not only the 'cultural anxieties' regarding the distinction between self and other mentioned above, but also, as McCormack points out in discussing organ donations in contemporary film, concerns about 'national boundaries of belonging and whether "different others" are to be welcomed or expelled'.[73] When they are interviewed as part of the documentary, the Levinsons make quite clear that they do not want Palestinians to be part of their community, and they have very stereotypical perceptions of Palestinians. Yaakov, the father of the family, makes statements such as, 'Some crazy Arabs are trying to kill Jews all the time,' before saying that he was surprised that their daughter received a kidney from a Palestinian, suggesting that it is unusual for Palestinians to be preserving Jewish lives.[74] The Levinsons' attitude exemplifies what Daniel Bar-Tal calls a 'siege mentality', which is 'a generalized mistrust of other groups and negative feelings towards them. It is based on a system of beliefs dictating that other groups have negative intentions to harm the collective.'[75] When asked as part of the documentary whether their children can have Palestinian friends, the father says, 'That's not the way we want them to grow up', which he elaborates on by saying that Palestinian children would be considered a bad influence on their children.[76] This shows quite clearly that Ismael's act of kindness did not change the Levinsons' opinions about Palestinians and that they still refuse any ideas of coexistence, even on a small scale.

When the Levinsons finally agree to meet with Ismael, the meeting is very awkward, not least because Ismael does not speak Hebrew, so his brother Mustafa and Yaakov converse over his head. The daughter, Menuha, while knowing who they are and who Ahmed was, is uncomfortable with seeing them and being embraced by Ismael. As Kristin Boudreau has argued in relation to sentimentalism in American literature, '[w]hen social bonds are figured as familial bonds, the fiction of shared blood must be managed by imaginary leaps across a space of difference.'[77] What becomes evident in the case of the Levinsons is that they are not prepared to make an 'imaginative leap' that would acknowledge that Palestinians have national aspirations to the same territory as them, and thus they are unable to extend sympathy to the Palestinians and their plight. This becomes particularly pronounced when Yaakov asks Mustafa why Ismael is not leaving Jenin if there is no work there, and Mustafa responds: 'But this is his home; his homeland is here. How can he leave?'[78] For Yaakov, Palestinians have no connection to the land, which is in some ways ironic, as Yaakov is an immigrant from the United States. More importantly, this statement exemplifies how Palestinian ties to the land are negated in order to validate Jewish biblical connections to the same land. Moreover, when Yaakov thanks them for what they have done, his words of gratitude seem flat and insincere. Mustafa responds by saying: 'We didn't ask whether the receiver was Arab or Jewish. We all have the same blood',[79] which takes up the idea of a shared humanity. The idea is, however, quickly dismissed by Yaakov's half-hearted response: 'If we had been in the same situation, we would also have . . .' – a sentence that is left unfinished.[80] Ismael, while not fluent in Hebrew, still reads the overall situation correctly, and in what looks like a deliberate gesture rather than an accident, forgets to open the gift that Menuha presents to him. The audience never sees what the gift is, which is contrasted with the reception of Samah's gift of school bags, whose arrival is celebrated by the children in Jenin.

The ending of *Das Herz von Jenin* could be described as bittersweet. On one hand, it shows Ismael's resilience and his attempts to cross boundaries, challenge stereotypes and educate the next generation of children at the Centre that he is the director of – making him the titular 'Heart of Jenin' in that he tries to model peace and coexistence on different levels. However, on the other hand, this emphasis on relationality is counteracted and refuted by his encounters with people like the Levinsons. While admittedly only representative of a small portion of the Israeli Jewish, and the Orthodox Jewish, population in Israel, their refusal to fully engage with and understand the Palestinian history of suffering and displacement offers quite a pessimistic outlook on the possibilities of acknowledging others as equal and the feasibility of a one-state solution, or any kind of solution, in the near future.

Sentimentalism and the Desire for Coexistence

If we read the encounters between Palestinians and Israelis in the works discussed in this chapter in light of sentimentalism, whose 'ideological work', as Russell notes, can be found in the ways in which 'social ties' are able 'to link people and to elide difference',[81] then it is important that the endings of both *Wenn ich dich je vergesse, Jerusalem* and *Das Herz in Jenin* – albeit to different degrees – refute exactly this type of sentimentalism. They emphasise that the difference between Israelis and Palestinians cannot simply be overcome by an act of kindness and behaving in a humane way, as there are underlying ideological differences and injustices that need to be acknowledged and taken responsibility for. Refuting the idea that organ and blood donation creates a network of kinships across divides also serves to comment on the fact that there are bigger underlying issues in encounters between Israelis and Palestinians, including the acknowledgment of the suffering characterised in Palestinian experiences of displacement and dispossession since 1947 and the ongoing occupation of the Palestinian territories. These issues make it impossible to envision a sense of kinship that is simply based on the concept of 'shared humanity' at this point in time.

However, both works' attempts to imagine encounters between Israelis and Palestinians can also be read in light of a sense of nostalgia for the 1990s when, in the wake of the Oslo Peace Accords of 1993, a solution to the occupation of Palestine seemed to be within reach – at least from a European perspective. Both works discussed in this chapter emphasise the shared values that should allow people to overcome their differences, which can be linked to a certain wishful thinking for a better future. In many ways, a resolution to the so-called Israeli–Palestinian conflict would absolve German people of their guilt, as it would mean that Germany would have to worry less about Israel's security. Interestingly, this extends the idea of Germany as unconditionally supporting Israel by not critically engaging with its occupation of the Palestinian people to imagining a resolution to this occupation. In many ways, then, these final examples of critical relationality are the ones whose critique is the most far-reaching. They expose the many hurdles that Palestinians and Israelis have to overcome in order to be able to share a state as equals, foregrounding the understanding that any dialogue and coexistence need to go hand in hand with, or rather be preceded by, ending the occupation.

The final chapter offers a critical outlook on the future of relationality, focusing on (Israeli) Jewish and Palestinian artists working in the diaspora, especially those that consider relations across the Israel–Palestine divide such as Israeli Jewish artist Oreet Ashery and Palestinian artist Larissa Sansour. Focusing on their co-authored mixed genre work *The Novel of Nonel and Vovel* (2009), I examine the more speculative genres that are becoming increasingly popular in Palestinian and Israeli culture. I ask how these genres might propose ways of transcending the political impasse between Israeli Jewish and Palestinian relations in the present by focusing on speculative relationalities that are situated in the future rather than in the present or the past.

Notes

1. Tamar Ashkenazi et al., 'A Bridge Between Hearts: Mutual Organ Donation by Arabs and Jews in Israel,' *Transplantation* 77, no. 1 (2004): 151, https://doi.org/10.1097/01.TP.0000103722.79951.DE.
2. Chris McGreal, 'Ahmed's Gift of Life,' *The Guardian*, 12 November 2005, https://www.theguardian.com/world/2005/nov/11/israel1. Similar rhetoric was employed by media outlets across the world. See, for example, Erich Follath and Christoph Schult's article entitled 'Das Herz des Feindes,' *Der Spiegel*, 21 December 2006, https://www.spiegel.de/politik/das-herz-des-feindes-a-ee47acaa-0002-0001-0000-000049976953.

3. Emily Russell, *Transplant Fictions: A Cultural Study of Organ Exchange* (Cham: Palgrave Macmillan, 2019), 13.
4. William Hughes, *Beyond Dracula: Bram Stoker's Fiction and its Cultural Context* (London: Palgrave Macmillan, 2020), 139.
5. Kath Weston, 'Kinship, Controversy, and the Sharing of Substance: The Race/Class Politics of Blood Transfusion,' in *Relative Values: Reconfiguring Kinship Studies*, ed. Sarah Franklin and Susan McKinnon (Durham, NC: Duke University Press, 2001), 153.
6. Hochberg, *In Spite of Partition*, 2.
7. Samuel P. Huntington, 'The Clash of Civilizations?' *Foreign Affairs* 72, no. 3 (1993): 22, https://doi.org/10.2307/20045621.
8. Ella Shohat, 'On Orientalist Genealogies,' 89.
9. Edward Said, *The End of the Peace Process: Oslo and After* (New York: Vintage Books, 2001), 319.
10. For an overview of Karmi's discussion, see Ghada Karmi, 'The One-State Solution: An Alternative Vision for Israeli-Palestinian Peace,' *Journal of Palestine Studies* 40, no. 2 (2011): 62–76, https://doi.org/10.1525/jps.2011.xl.2.62. For an in-depth discussion of the one-shared-state model, see Ali Abunimah, *One Country: A Bold Proposal to End the Israeli-Palestinian Impasse* (New York: Metropolitan Books, 2006) and for the parallel-state model, see Mark LeVine and Matthias Mossberg, ed., *One Land, Two States: Israel and Palestine as Parallel States* (Berkeley: University of California Press, 2014).
11. Said, *End of the Peace Process*, 319.
12. See Kotef, *Colonizing Self*, especially the introduction. Other works that have engaged with the impact of Israel's occupation on Israeli Jewish identities include Virginia Tilley's *The One-State Solution: A Breakthrough for Peace in the Israeli-Palestinian Deadlock* (Ann Arbor: University of Michigan Press, 2005) and Gil Z. Hochberg's *Visual Occupations: Violence and Visibility in a Conflict Zone* (Durham; London: Duke University Press, 2015).
13. Werner Sonne, *Wenn ich dich vergesse, Jerusalem* (Berlin: Bloomsbury Berlin, 2008), 285.
14. Cherine Hussein, *The Re-Emergence of the Single State Solution in Palestine/Israel: Countering an Illusion* (New York: Routledge, 2015), 1.
15. Sonne, *Jerusalem*, 285.
16. Both sites were nominated for a Nobel Peace Prize in 2005.
17. Kamal Husseini, 'The Hadassah Model,' *Ynet News*, 12 November 2011, https://www.ynetnews.com/articles/0,7340,L-4159504,00.html.

18. Ehud Kokia, 'The Hadassah Model: Diary of a Director General,' *Hadassah The Women's Zionist Organisation of America*, 2011, accessed 4 May 2021, http://hadassah.org/site/apps/nlnet/content3.aspx?c=keJNIWOvEIH&b=7874737&ct=11560719&notoc=1.
19. Piterberg, *Returns of Zionism*, 64.
20. Lockman, *Comrades and Enemies*, 9. Other examples include Ian Black, *Enemies and Neighbors: Arabs and Jews in Palestine and Israel, 1917–2017* (New York: Atlantic Monthly Press, 2017) and Abigail Jacobson and Moshe Naor, *Oriental Neighbors: Middle Eastern Jews and Arabs in Mandatory Palestine* (Waltham: Brandeis University Press, 2016).
21. Benz quoted in Pól Ó Dochartaigh, 'Philo-Zionism as a German Political Code,' 241.
22. It is a popular misconception that people with blood group AB can only receive blood from someone with the same blood group – in fact they can receive blood from all four blood groups but only donate to AB (Bruno Danic and Jean-Jacques Lefrère, 'Transfusion and Blood Donation on the Screen,' *Transfusion* 48 (2008): 1,027–31, https://doi.org/10.1111/j.1537-2995.2007.01634.x-i2).
23. Yiftachel, *Ethnocracy*, 104. Yiftachel applies the term 'ethnocracy' to Israel to highlight its discriminatory practices against non-Jewish minority groups within the state and to emphasise the fact that Israel is 'driven, first and foremost, by a sense of collective entitlement of the majority group to control "its" state and "its" homeland' (Yiftachel, *Ethnocracy*, 37).
24. Timothy Wright, 'Ecologies of Blood in Johannesburg Vampire Fiction,' *Safundi* 17, no. 4 (2016): 389, https://doi.org/10.1080/17533171.2016.1226729.
25. Sonne, *Jerusalem*, 21.
26. Bashir and Goldberg, 'Holocaust and the Nakba,' 2.
27. Hochberg, *In Spite of Partition*, 3.
28. Bashir Bashir and Amos Goldberg, 'Deliberating the Holocaust and the Nakba: Disruptive Empathy and Binationalism in Israel/Palestine,' *Journal of Genocide Research* 16, no. 1 (2014): 74, 78, http://dx.doi.org/10.1080/14623528.2014.878114. Grace Wermenbol makes a similar point, arguing that the 'persistence of Israeli and Palestinian exclusionary narratives . . . actively contributes to the conflict's continuation' (Wermenbol, *A Tale of Two Narratives*, 15).
29. Sonne, *Jerusalem*, 53. This is historically inaccurate since only inmates at Auschwitz were tattooed with their inmate number. At the Dachau concentration camp, the number was sewn onto their clothing together with different coloured triangles, indicating the category of prisoners they belonged to, which might

include 'political' or 'criminal' (Paul Berben, *Dachau, 1933–1945: The Official History* (London: Norfolk Press, 1975), Appendix 12 between pages 226 and 227.
30. Bar-On and Sarsar, 'Bridging the Unbridgeable,' 65.
31. Bar-On and Sarsar, 'Bridging the Unbridgeable,' 65.
32. Sonne, *Jerusalem*, 90.
33. Mahmood Mamdani, *When Victims Become Killers: Colonialism, Nativism, and the Genocide in Rwanda* (Princeton: Princeton University Press, 2001), 233.
34. Hanna Yablonka, *Survivors of the Holocaust: Israel After the War*, trans. Ora Cummings (Basingstoke: Macmillan, 1999), 82.
35. Diane Enns, *The Violence of Victimhood* (University Park: Penn State University Press, 2012), 45.
36. Sonne, *Jerusalem*, 182.
37. Weston, 'Kinship, Controversy, and the Sharing of Substance,' 153.
38. Sonne, *Jerusalem*, 184.
39. Cleary, *Literature, Partition and Nation-State*, 112.
40. Sonne, *Jerusalem*, 110.
41. Sonne, *Jerusalem*, 111.
42. Walid Khalidi, 'Plan Dalet: Master Plan for the Conquest of Palestine,' *Journal of Palestine Studies* 18, no. 1 (1988): 8, https://doi.org/10.2307/2537591.
43. Sonne, *Jerusalem*, 204.
44. Wright, 'Ecologies of Blood,' 389.
45. Sonne, *Jerusalem*, 218.
46. Sonne, *Jerusalem*, 234.
47. Sonne, *Jerusalem*, 239.
48. Sonne, *Jerusalem*, 237.
49. Elias Khoury, 'Foreword,' in Bashir and Goldberg, *New Grammar of Trauma and History*, xvi.
50. Stav, 'Nakba and Holocaust,' 89.
51. Wright, 'Ecologies of Blood,' 389.
52. Bashir and Goldberg, 'Holocaust and the Nakba,' 2.
53. A Jewish teenager received Ahmed's lungs, and his liver was divided between a seven-month-old Jewish girl and a fifty-eight-year-old woman (McGreal, 'Ahmed's Gift of Life'). The recipients of the heart (an Israeli Druze Girl) and the kidneys (a three-year-old Jewish girl and a five-year-old Bedouin boy) are depicted in the documentary.
54. EIKON describes itself as continually asking big questions in new ways and giving a voice to the weak and those without a voice ('Über uns,' accessed 20 July 2021, https://www.eikon-film.de/ueber-uns).

55. Marcus Vetter, 'Director Statement,' accessed 27 July 2021, https://marcusvetter.com/heart-of-jenin.
56. It is important to note that the groups depicted in the documentary are all to a certain extent minority groups in Israel rather than part of the mainstream: the Druze community that Samah is part of, which accounted for 1.6 per cent of Israel's population in 2019 (Central Bureau of Statistics, 'The Druze Population of Israel, 2019,' 23 April 2020, https://www.cbs.gov.il/en/mediarelease/Pages/2021/The-Druze-Population-of-Israel.aspx); the Bedouin community of Mohamed, which numbered around 190,000 people in 2004, making up 3.5 per cent of the population (The Knesset, 'Bedouins in the State of Israel,' *Lexicon of Terms*, 2010, accessed 28 July 2021, https://knesset.gov.il/lexicon/eng/bedouim_eng.htm); and the ultra-Orthodox Jewish community, which in 2010 accounted for 9 per cent of the Jewish population (Central Bureau of Statistics, 'The Social Survey. Israel, 2009–2010,' April 2012, https://www.cbs.gov.il/en/Statistical/seker-chevrati-e124.pdf#search=ultraorthodox, 3). Rather than visiting and creating links with mainstream Israeli Jewish society, Ismael's visits provide an insight into groups that might not be as well-known in European and German culture even though the lives of ultra-Orthodox Jews have recently been popularised by Netflix series set in Israel, such as *Shtisel*, and those set in the diaspora, such as *Unorthodox*.
57. After the Second Intifada, there was a decrease in organ donations among Palestinians, which Ashkenazi et al. mainly attribute to 'fear of ostracism or repercussion from the community' (Ashkenazi et al., 'Bridge Between Hearts,' 155).
58. *Das Herz von Jenin*, directed by Marcus Vetter and Leon Geller, featuring Ismael Khatib, 2009. Streamed via Vimeo, https://vimeo.com/ondemand/heardofjenin [15:33–15:46].
59. For an overview of the use of this rhetoric in relation to organ transplantation, see Chapter 5, '"The Gift of Life": Sentiment and the Family," in Russell, *Transplant Fictions*, 141–89.
60. Ashkenazi et al., 'Bridge Between Hearts,' 154. What is not mentioned in the documentary is that Ismael's brother died in 1983, aged twenty-two, due to kidney failure. After one of his kidneys stopped worked, Ismael witnessed his brother's steady decline until his death. He has explained that he 'lived the whole ordeal' and 'wanted to stop others suffering like that' (McGreal, 'Ahmed's Gift of Life').
61. Donna McCormack, 'Intimate Borders: The Ethics of Human Organ Transplantation in Contemporary Film,' *Review of Education, Pedagogy, and Cultural Studies* 34, no. 3–4 (2012): 171, https://doi.org/10.1080/10714413.2012.687290.
62. *Das Herz von Jenin* [00:21:36–00:21:38].

63. *Das Herz von Jenin* [00:41:50–00:42:24]. Ismael's wife, Abla, also expressed her hope that by donating their son's organs to Israeli Jews, they 'will think of [them] differently. Maybe just one Israeli will decide not to shoot' (McGreal, 'Ahmed's Gift of Life').
64. As Julia Chaitin argues, stereotyping and scapegoating play a key role in shaping each side's engagement with the other and result in 'delegitimation', which means 'blaming' the other side for all their problems. This attribution of blame to the opposing group 'also makes it easier to delegitimate the claims for certain (or all) civil, legal, and human rights' (Julia Chaitin, *Peace-Building in Israel and Palestine: Social Psychology and Grassroots Initiatives* (New York: Palgrave Macmillan: 2011), 45).
65. Russell, *Transplant Fictions*, 104.
66. Wright, 'Ecologies of Blood,' 388.
67. Mordecai Nisan, 'The Druze in Israel: Questions of Identity, Citizenship, and Patriotism,' *The Middle East Journal* 64, no. 4 (2010): 582. According to the Israel's Central Bureau of Statistics, 81 per cent of Druze people live in the North of Israel (Central Bureau of Statistics, 'The Druze Population of Israel, 2019,' 23 April 2020, https://www.cbs.gov.il/en/mediarelease/Pages/2021/The-Druze-Population-of-Israel.aspx).
68. Russell, *Transplant Fictions*, 149.
69. For an overview of the Druze community in Israel, see for example Mordecai Nisan, 'Druze in Israel.'
70. Russell, *Transplant Fictions*, 149.
71. Lesley A. Sharp, 'Organ Transplantation as a Transformative Experience: Anthropological Insights into the Restructuring of the Self,' *Medical Anthropology Quarterly* 9, no. 3 (1995): 378, https://doi.org/10.1525/maq.1995.9.3.02a00050.
72. Donna McCormack, 'Living with Others Inside the Self: Decolonising Transplantation, Selfhood and the Body Politic in Nalo Hopkinson's *Brown Girl in the Ring*,' *Medical Humanities* 42, no. 4 (2016): 252, https://doi.org/10.1136/medhum-2016-010917.
73. McCormack, 'Intimate Borders' 171.
74. *Das Herz von Jenin* [1:01:37–1:01:54]. Critics have taken the film to task for not showing an accurate representation of Israeli Jewish society as the Levinsons are the only Jewish people represented at some length in it (Ullrich W. Sahm, 'Das "Herz von Jenin,"' *HaGalil*, 12 July 2008, https://www.hagalil.com/01/de/Israel.php?itemid=2601). Conversely, the film has also been criticised for not discussing the location of the Levinsons' house in the Shuafat neighbourhood of East

Jerusalem as part of an illegal Jewish settlement (Susie Kneedler, 'In "Heart of Jenin", Injustice Finds Bromides,' *Mondoweiss*, 19 July 2019, https://mondoweiss.net/2009/07/the-divine-image-pbss-wide-angle-narrows-heart-of-jenin-to-zionist-line-and-all-must-love-the-human-form).

75. Daniel Bar-Tal et al., 'A Sense of Self-Perceived Victimhood in Intractable Conflicts,' *International Review of the Red Cross* 91, no. 874 (2009): 251, https://doi.org/10.1017/S1816383109990221.
76. *Das Herz von Jenin* [1:01:58–1:02:01].
77. Kristin Boudreau, *Sympathy in American Literature: Sentiments from Jefferson to the Jameses* (Gainesville: University of Florida Press, 2002), x.
78. *Das Herz von Jenin* [1:17:06–1:17:11].
79. *Das Herz von Jenin* [1:18:10–1:18:15].
80. *Das Herz von Jenin* [1:18:17–1:18:21].
81. Russell, *Transplant Fictions*, 163.

CONCLUSION: FUTURE RELATIONALITIES

After the documentary *Das Herz von Jenin*, Marcus Vetter and Ismael Khatib continued their collaboration and decided to rebuild the cinema in Jenin, which was once the biggest cinema in Palestine but which had been left in ruins since the First Intifada. This project became the subject of Vetter's next documentary *Cinema Jenin: The Story of a Dream* (2012). This project was widely lauded for its contribution to peace, and the reconstruction of the cinema was described as an important 'symbol' for 'the return of culture to a place, which has often been seen as being without culture'.[1] Putting aside this questionable assessment of Palestine as a place without culture, it is important to note the role that is attributed to culture in advancing peace, as we have seen throughout *Reimagining Israel and Palestine in Contemporary British and German Culture*.[2] However, in spite of the efforts of Vetter, Khatib and other local Palestinians, the cinema was not successful: Palestinian people suspected it to be too close to the Israeli state, and they could not accept the normalisation embedded in such a project while they were still living under Israeli occupation.[3]

I start my conclusion with this example of a failed German–Palestinian collaboration to emphasise that political powers outside of Israel and the Occupied Palestinian Territories play a key role in supporting Israel and Palestine and might contribute to ending Israel's occupation of Palestine and helping Palestinians achieve self-determination. However, the failure of this collaboration draws attention to the importance of considering how relationality, and especially critical relationality, is imagined not only by outsiders but also by people who are from Israel and the Occupied Palestinian Territories. This is why in this chapter I turn to the mixed-genre work *The Novel of Nonel and Vovel* (2009), a collaboration between Israeli Jewish artist Oreet Ashery and Palestinian artist Larissa Sansour, which brings together Israeli Jewish and Palestinian voices from outside the region. This approach challenges the idea that cultural works are only situated and read within one national or cultural context, an idea that is confirmed by both artists' location in the diaspora. *The Novel of Nonel and Vovel* extends the discussion started in the previous chapter, and opens up ideas that I have focused on throughout this book. It does this by examining the more speculative genres that are becoming increasingly popular in Palestinian and Israeli culture, to address relations between Palestinians and Israeli Jews and to transcend the political impasse that defines these relations in the present.[4]

The Novel of Nonel and Vovel was part of a collaboration between Ashery and Sansour, when Ashery was an Arts and Humanities Research Council Creative Research Fellow at Queen Mary University of London. Ashery is a visual artist who was born in West Jerusalem in 1966 and immigrated to the UK at the age of nineteen. Sansour, a Palestinian visual artist born in East Jerusalem in 1976, moved to the UK with her family during the First Intifada, a few years after Ashery. In the preface to the book, Ashery and Sansour write that, 'One important aim of this book is to address the problematic nature of the very kind of dialogue that we – as collaborating artists from opposite sides of the divide – are in some form or shape engaging in.'[5] Dialogue between Israeli Jews and Palestinians is something that is often praised and encouraged outside of Israel and the Occupied Palestinian Territories, especially as a means to solve the so-called conflict. However, one of the problems of this approach, as Omar Barghouti shows, is that these groups

> giv[e] the impression of symmetric, normal, even amicable relations between artists on the two sides of the divide. The inescapable implication is that all that is needed is to accumulate enough of such collaborations to eventually overcome the 'hatred' embedded in this 'conflict.'[6]

Hence, an important aspect of Sansour and Ashery's collaboration, as Ashery explains, is that 'the project presents one united perspective under the remits of resistance to the occupation of Palestine'.[7] As Ashery's statement indicates, and as *The Novel of Nonel and Vovel* itself confirms, the aim of their work is not to facilitate dialogue through their collaboration but to develop a 'unified perspective' to resist the occupation of Palestine. This approach foregrounds the importance of collaborative practices between Israeli Jews and Palestinians – both on an individual and collective level – that take into account the different power imbalances that govern encounters between them, encounters that are shaped by dispossession, settler-colonialism and histories of suffering that are perceived as incompatible. Visually, this development from two perspectives into a more unified perspective is illustrated through the different styles and genres used in each part of *The Novel of Nonel and Vovel*. The first part, which is entitled 'The Virus Story', is composed of seven chapters. The first section of each chapter sets up the narrative of the superhero comic, entitled 'Intergalactic Palestine: The Puppet Master's Reservoir', which constitutes the second part of the text. Unlike 'Intergalactic Palestine', 'The Virus Story' is not a straightforward graphic narrative, but combines different styles of comics with collages, photographs, crosswords and quizzes while the second section of each chapter focuses on larger questions related to representing Palestine and Israel, the involvement of international powers, and the relations between Israeli Jews and Palestinians. This pastiche illustrates the work of collaboration, of bringing together different styles and ideas, and of finding a common approach and perspective for the superhero graphic narrative, both aesthetically and theoretically.

In this conclusion, I will focus on 'Intergalactic Palestine', which, unlike other works that I have discussed in *Reimagining Israel and Palestine in Contemporary British and German Culture*, shows a desire to move beyond the past and the present. Instead, it imagines a future for Palestine. 'Intergalactic Palestine' is a graphic narrative that was illustrated by storyboard artist Hiro Enoki and written by Søren Lind, a Danish author, artist, director and scriptwriter and Sansour's partner. It uses the genre of the superhero narrative, which can be seen both as a form of escapism and as a key genre for commenting on the politics of its time, as critics have mentioned in their discussion of the proliferation of superhero narratives in the United States after 9/11.[8] And indeed, 'Intergalactic Palestine' is very much a product of its time: it was written a few years after the Second Intifada. Since then, as Mikko Joronen et al.

have suggested, 'there [has been] little realistic prospect of Israeli acquiescence to a Palestinian state of any kind'. Instead, 'a Palestinian future is tied to prolonged (and by now somewhat staid) debate around "conflict" resolution, be it a one- or two-state. In an important sense, discourses around state-level solutions (and dissolutions) function at the level of thought experiment.'[9] Using the superhero narrative and focusing on Palestinian liberation rather than Palestinian statehood are two of the ways in which Sansour and Ashery's work is a 'thought experiment' to raise concerns related to Palestinian representation and self-determination that need addressing before a Palestinian state can be established.

'Intergalatic Palestine' starts with newly minted superheroes Nonel and Vovel, the alter egos of Ashery and Sansour, flying to the Occupied Palestinian West Bank with the intention to use their superhero powers to end the Israeli occupation. At the end of Part 1 of *The Novel of Nonel and Vovel*, Nonel and Vovel find out that they have been infected with a virus and that they now have superpowers, but that this comes at the expense of their creativity, which is slowly diminishing.[10] Will Brooker has argued that, 'Superheroes are about wish fulfillment. They're about imagining a better world and creating an alternative vision of yourself – bigger, brighter, bolder than the real thing – to patrol and protect it.'[11] Read alongside a common trope in the twenty-first-century superhero narrative whereby the audience is encouraged to 'admire the psychological strength and perseverance of an ordinary individual . . . and to uphold the notion of how a single person can overcome what seem to be insurmountable obstacles and triumph in the end',[12] Ashery and Sansour's focus on ordinary characters as superheroes who play a key role in ending the occupation can be interpreted as 'creating an alternative vision' that critically responds to how political leaders have failed to achieve liberation and self-determination for the Palestinian people. This critique aligns with Beshara Doumani's point that the Palestinians 'have tolerated successive leaderships that have been largely co-opted, that have committed strategic blunders, and that have acquiesced in rules specifically designed to pre-empt substantive self-determination'.[13]

This disillusionment with Palestinian leadership is commented on further when Nonel and Vovel step outside of the narrative and we see them in their civilian clothes. Ashery and Sansour discuss being rescued from Israeli soldiers by a ninja, which Ashery is concerned is 'a little too Elia Suleiman',[14] referencing Palestinian filmmaker Elia Suleiman's 2002 film *Divine Intervention* in which a female ninja, who is also the love interest of the main character/director, fights off a group of Israeli soldiers in a similarly exaggerated manner to that depicted by 'Intergalactic Palestine'. Reflecting on the use of violence, Nonel says that, 'I'm not sure I feel comfortable practicing now what I never preached before ... I admit [violence]'s tempting, but aren't we supposed to, you know, come in peace?'[15] Vovel responds by asking what Nonel wants to do instead, 'pour a powerful love potion in the drinking water? Seduce the political leaders by spellbinding rhetoric? Or engage in some kind of sexy cross-border artistic dialogue, perhaps?'[16] These slightly over-the-top suggestions bring to the fore how ineffective past attempts aimed at achieving Palestinian liberation and statehood have been, especially those in the post-Oslo period, while constituting a nod to their own work through the reference to 'sexy cross-border artistic dialogue'. Nonel and Vovel suggest that relationality between the past and present does not bring about any tangible changes for Palestinians, and even though the British and German emphasis on relationality reflects an important change in thinking about Israel and Palestine, there is a sense that this relational engagement is not only belated in terms of changing the 'facts on the ground' for Palestinians but also that it has limitations as an approach for depicting traumatic experiences. This is especially so from a Palestinian perspective where the *nakba* is often only read in conjunction with, or through the lens of, Jewish suffering.

This idea is reflected in Hoda El Shakry's discussion of the use of Palestinian speculative fiction, which 'reveals both the conceptual limitations – and the imaginative possibilities – afforded by the ongoing nature of the occupation'.[17] However, while acknowledging the 'conceptual limitations' of a relational approach to depicting Jewish and Palestinian suffering for considering Palestinian futures, Ashery and Sansour explore the 'imaginative possibilities' of the superhero genre in depicting the future of Palestine. Aida,[18] the female ninja who saved Nonel and Vovel, explains that the wall around the West Bank has not been built to obscure Israel's occupation of the Palestinian Territories. Instead, it is part of a sinister plan by evil alien dictator Dharq Jhumpa, for whom '[t]he Wall around the Occupied Territories makes up a gigantic barrel. This is where they are going to store the fertilizer'.[19] The absurdity of this scenario reflects the absurdity of everyday life in the Palestinian West Bank, including the construction of a wall that is meant to enhance the security of Israel by protecting its citizens from suicide bombers coming from the West Bank, but which in fact is part of an Israeli drive to annex further territory and thus to make a coherent Palestinian state in the West Bank impossible.

In 'Intergalactic Palestine,' the plan of sealing off the West Bank is unsuccessful, which addresses on a figurative level how art contributes to breaking the isolation and 'sealing off' of Palestinians living in the West Bank (as well as Gaza and East Jerusalem) and to sharing stories of everyday and not-so-everyday life under occupation. Nonel and Vovel achieve this goal by being strapped to a gigantic slingshot to which they attach a big dynamite stick that will destroy the Fifth Planet, where the evil dictator Dharq Jhumpa resides. While the threat of the Palestinian West Bank being obliterated is averted in the superhero graphic narrative, stepping outside of the narrative in the final pages of *The Novel of Nonel and Vovel*, Nonel reflects that, 'It would seem a bit odd if we had actually managed to solve the Palestinian problem just by dressing up in capes and tight suits.'[20] The ending of *The Novel of Nonel and Vovel*, both that of the superhero narrative itself and Nonel's reflection on it, confirms that the current impasse that Israel and Palestine find themselves in necessitates the imagining of solutions that go beyond realist depictions. Instead, it emphasises utopian futures or dystopian visions that highlight the often absurd and surreal conditions of Palestinian life under occupation.

However, while Nonel and Vovel are able to stop the destruction of the West Bank, it is significant that their superhero comic situates ending the occupation, liberating Palestine and creating an independent Palestinian state in outer space, thus placing it beyond the reach of regional and international actors. Moreover, Ashery and Sansour do not imagine a future Palestinian state, drawing attention to the fact that ending the occupation is only the first step towards achieving this goal and that there are wider structures and infrastructures that need to be dismantled before Palestinian statehood can be realised. As such, we can read both of the parts that make up *The Novel of Nonel and Vovel* as addressing what Jacqueline Rose has aptly described as a 'radical asymmetry', since

> on the one hand, the Palestinian Arabs, and Arabs more widely, have had no choice but to engage with the Jews, who would build a nation-state in Palestine; on the other hand, the Jews who arrived in Israel and indeed in the

diaspora either failed to see Arabs completely or have mostly done so through a lens prescribed by the rules of national self-determination, then conquest and occupation.[21]

Hence, using genres that move Israeli Jews and Palestinians beyond the present time and space is essential in considering future relationalities between Israel and Palestine that address the radically different symmetries governing encounters between occupier and occupied.

In order to start addressing these asymmetries, as I have done throughout this book, it is important to consider the many productive avenues that are opened up by a relational approach to the histories of Israel and Palestine. The different types of relationality discussed in *Reimagining Israel and Palestine in Contemporary British and German Culture* – displaced relationality, libidinal relationality, disrupted relationality, relational memories and relational coexistence – have contributed to bringing ideas, peoples and narratives together, including those that are often occluded in more mainstream discourses. Following David Lloyd, who has argued that 'thinking of Israel/Palestine is . . . at once divided and indivisible',[22] I have shown that these relationalities have paradoxically but also productively emphasised both closeness and distance, relationality and separation. In this way, they have addressed some of the pitfalls and problems of thinking Palestine and Israel together. While they have demonstrated that solidarity with the Palestinians does not need to come at the expense of remembering the Holocaust, the reverse does not always hold true, as the spectre of the Holocaust often limits critical engagement with Israel and its treatment of the Palestinians, especially in a German context. Hence, the works under discussion have often drawn attention to the blind spots in contemporary British and German culture in terms of depicting Israel, Palestine and their relations, such as the role of the British Mandate in this context and the ways in which divided loyalties shape both the United Kingdom and Germany, most poignantly expressed on a cultural level through the use of (failed) libidinal relationships. But as *The Novel of Nonel and Vovel* reminds us, relationality is a promising approach for thinking about Israel and Palestine, and thinking about them together, but such thinking is often ambivalent and doomed to failure, especially if the relationality is motivated by a desire to be absolved of guilt about British or German actions or histories.

While relationality might not always be successful in achieving its full critical potential, it nevertheless offers a more nuanced portrait of Israel and Palestine as geopolitical and metaphorical spaces in the twenty-first century, and reveals the imaginative potential that culture has in thinking about the stories of Palestine and Israel together, as well as those of the Middle East and Europe. Thus, it allows us to reconsider ideas of victimhood and power, antagonism and separation, and to contemplate what it means to imagine Israel, Palestine, Germany and the United Kingdom as intimately connected, both on a political and a cultural level.

Notes

1. Christoph Gunkel, 'Wenn gespendete Organe Frieden spenden sollen,' *Der Spiegel*, 23 May 2021, https://www.spiegel.de/geschichte/israel-und-der-nahostkonflikt-wenn-gespendete-organe-frieden-spenden-sollen-a-98700ae8-c772-4426-a230-404186ecde16,
2. Unsurprisingly, this initiative was also funded by a wide range of public and governmental organisations in Germany, including the Goethe-Institute in the Occupied Palestinian Territories, the German Foreign Office and TV channels such as ARTE and SWR.
3. Gunkel, 'Wenn gespendete Organe Frieden spenden sollen.'
4. Some recent examples of texts available in English include Palestinian author Ibtisam Azem's *The Book of Disappearance*, the short story collection *Palestine +100*, edited by Basma Ghalayini, and Israeli Jewish writer Lavie Tidhar's 2016 book *Central Station*.
5. Oreet Ashery and Larissa Sansour, *The Novel of Nonel and Vovel* (New York: Charta, 2009), 7.
6. Barghouti, *Boycott, Divestment, Sanctions*, 103.
7. Oreet Ashery, 'The Novel of Nonel and Vovel,' Goldsmiths Research Online, 8 July 2013, https://research.gold.ac.uk/id/eprint/8623/1/The%20novel%20of%20N&V%20Goldsmiths%20resaerch.pdf.
8. Terence McSweeney, *The Contemporary Superhero Film: Projections of Power and Identity* (New York: Columbia University Press, 2020), 9.
9. Mikko Joronen et al., 'Palestinian Futures: Anticipation, Imagination, Embodiments: Introduction to Special Issue,' *Geografiska Annaler: Series B, Human Geography* 103, no. 4 (2021): 1, https://doi.org/10.1080/04353684.2021.2004196.
10. The archetypal evil scientist who relays this information to them explains that, 'We figured that artists always sought to influence the world. This is your chance

to do something real with your powers' (Ashery and Sansour, *Novel of Nonel and Vovel*). In spite of this quite stereotypical view of art and the difficulties of its making an impact in the world, this part of 'The Virus Story', alongside 'Intergalactic Palestine', asks serious questions about how effective art is in shaping society and politics. This, of course, is quite important in a context such as Palestine where culture plays a key role in challenging misrepresentation and stereotypes.

11. Will Brooker, 'We Could Be Heroes,' in *What is a Superhero?* ed. Robin S. Rosenberg and Peter Coogan (Oxford: Oxford University Press, 2013), 11.
12. Richard J. Gray and Betty Kaklamanidou, 'Introduction,' in *21st Century Superhero: Essays on Gender, Genre and Globalization in Film*, ed. Richard J. Gray and Betty Kaklamanidou (Jefferson: McFarland & Company, 2011), 5.
13. Doumani, 'Palestine versus the Palestinians?,' 60.
14. Ashery and Sansour, *Novel of Nonel and Vovel*.
15. Ashery and Sansour, *Novel of Nonel and Vovel*.
16. Ashery and Sansour, *Novel of Nonel and Vovel*.
17. Hoda El Shakry, 'Palestine and the Aesthetics of the Future Impossible,' *Interventions* 23, no. 5 (2021): 670, https://doi.org/10.1080/1369801X.2021.1885471.
18. Aida shares her name with one of the major refugee camps in Bethlehem.
19. Ashery and Sansour, *Novel of Nonel and Vovel*.
20. Ashery and Sansour, *Novel of Nonel and Vovel*.
21. Jacqueline Rose, 'Apocalypse/Enmity/Dialogue: Negotiating the Depths,' in Bashir and Farsakh, *Arab and Jewish Questions*, 201.
22. Lloyd, 'Settler Colonialism and the State of Exception,' 61.

BIBLIOGRAPHY

Abu-Lughod, Lila and Ahmad H. Sa'di. 'Introduction: The Claims of Memory.' In Ahmad H. Sa'di and Lila Abu-Lughod, *Nakba: Palestine, 1948, and the Claims of Memory*, 1–24.

Abunimah, Ali. *One Country: A Bold Proposal to End the Israeli-Palestinian Impasse*. New York: Metropolitan Books, 2006.

Achcar, Gilbert. *The Arabs and the Holocaust: The Arab-Israeli War of Narratives*. Translated by G. M. Goshgarian. London: Saqi, 2010.

Adel Sinno, Nadine. 'Family Sagas and Checkpoint Dramas: Tragedy, Humor, and Family Dynamics in Suad Amiry's *Sharon and My Mother-in Law: Ramallah Diaries*.' *Journal of Middle East Women's Studies* 9, no. 1 (2013): 30–53. https://www.muse.jhu.edu/article/493764.

Aderet, Ofer. 'I Was Afraid I'd Be Treated Like a Murderer.' *Haaretz*, 2 June 2008. http://www.haaretz.com/news/i-was-afraid-i-d-be-treated-like-a-murderer-1.247033.

Ahmed, Sara. *Strange Encounters Embodied Others in Post-Coloniality*. London: Routledge, 2000.

Alayan, Samira. 'The Holocaust in Palestinian Textbooks: Differences and Similarities in Israel and Palestine.' *Comparative Education Review* 60, no. 1 (2016): 80–104. https://doi.org/10.1086/684362.

Alcalay, Ammiel. *After Jews and Arabs: Remaking Levantine Culture*. Minneapolis: University of Minnesota Press, 1992.

Alexical. 'A Superb, Warm, Touching, Clever Novel.' Amazon UK, 12 September 2012. https://www.amazon.co.uk/gp/customer-reviews/RO5T25JCB9Q7D.

Altmann, Andreas. *Verdammtes Land: Eine Reise durch Palästina*. München: Piper, 2014.

Amiry, Suad. *Sharon and my Mother-in-Law: Ramallah Diaries*. London: Granta, 2005.

Amoruso, Francesco, Ilan Pappé and Sophie Richter-Devroe. 'Introduction: Knowledge, Power, and the "Settler Colonial Turn" in Palestine Studies.' *Interventions* 21, no. 4 (2019): 451–463. https://doi.org/10.1080/1369801X.2019.1581642.

Anderson, Perry. 'Agendas for Radical History.' *Radical History Review* 36 (1986): 32–7. https://doi.org/10.1215/01636545-1986-36-26.

Anidjar, Gil. *The Jew, the Arab: A History of the Enemy*. Stanford: Stanford University Press, 2003.

Anonymous. 'Palestine Between German Memory Politics and (De-)Colonial Thought.' *Journal of Genocide Research* 23, no. 3 (2021): 374–82. https://doi.org/10.1080/14623528.2020.1847852.

Ashery, Oreet and Larissa Sansour. *The Novel of Nonel and Vovel*. New York: Charta, 2009.

Ashery, Oreet. 'The Novel of Nonel and Vovel.' Goldsmiths Research Online, 8 July 2013. https://research.gold.ac.uk/id/eprint/8623/1/The%20novel%20of%20N&V%20Goldsmiths%20resaerch.pdf.

Ashkenazi, Tamar, Marius Berman, Sharona Ben Ami, Abed Fadila and Dan Aravot. 'A Bridge Between Hearts: Mutual Organ Donation by Arabs and Jews in Israel.' *Transplantation* 77, no. 1 (2004): 151–61. https://doi.org/10.1097/01.TP.0000103722.79951.DE.

Assmann, Aleida. *Das neue Unbehagen an der Erinnerungskultur: Eine Intervention*. München: C. H. Beck, 2013.

Associated Press. 'Life on the Beaches of Tel Aviv and Gaza City – in Pictures.' *The Guardian*, 3 November 2021. https://www.theguardian.com/artanddesign/2021/nov/03/life-on-the-beaches-of-tel-aviv-and-gaza-city-in-pictures.

Atshan, Sa'ed, and Katharina Galor. *The Moral Triangle: Germans, Israelis, Palestinians*. Durham, NC: Duke University Press, 2020.

Auron, Yair. *The Holocaust, Rebirth, and the Nakba: Memory and Contemporary Israeli-Arab Relations*. Lanham: Lexington Books, 2017.

Azem, Ibtisam. *The Book of Disappearance: A Novel*. Translated by Sinan Antoon. Syracuse: Syracuse University Press, 2019.

Azoulay, Ariella and Adi Ophir. *The One-State Condition: Occupation and Democracy in Israel/Palestine*. Palo Alto: Stanford University Press, 2012.

Bar-On, Dan and Saliba Sarsar. 'Bridging the Unbridgeable: The Holocaust and Al-Nakba.' *Palestine-Israel Journal of Politics, Economics and Culture* 11, no. 1 (2004): 63–70. https://www.pij.org/articles/17.

Bar-Tal Daniel, Lily Chernyak-Hai, Noa Schori and Ayelet Gundar. 'A Sense of Self-Perceived Victimhood in Intractable Conflicts.' *International Review of the Red Cross* 91, no. 874 (2009): 229–58. https://doi.org/10.1017/S1816383109990221.

Bar-Yosef, Eitan. *The Holy Land in English Culture 1799-1917: Palestine and the Question of Orientalism*. Oxford: Clarendon Press, 2005.

Barghouti, Omar. *Boycott, Divestment, Sanctions: The Global Struggle for Palestinian Rights*. Chicago: Haymarket Books, 2011.

Bashir, Bashir and Leila Farsakh, ed. *The Arab and Jewish Questions: Geographies of Engagement in Palestine and Beyond*. New York: Columbia University Press, 2020.

Bashir, Bashir and Leila Farsakh. 'Introduction: Three Questions that Make One.' In Bashir and Farsakh, *Arab and Jewish Questions*, 1–22.

Bashir, Bashir and Amos Goldberg, *The Holocaust and the Nakba: A New Grammar of Trauma and History*. New York: Columbia University Press, 2018.

Bashir, Bashir and Amos Goldberg. 'Deliberating the Holocaust and the Nakba: Disruptive Empathy and Binationalism in Israel/Palestine.' *Journal of Genocide Research* 16, no. 1 (2014): 77–99. http://dx.doi.org/10.1080/14623528.2014.878114.

Bashir, Bashir and Amos Goldberg. 'Introduction: The Holocaust and the Nakba: A New Syntax of History, Memory, and Political Thought.' In Bashir and Goldberg, *New Grammar of Trauma and History*, 1–42.

Bäuerlein, Theresa. 'Mein Freund, der Jude: Lieben in Tel Aviv.' *Jetzt.de,* 13 May 2007. http://www.jetzt.de/jetztgedruckt/mein-freund-der-jude-lieben-in-tel-aviv-381130.

Bäuerlein, Theresa. *Das war der gute Teil des Tages*. Frankfurt: Fischer, 2008.

Behar, Marianne. 'Rencontre avec Peter Kosminsky, Réalisateur Du "Serment".' *L'Humanité*, 22 March 2011. https://www.humanite.fr/rencontre-avec-peter-kosminsky-realisateur-du-serment.

Behdad, Ali. *Belated Travelers: Orientalism in the Age of Colonial Dissolution*. Durham, NC: Duke University Press, 1994.

Ben-Natan, Asher. 'Ansprache.' In *Israel und die Bundesrepublik Deutschland: Dreißig Jahre diplomatische Beziehungen*, edited by Renate Schlief-Ehrismann, 19–25. Berlin: Argon, 1995.

Benbassa, Esther. *Suffering as Identity: The Jewish Paradigm*. Translated by G. M. Goshgarian. London; New York: Verso, 2010.

Berben, Paul. *Dachau, 1933–1945: The Official History*. London: Norfolk Press, 1975.

Berger, Arthur Asa. 'The Politics of Laughter.' In *The Social Faces of Humour: Practices and Issues*, edited by George E. C. Paton, Chris Powell and Stephen Wagg, 15–28. Aldershot: Ashgate Publishing, 1996.

Berger, Stefan. *Germany*. London: Hodder Headline, 2004.

Berman, Nina. *German Literature on the Middle East: Discourses and Practices, 1000–1989*. Ann Arbor: University of Michigan Press, 2011.

Bergmann, Michel. *Herr Klee und Herr Feld*. München: dtv, 2014.

Bernard, Anna. 'Another Black September? Palestinian Writing after 9/11.' *Journal of Postcolonial Writing* 46, no. 3 (2010): 349–58. http://dx.doi.org/10.1080/17449855.2010.482409.

Bernard, Anna. 'Forms of Memory: Partition as a Literary Paradigm.' *Alif: Journal of Comparative Poetics* 30 (2010): 9–33. https://www.jstor.org/stable/27929845.

Bernard, Anna. 'Taking Sides: Palestinian Advocacy and Metropolitan Theatre.' *Journal of Postcolonial Writing* 50, no. 2 (2014): 163–75. https://doi.org/10.1080/17449855.2014.883174.

Bernard, Anna. *Rhetorics of Belonging: Nation, Narration, and Israel/Palestine*. Liverpool: Liverpool University Press, 2013.

Bernie, Pit. *So könnte es gehen*. Hamburg: Tredition, 2017.

Bhattacharyya, Gargi. 'Globalizing Racism and Myths of the Other in the "War on Terror".' In *Thinking Palestine*, edited by Ronit Lentin, 46–61. London: Zed Books, 2008.

Billig, Michael. *Laughter and Ridicule: Towards a Social Critique of Humour*. London: Sage, 2005.

Black, Ian. *Enemies and Neighbors: Arabs and Jews in Palestine and Israel, 1917–2017*. New York: Atlantic Monthly Press, 2017.

Blick, Hugo, dir. *The Honourable Woman*. Episode 1, 'The Empty Chair.' Featuring Maggie Gyllenhal, Lubna Azabal and Andrew Buchan. Aired 3 July 2014, on BBC Two. Streamed via Stan. https://play.stan.com.au/programs/1333466/play.

Blick, Hugo dir. *The Honourable Woman*. Episode 4, 'The Ribbon Cutter.' Featuring Maggie Gyllenhal, Lubna Azabal and Stephen Rea. Aired 24 July 2014, on BBC Two. Streamed via Stan. https://play.stan.com.au/programs/1333469/play.

Blick, Hugo, dir. *The Honourable Woman*. Episode 8, 'The Paring Knife.' Featuring Maggie Gyllenhal, Lubna Azabal and Eve Best. Aired 21 August 2014, on BBC Two. Streamed via Stan. https://play.stan.com.au/programs/1333473/play.

Blick, Hugo. 'Q&A with Hugo Blick, Writer, Producer and Director of *The Honourable Woman*.' *BBC Writers Room*, 3 July 2014. https://www.bbc.co.uk/blogs/writersroom/entries/cc86b976-3937-3b4e-accb-dce2e7f2e77b.

Boudreau, Kristin. *Sympathy in American Literature: Sentiments from Jefferson to the Jameses*. Gainesville: University of Florida Press, 2002.

Braach-Maksvytis, Martin. 'Germany, Palestine, Israel, and the (Post)Colonial Imagination.' In *German Colonialism: Race, the Holocaust, and Postwar Germany*, edited by Volker Langbehn and Mohammad Salama, 294–313. New York: Columbia University Press, 2011.

Brenner, Rachel Feldhay. *Inextricably Bonded: Israeli Jewish and Arab Writers Re-Visioning Culture*. Madison: University of Wisconsin Press, 2003.

Brockhaus, Gudrun. 'The Emotional Legacy of the National Socialist Past in Post-War Germany.' In *Memory and Political Change*, edited by Aleida Assmann and Linda Shortt, 34–49. Basingstoke: Palgrave Macmillan, 2012.

Brooker, Will. 'We Could Be Heroes.' In *What is a Superhero?*, edited by Robin S. Rosenberg and Peter Coogan, 11–17. Oxford: Oxford University Press, 2013.

Burleigh, Michael and Wolfgang Wippermann. *The Racial State: Germany 1933–1945*. Cambridge: Cambridge University Press, 1991.

Busbridge, Rachel. 'Israel-Palestine and the Settler Colonial "Turn": From Interpretation to Decolonization.' *Theory, Culture & Society* 35, no. 1 (2018): 91–115. https://doi.org/10.1177/0263276416688544.

Butler, Judith. *Parting Ways: Jewishness and the Critique of Zionism*. New York: Columbia University Press, 2012.

Cahill, Ann J. *Rethinking Rape*. Ithaca: Cornell University Press, 2001.

Capdepón, Ulrike and A. Dirk Moses. 'Introduction.' *Journal of Genocide Research* 23, no. 3 (2021): 371–3. https://doi.org/10.1080/14623528.2020.1847851.

Central Bureau of Statistics, 'The Social Survey. Israel, 2009–2010.' April 2012. https://www.cbs.gov.il/en/Statistical/seker-chevrati-e124.pdf#search=ultraorthodox, 1–8.

Central Bureau of Statistics. 'The Druze Population of Israel, 2019.' 23 April 2020. https://www.cbs.gov.il/en/mediarelease/Pages/2021/The-Druze-Population-of-Israel.aspx.

Cesarani, David. 'Seizing the Day: Why Britain Will Benefit from Holocaust Memorial Day.' *Patterns of Prejudice* 34, no. 4 (2000): 61–6. https://doi.org/10.1080/003132200128811008.

Chaitin, Julia. *Peace-Building in Israel and Palestine: Social Psychology and Grassroots Initiatives*. New York: Palgrave Macmillan: 2011.

Charney, Marc D. 'The World: Arab and Israeli – The Roots of the Conflict.' *The New York Times*, 28 February 1998. https://www.nytimes.com/1988/02/28/weekinreview/world-arab-israeli-roots-conflict-battleground-jordan-sea.html.

Chatterjee, Sreya. *Family Fictions and World Making: Irish and Indian Women's Writing in the Contemporary Era*. New York: Routledge, 2021.

Cleary, Joe. *Literature, Partition and Nation-State: Culture and Conflict in Ireland, Israel and Palestine*. Cambridge: Cambridge University Press, 2002.

Cohen, Hella Bloom. *The Literary Imagination in Israel-Palestine: Orientalism, Poetry, and Biopolitics*. New York: Palgrave Macmillan, 2016.

Cohen, Hillel. 'The Internal Refugees in the State of Israel; Israeli Citizens, Palestinian Refugees.' *Palestine – Israel Journal of Politics, Economics and Culture* 9, no. 2 (2002): 43–51. https://pij.org/articles/159/the-internal-refugees-in-the-state-of-israel---israeli-citizens-palestinian-refugees.

Cohen, Nir. 'Love and Surveillance: Politicized Romance in Peter Kosminsky's *The Promise*.' *Jewish Film & New Media* 1, no. 1 (2013): 44–63. https://www.jstor.org/stable/10.13110/jewifilmnewmedi.1.1.0044.

Collins, John. *Global Palestine*. London: Hurst, 2011.

Conrad, Sebastian. *German Colonialism: A Short History*. Translated by Sorcha O'Hagan. Cambridge: Cambridge University Press, 2012.

Critchley, Simon. *On Humour*. London: Routledge, 2002.

Crossman, Richard. *Palestine Mission: A Personal Record*. New York: Harper & Brothers Publishing, 1947.

Danic, Bruno and Jean-Jacques Lefrère. 'Transfusion and Blood Donation on the Screen.' *Transfusion* 48 (2008): 1,027–31. https://doi.org/10.1111/j.1537-2995.2007.01634.x-i2.

Deckard, Sharae, Nick Lawrence, Neil Lazarus, Graeme Macdonald, Upamanyu Pablo Mukherjee, Benita Parry and Stephen Shapiro (Warwick Research Collective). *Combined and Uneven Development: Towards a New Theory of World-Literature*. Liverpool: Liverpool University Press, 2015.

Denning, Michael. *Cover Stories: Narrative and Ideology in the British Spy Thriller*. London: Routledge & Kegan Paul, 1987.

Dennison, Stephanie and Song Hwee Lim. 'Introduction: Situating World Cinema as a Theoretical Problem.' In *Remapping World Cinema: Identity, Culture and Politics in Film*, edited by Stephanie Dennison and Song Hwee Lim, 1–15. London; New York: Wallflower Press, 2006.

Dentler, Ina. *Zerbrochenes Deutsch: Zweimal Berlin-Haifa*. Berlin: AphorismA, 2014.

Department for Culture, Media and Sport, Helen Grant, and the Rt Hon. Sajid Javid MP. *Policy Paper: 2010 to 2015 Government Policy: National Events and Ceremonies*. 27 February 2013, updated 8 May 2015. https://www.gov.uk/government/publications/2010-to-2015-government-policy-national-events-and-ceremonies.

Deutscher Bundestag, 'Bundestag verurteilt Boykottaufrufe gegen Israel.' 17 May 2019. https://www.bundestag.de/dokumente/textarchiv/2019/kw20-de-bds-642892.

'Documenta-Gesellschafter benennen Expertengremium zur Aufarbeitung.' *Der Spiegel Online*, 1 August 2022. https://www.spiegel.de/kultur/documenta-expertengremium-soll-antisemitismus-skandale-aufarbeiten-a-3e03b833-0b5f-4216-ae1e-04ef75b0126d.

Dotan-Dreyfus, Tomer. *Birobidschan*. Berlin: Voland & Quist, 2023.

Doumani, Beshara. 'Palestine versus the Palestinians? The Iron Laws and Ironies of a People Denied.' *Journal of Palestine Studies* 36, no. 4 (2007): 49–64. https://doi.org/10.1525/jps.2007.36.4.49.

East, Ben. 'Claire Hajaj's novel *Ishmael's Oranges* Is a Love Story Set Against Unrest in the Middle East.' *The National*, 19 July 2014. https://www.thenational.ae/arts-culture/books/claire-hajaj-s-novel-ishmael-s-oranges-is-a-love-story-set-against-unrest-in-the-middle-east-1.307044.

Ebbrecht-Hartmann, Tobias. *Übergänge: Passagen durch eine deutsch-israelische Filmgeschichte*. Berlin: Neofelis Verlag, 2014.

Eiermacher, Martin. 'Eine echte Causa.' *Die Zeit*, 22 April 2020. https://www.zeit.de/2020/18/achille-mbembe-antsemitismus-vorwurf-israel.

EIKON Film. 'Über uns.' Accessed 20 July 2021. https://www.eikon-film.de/ueber-uns.

El Shakry, Hoda. 'Palestine and the Aesthetics of the Future Impossible.' *Interventions* 23, no. 5 (2021): 669–90. https://doi.org/10.1080/1369801X.2021.1885471.

Elm, Michael. 'The Making of Holocaust Trauma in German Memory: Some Reflection about Robert Thalheim's Film *And Along Come Tourists*.' In *Being Jewish in 21st-Century Germany*, edited by Haim Fireberg and Olaf Glöckner, 31–45. Berlin: De Gruyter, 2015.

Enns, Diane. *The Violence of Victimhood*. University Park: Penn State University Press, 2012.

Eshel, Amir. 'Vom eigenen Gewissen: Die Walser-Bubis-Debatte und der Ort des Nationalsozialismus im Selbstbild der Bundesrepublik.' *Deutsche Vierteljahrsschrift für Literaturwissenschaft und Geistesgeschichte* 74, no. 2 (2000): 333–60. https://doi.org/10.1007/BF03375544.

Esposti, Emanuelle Degli. 'Conspiracy in the Holy Land.' Review of *Shake Off*, by Michel Hiller. *The Arab Review*. http://www.thearabreview.org/shake-off-mischa-hiller-review.

Farsoun, Sami K. and Naseer H. Aruri. *Palestine and the Palestinians*, 2nd ed. New York: Routledge, 2018.

Faulenbach, Bernd and Helmuth Schütte. 'Zur Einführung.' In *Deutschland, Israel und der Holocaust: Zur Gegenwartsdeutung der Vergangenheit*, edited by Bernd Faulenbach and Helmuth Schütte, 7–10. Essen: Klartext, 1998.

Fink, Carole. *West Germany and Israel: Foreign Relations, Domestic Politics, and the Cold War, 1965–1974*. Cambridge: Cambridge University Press, 2019.

Finkelstein, Norman G. 'Solution for Israel-Palestine Conflict.' *Website of Norman G. Finkelstein*, 4 August 2014. https://www.normanfinkelstein.com/solution-for-israel-palestine-conflict%e2%80%8f.

Fischer, Leandros. 'Deciphering Germany's Pro-Israel Consensus.' *Journal of Palestine Studies* 48, no. 2 (2019): 26–42. https://doi.org/10.1525/jps.2019.48.2.26.

Fleischer, Tzvi. 'The Promise.' *Australia/Israel & Jewish Affairs Council*, 29 November 2011. https://aijac.org.au/update/the-promise.

Flohr, Markus. 'Warum bist du bloß so deutsch?' *Der Spiegel,* 19 October 2009. http://www.spiegel.de/spiegel/unispiegel/d-67414810.html.

Flohr, Markus. *Wo samstags immer Sonntag ist: Ein deutscher Student in Israel.* Hamburg: Rowohlt, 2011.

Follath, Erich and Christoph Schult. 'Das Herz des Feindes.' *Der Spiegel,* 21 December 2006. https://www.spiegel.de/politik/das-herz-des-feindes-a-ee47acaa-0002-0001-0000-000049976953.

Fox, Thomas C. *Stated Memory: East Germany and the Holocaust.* New York: Camden House, 1999.

Free Speech on Israel. 'FSOI Supports Global Jewish Initiative against Demonising Criticism of Israel.' 17 July 2018. https://freespeechonisrael.org.uk/globaljewishstatement/#defn.

Fuchs, Anne. *Phantoms of War in Contemporary German Literature, Films and Discourse: The Politics of Memory.* Basingstoke: Palgrave Macmillan, 2008.

Gardier, Tomer. *Broken German.* Graz: Literaturverlag Groschl, 2016.

Gan, Alon. 'The Tanks of Tammuz and The Seventh Day: The Emergence of Opposite Poles of Israeli Identity after the Six Day War.' *The Journal of Israeli History* 28, no. 2 (2009): 155–73. https://doi.org/10.1080/13531040903169727.

Gehrcke, Wolfgang, Jutta von Freyberg and Harri Grünberg. *Die deutsche Linke, der Zionismus und der Nahost-Konflikt: Eine notwendige Debatte.* Köln: Papyrossa, 2009.

Ghalayini, Basma, ed. *Palestine +100: Stories from a Century after the Nakba.* Manchester: Comma Press, 2019.

Ghanim, Honaida. 'When Yaffa Met (J)Yaffa: Intersections Between the Holocaust and the Nakba in the Shadow of Zionism.' In Bashir and Goldberg, *New Grammar of Trauma and History,* 92–113.

Giblett, Kylie. '"Was ich nicht sehen kann muss ich erfinden": Third generation narratives of Nazi Herkunft in Tanja Ducker's "Himmelskörper" and Marcel Beyer's "Spione".' *Limbus: Australisches Jahrbuch für germanistische Literatur- und Kulturwissenschaft* 11 (2018): 175–92. https://doi.org/10.5771/9783968218588-175.

Gilroy, Paul. *After Empire: Melancholia or Convivial Culture?* Abingdon: Routledge, 2004.

Glöckner, Olaf and Julius H. Schoeps, ed. *Deutschland, die Juden und der Staat Israel: Eine politische Bestandsaufnahme.* Hildesheim: Georg Olms Verlag, 2016.

Glöckner, Olaf and Julius H. Schoeps. 'Vorwort.' In Glöckner and Schoeps, *Deutschland, die Juden und der Staat Israel,* 9–15.

Gordon, Michelle. 'Selective Histories: Britain, the Empire and the Holocaust.' In Lawson and Pierce, *Palgrave Handbook of Britain and the Holocaust,* 219–40.

Gorelik, Lena. *Hochzeit in Jerusalem*. München: SchirmerGraf Verlag, 2007.

Goschler, Constantin. *Schuld und Schulden: Die Politik der Wiedergutmachung für NS-Verfolgte seit 1945*. Göttingen: Wallstein, 2005.

Gover, Yerach. *Zionism: The Limits of Moral Discourse in Israeli Hebrew Fiction*. Minneapolis; London: The University of Minnesota Press, 1994.

Government of the United Kingdom. 'David Cameron's Speech to the Knesset in Israel.' 12 March 2013, last modified 13 March 2014. https://www.gov.uk/government/speeches/david-camerons-speech-to-the-knesset-in-israel.

Grant, Linda. *The People on the Street: A Writer's View of Israel*. London: Virago, 2006.

Grant, Linda. *When I Lived in Modern Times*. London: Granta, 2000.

Grass, Günter. 'Was gesagt werden muss.' *Spiegel Online*, 4 April 2012. https://www.spiegel.de/kultur/gesellschaft/dokumentation-gedicht-was-gesagt-werden-muss-von-guenter-grass-a-825744.html.

Gray, Richard J. and Betty Kaklamanidou. 'Introduction.' In *21st Century Superhero: Essays on Gender, Genre and Globalization in Film*, edited by Richard J. Gray and Betty Kaklamanidou, 1–13. Jefferson: McFarland & Company, 2011.

Greene, Toby. *Blair, Labour, and Palestine: Conflicting Views on Middle East Peace After 9/11*. New York: Bloomsbury Academic, 2013.

Greene, Toby and Yossi Shain. 'The Israelization of British Jewry: Balancing Between Home and Homeland.' *The British Journal of Politics and International Relations* 18, no. 4 (2016): 848–65. https://doi.org/10.1177/1369148116669061.

Grossman, David. *Writing in the Dark: Essays on Literature and Politics*. Translated by Jessica Cohen. London: Bloomsbury, 2009.

Gunkel, Christoph. 'Wenn gespendete Organe Frieden spenden sollen.' *Der Spiegel*, 23 May 2021. https://www.spiegel.de/geschichte/israel-und-der-nahostkonflikt-wenn-gespendete-organe-frieden-spenden-sollen-a-98700ae8-c772-4426-a230-404186ecde16.

Guy, Veronica. 'The Glue that Bonds Human Relationships.' Amazon UK, 31 July 2010. https://www.amazon.co.uk/gp/customer-reviews/R25G4QCCPWRNB1.

Habermas, Jürgen. 'A Kind of Settlement of Damages (Apologetic Tendencies).' Translated by Jeremy Leaman. *New German Critique*, no. 44 (1988): 25–39. https://doi.org/10.2307/488144.

Hajaj, Claire. *Ishmael's Oranges*. London: Oneworld, 2014.

Hanika, Iris. *Das Eigentliche*. Graz: Droschl, 2010.

Hardt, Jürgen. 'Israels Sicherheit ist für uns nicht verhandelbar.' *CDU/CSU*, 30 June 2020. https://www.cducsu.de/presse/pressemitteilungen/israels-sicherheit-ist-fuer-uns-nicht-verhandelbar.

Harwood, Sarah. *Family Fictions: Representations of the Family in 1980s Hollywood Cinema*. New York: St. Martin's Press, 1997.

Hayot, Eric. *On Literary Worlds*. Oxford: Oxford University Press, 2012.

Hepperle, Sabine. *Die SPD und Israel. Von der großen Koalition 1966 bis zur Wende 1982*. Frankfurt: Peter Lang, 2000.

Herbert, Martin. *The Unilever Series: Doris Salcedo: Shibboleth*. London: Tate Publishing, 2007. Exhibition Brochure.

Herrmann, Meike. 'Spurensuche in der dritten Generation. Erinnerung an den Nationalsozialismus und Holocaust in der jüngsten Literatur.' In *Repräsentation des Holocaust im Gedächtnis der Generationen*, edited by Margrit Fröhlich, Yariv Lapid and Christian Schneider, 139–57. Frankfurt: Brandes und Apsel, 2004.

Hesse, Isabelle. *The Politics of Jewishness in Contemporary World Literature: The Holocaust, Zionism and Colonialism*. London: Bloomsbury Academic, 2016.

Hestermann, Jenny, Roby Nathanson and Stephan Stetter. *Deutschland und Israel heute: Zwischen Verbundenheit und Entfremdung*. Gütersloh: Bertelsmann Stiftung, 2 September 2022. https://doi.org/10.11586/2022125.

Hjorth, Ronnie. *Equality in International Society: A Reappraisal*. London: Palgrave Macmillan, 2014.

Hochberg, Gil Z. *In Spite of Partition: Jews, Arabs, and the Limits of Separatist Imagination*. Princeton: Princeton University Press, 2007.

Hochberg, Gil Z. *Visual Occupations: Violence and Visibility in a Conflict Zone*. Durham; London: Duke University Press, 2015.

Holland, Patrick and Graham Huggan. *Tourists with Typewriters: Critical Reflections on Contemporary Travel Writing*. Ann Arbor: University of Michigan Press, 2000.

Holm, Nicolas. *Humour as Politics: The Political Aesthetics of Contemporary Comedy*. Cham: Palgrave Macmillan, 2017.

Hughes, William. *Beyond Dracula: Bram Stoker's Fiction and its Cultural Context*. London: Palgrave Macmillan, 2020.

Huntington, Samuel P. 'The Clash of Civilizations?' *Foreign Affairs* 72, no. 3 (1993): 22–49. https://doi.org/10.2307/20045621.

Hussein, Cherine. *The Re-Emergence of the Single State Solution in Palestine/Israel: Countering an Illusion*. New York: Routledge, 2015.

Husseini, Kamal. 'The Hadassah Model.' *Ynet News*, 12 November 2011. https://www.ynetnews.com/articles/0,7340,L-4159504,00.html.

Huyssen, Andreas. *Urban Palimpsests and the Politics of Memory*. Stanford: Stanford University Press, 2003.

Jacobson, Abigail, and Moshe Naor. *Oriental Neighbors: Middle Eastern Jews and Arabs in Mandatory Palestine.* Waltham: Brandeis University Press, 2016.

Jaeger, Kinan. *Quadratur des Dreiecks: die deutsch-israelischen Beziehungen und die Palästinenser.* Schwalbach: Wochenschau Verlag, 1997.

Joffee, Linda. 'Acting Stint Transforms Arab's View of Israelis.' *The Christian Science Monitor*, 18 August 1992. https://search-proquest-com.ezproxy1.library.usyd.edu.au/docview/291194727/fulltext/673250E5D5F04B5FPQ/1?accountid=14757.

Joffee, Linda. 'An Interview With the Akko Theater's Artistic Director.' *The Christian Science Monitor*, 18 August 1992. https://search-proquest-com.ezproxy1.library.usyd.edu.au/docview/291196332/fulltext/F99DA54126F548CEPQ/1?accountid=14757.

Jones, Andrew. *Memory and Material Culture.* Cambridge; New York: Cambridge University Press, 2007.

Joronen, Mikko, Helga Tawil-Souri, Merav Amir and Mark Griffiths. 'Palestinian Futures: Anticipation, Imagination, Embodiments: Introduction to Special Issue.' *Geografiska Annaler: Series B, Human Geography* 103, no. 4 (2021): 1–7. https://doi.org/10.1080/04353684.2021.2004196.

Jureit, Ulrike. 'Opferidentifikation und Erlösungshoffnung: Beobachtungen im erinnerungspolitischen Rampenlicht.' In *Gefühlte Opfer: Illusionen der Vergangenheitsbewältigung* by Ulrike Jureit and Christian Schneider, 19–104. Stuttgart: Klett-Cotta, 2011.

Kadelbach, Philipp, dir. *Unsere Mütter, unsere Väter.* Aired 17, 18 and 20 March 2013 on ZDF. Hamburg: Studio Hamburg Enterprises, 2013, DVD.

Kalb, Deborah. 'Q&A with author Claire Hajaj.' *Book Q&As with Deborah Kalb*, 31 July 2014. https://deborahkalbbooks.blogspot.com/2014/07/q-with-author-claire-hajaj.html.

Karim, Sameena. 'The Co-Existence of Globalism and Tribalism: A Review of the Literature.' *Journal of Research in International Education* 11, no. 2 (2012): 137–151. https://doi.org/10.1177/1475240912452465.

Karmi, Ghada. 'The One-State Solution: An Alternative Vision for Israeli-Palestinian Peace.' *Journal of Palestine Studies* 40, no. 2 (2011): 62–76. https://doi.org/10.1525/jps.2011.xl.2.62.

Kattago, Siobhan. *Ambiguous Memory: The Nazi Past and German National Identity.* Westport, Connecticut: Praeger, 2001.

Kelemen, Paul. *The British Left and Zionism: History of a Divorce.* Manchester: Manchester University Press, 2012.

Khalidi, Walid. 'Plan Dalet: Master Plan for the Conquest of Palestine.' *Journal of Palestine Studies* 18, no. 1 (1988): 4–33. https://doi.org/10.2307/2537591.

Khalili, Laleh. *Heroes and Martyrs of Palestine: The Politics of National Commemoration.* Cambridge: Cambridge University Press, 2007.

Khoury, Elias. 'Foreword.' In Bashir and Goldberg, *New Grammar of Trauma and History*, ix–xvi.

Kim, Claire Jean. 'Moral Extensionism or Racist Exploitation? The Use of the Holocaust and Slavery Analogies in the Animal Liberation Movement.' *New Political Science* 33, no. 3 (2011): 311–33. https://doi.org/10.1080/07393148.2011.592021.

Kloke, Martin. 'Zwischen Lobpreisung und Verteufelung: Die Haltung der deutschen Linken gegenüber Israel.' In *Israel in den neunziger Jahren und die deutsch-israelischen Beziehungen*, edited by Karl Schmitt and Michael Edinger, 55–67. Jena: Universitätsverlag Jena, 1996.

Klug, Brian. 'An Emblematic Embrace: New Europe, the Jewish State, and the Palestinian Question.' In Bashir and Farsakh, *Arab and Jewish Questions*, 47–67.

Kneedler, Susie. 'In "Heart of Jenin", Injustice Finds Bromides.' *Mondoweiss*, 19 July 2019. https://mondoweiss.net/2009/07/the-divine-image-pbss-wide-angle-narrows-heart-of-jenin-to-zionist-line-and-all-must-love-the-human-form.

Knesset, The. 'Bedouins in the State of Israel.' *Lexicon of Terms*. 2010. Accessed 28 July 2021. https://knesset.gov.il/lexicon/eng/bedouim_eng.htm.

Kokia, Ehud. 'The Hadassah Model: Diary of a Director General.' *Hadassah The Women's Zionist Organisation of America*, 2011. Accessed 4 May 2021. https://archive.ph/20130414225231/http://www.hadassah.org/site/apps/nlnet/content3.aspx?c=keJNIWOvElH&b=7874737&ct=11560719&notoc=1.

Kosminsky, Peter. 'A Film-Maker's Eye on the Middle East.' *The Guardian*, 28 January 2011. http://www.theguardian.com/world/2011/jan/28/the-promise-peter-kosminsky-middle-east.

Kosminsky, Peter. 'Audio Commentary.' *The Promise*. Directed by Peter Kosminsky. London: Daybreak Pictures, 2011. DVD.

Kosminsky, Peter, dir. *Britz*. Aired 31 October and 1 November 2007 on Channel 4. London: Daybreak Pictures, 2007. DVD.

Kosminsky, Peter, dir. *The Promise*, Part 1. Aired 6 February 2011, on Channel 4. London: Daybreak Pictures, 2011. DVD.

Kosminsky, Peter, dir. *The Promise*, Part 2. Aired 13 February 2011, on Channel 4. London: Daybreak Pictures, 2011. DVD.

Kosminsky, Peter, dir. *The Promise*, Part 4. Aired 27 February 2011, on Channel 4. London: Daybreak Pictures, 2011. DVD.

Kosminsky, Peter, dir. *Warriors*. Aired 20 and 21 November 1999 on BBC One. London: BBC Films, 1999. DVD.

Kotef, Hagar. *The Colonizing Self: or, Home and Homelessness in Israel/Palestine.* Durham, NC: Duke University Press, 2020.
Krieg, Robert, dir. *Intifada – Auf dem Weg nach Palästina.* Vimeo Video. Uploaded 4 January 2018 by Krieg & Nolte. https://vimeo.com/249684117.
Kunze, Sebastian. 'Deutschland, Israel und der Nahost Konflikt.' In Glöckner and Schoeps, *Deutschland, die Juden und der Staat Israel*, 247–64.
Lakoff, George. *Moral Politics: What Conservatives Know That Liberals Don't.* Chicago: University of Chicago Press, 1996.
Landgraf, Stefanie und Johannes Gulde, dirs. *Wir weigern uns Feinde zu sein.* YouTube Video. Uploaded 12 April 2015 by GOOD Morning Vietnam. https://www.youtube.com/watch?v=lWwxJs2r2K8.
Lavy, George. *Germany and Israel: Moral Debt and National Interest.* London: Frank Cass, 1996.
Lawson, Tom and Andy Pearce. 'Britain and the Holocaust: An Introduction.' In Lawson and Pierce, *Palgrave Handbook of Britain and the Holocaust*, 1–34.
Lawson, Tom and Andy Pearce, ed. *The Palgrave Handbook of Britain and the Holocaust.* Cham: Palgrave Macmillan, 2020.
LeVine, Mark and Matthias Mossberg, ed. *One Land, Two States: Israel and Palestine as Parallel States.* Berkeley: University of California Press, 2014.
Levy, Daniel and Natan Sznaider. *The Holocaust and Memory in the Global Age.* Translated by Assenka Oksiloff. Philadelphia: Temple University Press, 2006.
Levy, Dany, dir. *Mein Führer: Die wirklich wahrste Wahrheit über Adolf Hitler.* 2007. Burbank, CA: Warner Home Video, 2007. DVD.
Levy, Lital. *Poetic Trespass: Writing Between Hebrew and Arabic in Israel/Palestine.* Princeton: Princeton University Press, 2014.
Lewycka, Marina, Raja Shehadeh and Jean Seaton. 'Two Walks: Palestine and the Peak District. A Conversation between Raja Shehadeh and Marina Lewycka, September 2008.' *The Political Quarterly* 80, no. 1 (2009): 4–16. https://doi.org/10.1111/j.1467-923X.2009.01966.x.
Lewycka, Marina. *We Are All Made of Glue.* London: Penguin, 2010.
Lionis, Chrisoula. *Laughter in Occupied Palestine: Comedy and Identity in Art and Film.* London: I. B. Tauris, 2016.
Lisle, Debbie. *The Global Politics of Contemporary Travel Writing.* Cambridge: Cambridge University Press, 2006.
Livingstone, Ken. 'Naz Shah "Not Anti-Semitic".' Interview by Vanessa Feltz. *BBC News*, 28 April 2016. http://www.bbc.com/news/uk-politics-36163432.
Lloyd, David. 'Settler Colonialism and the State of Exception: The Example of Palestine/Israel.' *Settler Colonial Studies* 2, no. 1 (2012): 59–80. https://doi.org/10.1080/2201473x.2012.10648826.

Lockman, Zachary. *Comrades and Enemies: Arab and Jewish Workers in Palestine, 1906–1948*. Berkeley: University of California Press, 1996.

Loshitzky, Yosefa. *Identity Politics on the Israeli Screen*. Austin: University of Texas Press, 2001.

Mamdani, Mahmood. *When Victims Become Killers: Colonialism, Nativism, and the Genocide in Rwanda*. Princeton: Princeton University Press, 2001.

Martin, Rod A. *The Psychology of Humour: An Integrative Approach*. Burlington: Elsevier Academic Press, 2007.

Marwecki, Daniel. *Germany and Israel: Whitewashing and Statebuilding*. London: Hurst, 2020.

Masalha, Nur. *The Palestine Nakba: Decolonising History, Narrating the Subaltern, Reclaiming Memory*. London: Zed Books, 2012.

McClintock, Anne. 'Family Feuds: Gender, Nationalism and the Family.' *Feminist Review* 44 (1993): 61–80. https://doi.org/10.2307/1395196.

McClintock, Anne. *Imperial Leather: Race, Gender and Sexuality in the Colonial Conquest*. New York: Routledge, 1995.

McCormack, Donna. 'Intimate Borders: The Ethics of Human Organ Transplantation in Contemporary Film.' *Review of Education, Pedagogy, and Cultural Studies* 34, no. 3–4 (2012): 170–83. https://doi.org/10.1080/10714413.2012.687290.

McCormack, Donna. 'Living with Others Inside the Self: Decolonising Transplantation, Selfhood and the Body Politic in Nalo Hopkinson's *Brown Girl in the Ring*.' *Medical Humanities* 42, no. 4 (2016): 252–8. https://doi.org/10.1136/medhum-2016-010917.

McGreal, Chris. 'Ahmed's Gift of Life.' *The Guardian*, 12 November 2005. https://www.theguardian.com/world/2005/nov/11/israel1.

McSweeney, Terrence. *The Contemporary Superhero Film: Projections of Power and Identity*. New York: Columbia University Press, 2020.

Milton-Edwards, Beverley. *Contemporary Politics in the Middle East*. Cambridge: Polity, 2011.

Mintz, Lawrence E. 'American Humor as Unifying and Divisive.' *Humor – International Journal of Humor Research* 12, no. 3. (1999): 237–52. https://doi.org/10.1515/humr.1999.12.3.237.

Moore-Gilbert, Bart. 'Palestine, Postcolonialism and Pessoptimism.' *Interventions* 20, no. 1 (2018): 7–40. https://doi.org/10.1080/1369801X.2016.1156555.

Morreall, John. *Taking Laughter Seriously*. Albany: State University of New York, 1983.

Ms Sally Kirkman. 'We Are All Made of Glue.' Amazon UK, 11 May 2012. https://www.amazon.co.uk/gp/customer-reviews/R2QGQ505H2S8BU.

Mulkay, Michael. *On Humour: Its Nature and its Place in Modern Society.* Cambridge: Polity Press, 1988.

Neeves, Mairi. 'The Pursuit of Selfhood: Writing the Absurd in Palestinian Life Narratives.' In *Life Writing: The Spirit of the Age and the State of the Art*, edited by Meg Jensen and Jane Jordan, 52–61. Newcastle-upon-Tyne: Cambridge Scholars Publishing, 2009.

Nimni, Ephraim, ed. *The Challenge of Post-Zionism: Alternatives to Israeli Fundamentalist Politics.* London: Zed Books, 2003.

Ninio, Roni and Shai Capon, dirs. *'Avodah 'Aravit.* Aired 2007–2013 on Keshet Channel 2. DVD.

Niroumand, Mariam. 'Ein Encounter, eine Art Entlastung.' *TAZ*, 21 April 1994. https://taz.de/Ein-Encounter-eine-Art-Entlastung/!1566321.

Nisan, Mordecai. 'The Druze in Israel: Questions of Identity, Citizenship, and Patriotism.' *The Middle East Journal* 64, no. 4 (2010): 575–96.

Niven, Bill. *Facing the Nazi Past: United Germany and the Legacy of the Third Reich.* London: Routledge, 2002.

Novak, David. *The Jewish Social Contract: An Essay in Political Theology.* Princeton: Princeton University Press, 2005.

Ó Dochartaigh, Pól. 'Philo-Zionism as a German Political Code: Germany and the Israeli-Palestinian Conflict Since 1987.' *Debatte: Journal of Contemporary Central and Eastern Europe* no. 2 (2007): 233–55. https://doi.org/10.1080/09651560701508547.

Ofer, Dalia. 'The Past that Does Not Pass: Israelis and Holocaust Memory.' *Israel Studies* 14, no. 1 (2009): 1–35. https://www.jstor.org/stable/30245842.

Oz, Amos. *Israel und Deutschland: Vierzig Jahre nach Aufnahme diplomatischer Beziehungen.* Translated by Lydia Böhmer. Frankfurt: Suhrkamp, 2005.

Ozacky-Lazar, Sarah. 'Holocaust Memory Among Palestinian Arab Citizens in Israel: Personal Sympathy and National Antagonism.' In *Holocaust Memory in a Globalizing World*, edited by Jacob S. Eder, Philipp Gassert and Alan E. Steinweis, 140–52. Göttingen: Wallstein Verlag, 2017.

Pappé, Ilan. 'Post-Zionism and its Popular Cultures.' In *Palestine, Israel, and the Politics of Popular Culture*, edited by Rebecca L. Stein and Ted Swedenburg, 77–95. Durham, NC: Duke University Press, 2005.

Pearce, Andy. *Holocaust Consciousness in Contemporary Britain.* New York; London: Routledge, 2014.

Pearce, Caroline. *Contemporary Germany and the Nazi Legacy: Remembrance, Politics and the Dialectic of Normality.* Basingstoke: Palgrave Macmillan, 2008.

Pellegrino, Nicky. 'The Best of Both Worlds.' *The New Zealand Herald*, 2 August 2009. http://www.nzherald.co.nz/entertainment/news/article.cfm?c_id=1501119&objectid=10587866.

Perry, Ruth. *Novel Relations: The Transformation of Kinship in English Literature and Culture, 1748–1818.* Cambridge: Cambridge University Press, 2004.

Piterberg, Gabriel. *The Returns of Zionism: Myths, Politics and Scholarship in Israel.* London: Verso, 2008.

Polak, Oliver with Jens Oliver Haas. *Ich darf das, ich bin Jude.* 9th ed. Köln: Kiepenheuer & Witsch, 2012.

Pollock, Griselda. 'Introduction: A Concentrationary Imaginary?' In *Concentrationary Imaginaries: Tracing Totalitarian Violence in Popular Culture*, edited by Griselda Pollock and Maxim Silverman, 1–43. London: I. B. Tauris, 2015.

PRIME (Peace Research Institute in the Middle East). '"Learning Each Other's Historical Narrative" in Israeli and Palestinian Schools.' Accessed 18 October 2022. http://www.vispo.com/PRIME/leohn.htm.

Raphael, T. J. and Mythili Rao. 'Her Mom is Jewish. Her Dad is Palestinian. She Sees Both Sides.' *The Takeaway*, 31 July 2014. https://www.pri.org/stories/2014-07-31/her-mom-jewish-her-dad-palestinian-she-sees-both-sides.

Rapp, Tobias. 'Macht uns das Gedenken an den Holocaust blind für andere deutsche Verbrechen?' *Der Spiegel*, 12 February 2021. https://www.spiegel.de/geschichte/holocaust-macht-uns-das-gedenken-blind-fuer-andere-deutsche-verbrechen-a-00000000-0002-0001-0000-000175304219.

Reinecke, Stefan. 'Laudatio anlässlich der Verleihung des Konrad-Wolf-Preises 2005.' In *Andres Veiel: Edition der Filmemacher* – DVD booklet, 14–22. Berlin: Neue Visionen Medien, 2006.

Reinhart, Tanya. *Israel/Palestine: How to End the War of 1948.* 2nd ed. Crow's Nest: Allen & Unwin, 2003.

Rich, Dave. *The Left's Jewish Problem: Jeremy Corbyn, Israel and Anti-Semitism.* London: Biteback Publishing, 2016.

Rogers, Robert. *The Double in Literature: A Psychoanalytic Study.* Detroit: Wayne State University Press, 1970.

Rokem, Freddie. *Performing History: Theatrical Representations of the Past in Contemporary Theatre.* Iowa City: University of Iowa Press, 2000.

Rose, Jacqueline. 'Apocalypse/Enmity/Dialogue: Negotiating the Depths.' In Bashir and Farsakh, *Arab and Jewish Questions*, 201–19.

Rose, Jacqueline. *The Question of Zion.* Princeton: Princeton University Press, 2005.

Rosenfeld, Gavriel D. *Hi Hitler!: How the Nazi Past is Being Normalized in Contemporary Culture.* Cambridge: Cambridge University Press, 2015.

Rothberg, Michael. 'From Gaza to Warsaw: Mapping Multidirectional Memory.' *Criticism* 53, no. 4 (2011): 523–48. https://doi.org/10.1353/crt.2011.0032.

Rothberg, Michael. *Multidirectional Memory: Remembering the Holocaust in the Age of Decolonization*. Stanford: Stanford University Press, 2009.

Rothberg, Michael. *The Implicated Subject: Beyond Victims and Perpetrators*. Stanford: Stanford University Press, 2019.

Rovit, Rebecca. 'Emerging from the Ashes: The Akko Theatre Center Opens the Gates to Auschwitz.' *The Drama Review* 37, no. 2 (1993): 161–73. https://www.jstor.org/stable/1146255.

Rovner, Adam. *In the Shadow of Zion: Promised Lands Before Israel*. New York: New York University Press, 2014.

Rubens, Bernice. *The Sergeants' Tale*. London: Little Brown, 2003.

Runge, Evelyn. 'Roman-Debütantin Bäuerlein: Wo die Liebe stolpert.' *Spiegel Online*, 8 October 2008. http://www.spiegel.de/kultur/literatur/roman-debuetantin-baeuerlein-wo-die-liebe-stolpert-a-582833.html.

Russell, Emily. *Transplant Fictions: A Cultural Study of Organ Exchange*. Cham: Palgrave Macmillan, 2019.

Sa'di, Ahmad H. and Lila Abu-Lughod, ed. *Nakba: Palestine, 1948, and the Claims of Memory*. New York: Columbia University Press, 2007.

Sahm, Ullrich W. 'Das "Herz von Jenin".' *HaGalil*, 12 July 2008. https://www.hagalil.com/01/de/Israel.php?itemid=2601.

Said, Edward. 'Arabs and Jews.' *Journal of Palestine Studies* 3, no. 2 (1974): 3–14. https://doi.org/10.2307/2535796.

Said, Edward. *Orientalism*. New York: Vintage Books, 1994.

Said, Edward. *The End of the Peace Process: Oslo and After*. New York: Vintage Books, 2001.

Said, Edward. *The World, the Text and the Critic*. London: Vintage, 1991.

Schäuble, Martin. *Zwischen den Grenzen: Zu Fuss durch Israel und Palästina*. München: Carl Hanser Verlag, 2013.

Schmid, Thomas. 'Die Holocaust-Frage.' *Die Welt*, 28 February 2021. https://www.welt.de/kultur/literarischewelt/plus226821125/Multidirektionale-Erinnerung-Die-Holocaust-Frage.html.

Schrader, Maria, dir. *Unorthodox*. Featuring Shira Haas, Amit Rav and Jeff Wilbusch, 2020. Streamed via Netflix. https://www.netflix.com/au/title/81019069.

Schrobsdorff, Angelika. *Wenn ich dich je vergesse, oh Jerusalem ...* München: dtv, 2004.

Schrobsdorff, Angelika. *Jerusalem war immer eine schwere Adresse*. München: dtv, 1991.

Schuhmann, Antje. 'Whose Burden? The Significance of the Israel-Palestine Conflict in German Identity Politics.' In *Nationalist Myths and Modern Media: Contested*

Identities in the Age of Globalization, edited by Jan Herman Brinks, Stella Rock and Edward Timms, 163–172. London: I. B. Tauris, 2006.

Seidl, Claudius. 'War der Holocaust eine koloniale Tat?' *Frankfurter Allgemeine Zeitung*, 1 March 2021. https://www.faz.net/aktuell/feuilleton/streit-um-gedenkkultur-war-der-holocaust-eine-koloniale-tat-17217645.html.

Sharp, Lesley A. 'Organ Transplantation as a Transformative Experience: Anthropological Insights into the Restructuring of the Self.' *Medical Anthropology Quarterly* 9, no. 3 (1995): 357–89. https://doi.org/10.1525/maq.1995.9.3.02a00050.

Sheehan, Jack G. *Reel Bad Arabs: How Hollywood Vilifies a People*. New York: Olive Branch Press, 2001.

Sherman, A. J. *Mandate Days: British Lives in Palestine, 1918–1948*. New York: Thames and Hudson, 1998.

Shih, Shu-mei. 'Comparison as Relation.' In *Comparison: Theories, Approaches, Uses*, edited by Rita Felski and Susan Stanford Friedman, 78–98. Baltimore: Johns Hopkins University Press, 2013.

Shih, Shu-mei. 'Theory in a Relational World.' *Comparative Literature Studies* 53, no. 4 (2016): 722–746. https://doi.org/10.5325/complitstudies.53.4.0722.

Shindler, Colin. 'The Reflection of Israel Within British Jewry.' In *Israel, the Diaspora and Jewish Identity*, edited by Danny Ben-Moshe and Zohar Segev, 227–34. Brighton; Portland: Sussex Academic Press, 2007.

Shlaim, Avi. *Israel and Palestine. Reappraisals, Revisions, Refutations*. London; New York: Verso, 2009.

Shohat, Ella, and Robert Stam. *Unthinking Eurocentrism: Multiculturalism and the Media*. London: Routledge, 2014.

Shohat, Ella. 'On Orientalist Genealogies: The Split Arab/Jew Figure Revisited.' In Bashir and Farsakh, *Arab and Jewish Questions*, 89–121.

Shulman, Ken. 'Youth and the Legacy of the Holocaust.' *The New York Times*, 15 January 1995. https://www.nytimes.com/1995/01/15/movies/film-youth-and-the-legacy-of-the-holocaust.html.

Shwayder, Maya. 'Jpost conference preview: Ron Prosor on Israel and the United Nations.' *The Jerusalem Post*, 2 March 2014. https://www.jpost.com/features/in-thespotlight/jpost-conference-preview-ron-prosor-on-israel-and-the-united-nations-344030.

Silverman, Maxim. *Palimpsestic Memory: The Holocaust and Colonialism in French and Francophone Literature and Film*. New York: Berghahn, 2013.

Smith, Piers Michael. 'Culture of the Turnip: Humour in the Travel Writing of Alexander Kinglake (1844) and Wilfred Gifford Palgrave (1865).' *Arab Journal for the Humanities* 25, no. 97 (2007): 205–22.

Sommer, Doris. *Foundational Fictions: The National Romances of Latin America*. Berkeley: University of California Press, 1991.

Sonne, Werner. *Wenn ich dich vergesse, Jerusalem*. Berlin: Bloomsbury Berlin, 2008.

Sontag, Susan. *On Photography*. London: Penguin, 1979.

Spivak, Gayatri Chakravorty. *A Critique of Postcolonial Reason: Toward a History of the Vanishing Past*. Cambridge, MA: Harvard University Press, 1999.

Spurr, David. *The Rhetoric of Empire: Colonial Discourse in Journalism, Travel Writing, and Imperial Administration*. Durham, NC: Duke University Press, 1993.

Stav, Shira. 'Nakba and Holocaust: Mechanisms of Comparison and Denial in the Israeli Literary Imagination.' *Jewish Social Studies* 18, no. 3 (2012): 85–98. https://www.jstor.org/stable/10.2979/jewisocistud.18.3.85.

Steenken, Charlotte. 'Als würde Bassum Raketen auf Syke schießen.' *Kreiszeitung*, 18 January 2011. https://www.kreiszeitung.de/laeuft/als-wuerde-bassum-raketen-syke-schiessen-1086696.html.

Stein, Arlene. 'Whose Memories? Whose Victimhood? Contests for the Holocaust Frame in Recent Social Movement Discourse.' *Sociological Perspectives* 41, no. 3 (1998): 519–540. https://doi.org/10.2307/1389562.

Steir-Livny, Liat. 'Holocaust Humour, Satire and Parody on Israeli Television.' *Jewish Film & New Media* 3, no. 2 (2015): 193–219. https://doi.org/10.13110/jewifilmnewmedi.3.2.0193.

Steir-Livny, Liat. *Is it OK to Laugh About it?: Holocaust Humour, Satire and Parody in Israeli Culture*. Elstree: Vallentine Mitchell, 2017.

Stevenson, Catherine. 'Mary Kingsley's Travel Writings: Humor and the Politics of Style.' *Exploration* 8 (1980): 1–13.

Stone, Dan. 'Day of Remembrance or Day of Forgetting? Or, Why Britain Does Not Need a Holocaust Memorial Day.' *Patterns of Prejudice* 34, no. 4 (2000): 53–9. https://doi.org/10.1080/003132200128810991.

Styron, William. *Sophie's Choice*. London: Cape, 1979.

Suleiman, Elia, dir. *Divine Intervention*. Featuring Elia Suleiman and Manal Khader. 2002. Streamed via Netflix. https://www.netflix.com/au/title/60026107.

Sutcliffe, Tom. 'The Weekend's TV: *The Promise*, Sun, Channel 4 Faulks on Fiction, Sat, BBC 2.' *The Independent*, 7 February 2011. http://www.independent.co.uk/arts-entertainment/tv/reviews/the-weekends-tv-the-promise-sun-channel-4brfaulks-on-fiction-sat-bbc2-2206220.html.

Taberner, Stuart 'Was gesagt werden muss: Günter Grass's "Israel/Iran" Poem of April 2012.' *German Life and Letters* 65, no. 4 (2012): 518–31. https://doi.org/10.1111/j.1468-0483.2012.01586.x.

Tawil-Souri, Helga. 'Media, Globalization, and the (Un)Making of the Palestinian Cause.' *Popular Communication* 13, no. 2 (2015): 145–57. https://doi.org/10.10 80/15405702.2015.1021470.

Thomas, Mark. *Extreme Rambling: Walking Israel's Separation Barrier. For Fun.* London: Ebury Press, 2011.

Thompson, Carl. *Travel Writing.* New York: Routledge, 2011.

Thompson, Gardner. *Legacy of Empire: Britain's Support of Zionism and the Creation of Israel.* London: Saqi Books, 2019.

Tidhar, Lavie. *Central Station.* San Francisco: Tachyon, 2006.

Tilley, Virginia. *The One-State Solution: A Breakthrough for Peace in the Israeli-Palestinian Deadlock.* Ann Arbor: University of Michigan Press, 2005.

Timm, Angelika. *Hammer, Zirkel, Davidstern: Das gestörte Verhältnis der DDR zu Zionismus und Staat Israel.* Bonn: Bouvier, 1997.

Torpey, John. *Making Whole What Has Been Smashed: On Reparation Politics.* Cambridge, MA: Harvard University Press, 2006.

Tuchman, Barbara W. *Bible and Sword; England and Palestine from the Bronze Age to Balfour.* New York: New York University Press, 1956.

Ullrich, Peter. 'Antisemitismus, Antizionismus und Kritik an Israel in Deutschland. Dynamiken eines diskursiven Feldes.' In *Jahrbuch für Antisemitismusforschung 23*, edited by Stefanie Schüler-Springorum, 105–20. Berlin: Metropol Verlag 2012.

Urry, John and Jonas Larsen. *The Tourist Gaze 3.0.* 3rd ed. Los Angeles: SAGE, 2011.

Van Teeffelen, Toine. 'Racism and Metaphor: The Palestinian-Israeli Conflict in Popular Culture,' *Discourse and Society* 5, no. 38 (1994): 381–405. www.jstor.org/stable/42887929.

Veiel, Andres, dir. *Balagan.* Featuring Madi Maayan, Khaled Abu Ali and Moni Yosef, 1993. Streamed via Vimeo. https://vimeo.com/ondemand/balagan.

Vermes, Timur. *Er ist wieder da.* Köln: Eichborn, 2012.

Vetter, Marcus, dir. *Cinema Jenin: The Story of a Dream.* Featuring Ismael Khatib, Fahkri Hamad and Marcus Vetter, 2011. Berlin: Senator Home Entertainment, 2012. DVD.

Vetter, Marcus and Leon Geller, dirs. *Das Herz von Jenin.* Featuring Ismael Khatib, 2009. Streamed via Vimeo. https://vimeo.com/ondemand/heardofjenin.

Vetter, Marcus. 'Director Statement.' Accessed 27 July 2021. https://marcus-vetter.com/heart-of-jenin.

Von Heinz, Julia. *Hannas Reise.* Featuring Karoline Schuch, Doron Amit and Leah König. 2013. Köln: 2Pilots Filmproduction, 2014. DVD.

Walser, Martin. 'Dankesrede von Martin Walser zur Verleihung des Friedenspreises des Deutschen Buchhandels in der Frankfurter Paulskirche am 11. Oktober 1998.' In

Friedenspreis des Deutschen Buchhandels 1998. Ansprachen aus Anlaß der Verleihung. Frankfurt: Börsenverein des Deutschen Buchhandels, 1998.

Webber, Andrew J. *The Doppelgänger: Double Visions in German Literature*. Oxford: Clarendon Press, 1996.

Weingardt, Markus A. *Deutsche Israel- und Nahostpolitik: Die Geschichte einer Gratwanderung seit 1949*. Frankfurt: Campus, 2002.

Weiss, Phil and Annie Robbins. 'Robust Debate? Murdoch Apologizes for London "Times" Cartoon of Netanyahu as Bloody Obstructionist.' *Mondoweiss*, 29 January 2013. https://mondoweiss.net/2013/01/apologizes-netanyahu-obstructionist.

Weston, Kath. 'Kinship, Controversy, and the Sharing of Substance: The Race/Class Politics of Blood Transfusion.' In *Relative Values: Reconfiguring Kinship Studies*, edited by Sarah Franklin and Susan McKinnon, 147–174. Durham, NC: Duke University Press, 2001.

Wolff, Fabian. 'Nur in Deutschland.' *Die Zeit*, 2 May 2021. https://www.zeit.de/kultur/2021-04/judentum-antisemitismus-deutschland-israel-bds-fabian-wolff-essay.

Wright, Timothy. 'Ecologies of Blood in Johannesburg Vampire Fiction.' *Safundi* 17, no. 4 (2016): 384–406. https://doi.org/10.1080/17533171.2016.1226729.

Yablonka, Hanna. *Survivors of the Holocaust: Israel After the War*. Translated by Ora Cummings. Basingstoke: Macmillan, 1999.

Yiftachel, Oren. *Ethnocracy: Land and Identity Politics in Israel/Palestine*. Philadelphia: University of Pennsylvania Press, 2006.

Younes, Anna-Esther. 'Fighting Anti-Semitism in Contemporary Germany.' *Islamophobia Studies Journal* 5, no. 2 (2020): 250–66. https://doi.org/10.13169/islastudj.5.2.0249.

Youngs, Tim. *The Cambridge Introduction to Travel Writing*. Cambridge: Cambridge University Press, 2013.

Zandberg, Eyal. 'Critical Laughter: Humour, Popular Culture and Israeli Commemoration.' *Media, Culture & Society* 25, no. 4 (2006): 561–79. https://doi.org/10.1177/0163443706065029.

Zingman, Alon, dir. *Shtisel*. Featuring Doval'e Glickman and Michael Aloni, 2013–2021. Streamed via Netflix. https://www.netflix.com/au/title/81004164.

Zreik, Raef. 'Palestine, Apartheid, and the Rights Discourse.' *Journal of Palestine Studies* 34, no. 1 (2004): 68–80. https://doi.org/10.1525/jps.2004.34.1.68.

INDEX

9/11, 20, 24–5, 174
1948 war, 52, 77–8, 80, 147, 150, 153–6; see also *nakba*
1967 war, 7, 16
1968 generation, 15, 16, 42, 56–7
1973 war (Yom Kippur war), 149

Absentee Property Law, 125–6
Abu-Lughod, Lila, 129
affiliation and filiation, 124
Ahmed, Sara, 21–2
Akko Theatre Company, 45, 46, 48, 49
aliyah (Jewish immigration to Palestine), 61
Amiry, Suad
    Sharon and My Mother-in-Law: Ramallah Diaries, 95
Anderson, Perry, 23
Anidjar, Gil, 24
anti-apartheid movement, 21
anti-Semitism, 127
    and Germany, 18–19
    and Great Britain, 9, 10–11
    and International Holocaust Remembrance Alliance (IHRA), 10
    and philo-Semitism, 17, 18, 44
    and *Zerbrochenes Deutsch: Zweimal Berlin-Haifa*, 56, 57, 58
apartheid, 3–4, 18, 21
Arafat, Yasser, 149
Arendt, Hannah, 14
Ashery, Oreet, 30, 165, 173–9
Ashkenazi Jews, 46
Assmann, Aleida, 42
atonement, 17–18, 43, 56, 82, 103, 109
Auschwitz (camp), 11, 12, 49, 58
Auschwitz trials (1963–7), 11
'Avodah 'Aravit (*Arab Labour*) (sitcom), 95
Azoulay, Ariella, 122

Balagan (documentary, 1993), 27–8, 44–54, 63
Balfour Declaration, 6–7, 32n21
Bar-On, Dan, 130
Bar-Tal, Daniel, 162–3
Bar-Yosef, Eitan, 6
Barghouti, Omar, 53, 173

Bashir, Bashir, 4, 24, 72–3, 82, 152, 157
Bäuerlein, Theresa, 28, 90, 95–6, 97, 99–105, 112–13
Behdad, Ali, 97
Ben-Natan, Asher, 117n40
Benbassa, Esther, 50
Bergen Belsen (camp), 75–6, 83–4
Berger, Arthur Asa, 95–6
Berlin Wall, 17
Bernard, Anna, 9, 20, 131
Black September, 36n68
Blair, Tony, 7–8
Blick, Hugo, 29, 113–14, 121, 122, 123–4, 132–9
blood donation, 29, 140, 145–6, 164
   and *Wenn ich dich vergesse, Jerusalem*, 151–2, 154, 155–6
Boudreau, Kristin, 163
Boycott, Divestment and Sanctions (BDS) movement, 21
Braach-Maksvytis, Martin, 19
Brandt, Willy, 15
Britain *see* Great Britain
British Empire, 8–9, 12
British Mandate, 5, 6–7, 8–9
   and the Holocaust, 12–13
   and *The Honourable Woman*, 138
   and *Ishmael's Oranges*, 125–6, 132
   and literature, 33n30
   and *The Promise*, 74–5, 76–83, 92n17, 92n23
   and *We Are All Made of Glue*, 85
   and *Wenn ich dich vergesse, Jerusalem*, 150, 152, 154
British Muslims, 7, 74
Britz (TV series, 2007), 74
Brockhaus, Gudrun, 111
Brooker, Will, 175
Butler, Judith, 21

Cahill, Ann J., 135
Cameron, David, 8
Césaire, Aimé, 14
Cesarani, David, 12
Chatterjee, Shreya, 121
children, 124, 128, 129, 131, 135–6, 138
cinema, 25, 26–7; *see also Balagan*; *Das Herz von Jenin*
Cinema Jenin: The Story of a Dream (documentary, 2012), 172–3
Cleary, Joe, 96, 111
coexistence, 29–30, 140, 146, 147–8, 164–5, 178
   and *Das Herz von Jenin*, 158–64
   and Hadassah hospital, 149–50
   and *Wenn ich dich vergesse, Jerusalem*, 150–2
Cohen, Hella Bloom, 123, 124, 128, 129, 135
Cohen, Nir, 82
collaboration, 172–4
colonialism
   and Germany, 43
   and Great Britain, 3, 5
   and the Holocaust, 12–14
   and *Ishmael's Oranges*, 123
   and memory, 22–3
   and Palestine, 6, 7, 8
   and stereotypes, 19–20
   and travel writing, 104–5
   and *We Are All Made of Glue*, 85
   see also settler-colonialism
concentration camps *see* Auschwitz; Bergen Belsen; Dachau
Corbyn, Jeremy, 10
Critchley, Simon, 109
Crossman, Richard, 81

Dachau (camp), 149, 151, 153, 155–6, 167n29
Das Herz von Jenin (*The Heart of Jenin*)
  (documentary, 2008), 29, 140, 146,
  147, 158–64
  and critics, 170n74
Das war der gute Teil des Tages (*That Was
  The Good Part of the Day*) (Bäuerlein),
  28, 90, 95–6, 97, 99–105, 112–13
Deir Yassin massacre, 147, 150, 155, 156
Denning, Michael, 137
Dennison, Stephanie, 25
Dentler, Ina, 27–8, 42, 44, 45, 55–63, 75
dialogue, 2, 22–3, 25, 53, 132, 165
  and *The Honourable Woman*, 138
  and kinship, 121
  and *The Novel of Nonel and Vovel*, 173–4,
    176
  and *We Are All Made of Glue*, 87, 88
  and *Zerbrochenes Deutsch: Zweimal
    Berlin-Haifa*, 62, 70n87
displaced relationality, 44–5, 52–3, 56,
  63–4, 178
disrupted familial relationality, 113–14, 121,
  178
  and *The Honourable Woman*, 123–4,
    133–4, 135–7, 138–9
  and *Ishmael's Oranges*, 122–3, 126–7,
    129–32
Divine Intervention (film, 2002), 176
documentary, 26, 67n43; see also *Balagan*;
  Das Herz von Jenin
donation *see* blood donation; organ
  donation
doubling, 56, 58
Doumani, Beshara, 20, 175
Druze, 161–2, 169n56

East Germany *see* German Democratic
  Republic
East Jerusalem, 3, 9, 148

Ebbrecht-Hartmann, Tobias, 48
Eichmann trial, 11
El Shakry, Hoda, 176
Elm, Michael, 58
Enns, Diane, 154
ethnicity, 124, 127–8, 130, 154–5, 161
  and blood/organ donation, 145–6, 151–2
Europe *see* France; Germany; Great Britain

families, 29, 113–14, 120–4
  and *Das Herz von Jenin*, 158–64
  and *The Honourable Woman*, 133–4,
    135–6, 138
  and *Ishmael's Oranges*, 126–7, 130–2
  and metaphors for the nation, 139
  and *Zerbrochenes Deutsch: Zweimal
    Berlin-Haifa*, 55, 56–9, 60–1,
    62
Farsakh, Leila, 4
  The Arab and Jewish Questions, 24
Farsoun, Sami K., 20–1
Faulenbach, Bernd, 110
Federal Republic of Germany (FRG), 13,
  14–17, 19–20
filiation and affiliation, 124
film *see* cinema
Fink, Carole, 15
First Intifada, 7, 16, 49, 134
  and *Balagan*, 63
  and *Das Herz von Jenin*, 160–1
  and victimhood, 20–1
Fischer, Leandros, 18
Flohr, Markus, 28, 90, 95–6, 97–8,
  105–13
Fox, Thomas, 14–15
France, 25
Freyberg, Jutta von, 112
FRG *see* Federal Republic of Germany
Fuchs, Anne, 42, 55
future relationality, 27, 172–9

Gan, Alon, 60
Gaza Strip, 1–2, 9, 63, 148
   and *The Honourable Woman*, 134–5, 136
   and *The Promise*, 75, 82
   and *Zerbrochenes Deutsch: Zweimal Berlin-Haifa*, 61, 62
GDR *see* German Democratic Republic
Gehrcke, Wolfgang, 112
Geller, Leon, 29, 140, 146, 147, 158–64
generations, 41–2; *see also* second generation; third generation
genocide, 43; *see also* Holocaust
German Democratic Republic (GDR), 13, 14–17
German South West Africa (Namibia), 43
Germany, 2, 3, 4–5, 9
   and colonialism, 43
   and divided loyalties, 178
   and guilt, 165
   and the Holocaust, 13–14, 27–8, 41–3
   and Israel, 17–19, 43–4, 96–7
   and Jenin cinema project, 179n2
   and normalisation, 14, 16, 18, 45–6, 101–3, 105, 111–12, 148
   and Palestine, 14–19
   see also *Balagan*; *Das Herz von Jenin* (*The Heart of Jenin*); *Das war der gute Teil des Tages*; Federal Republic of Germany (FRG); German Democratic Republic (GDR); *Wenn ich dich vergesse, Jerusalem* (*If I Forget You, Jerusalem*); *Wo samstags immer Sonntag ist*; *Zerbrochenes Deutsch: Zweimal Berlin-Haifa*
Ghanim, Honaida, 86
Giblett, Kylie, 57
Gilroy, Paul, 8–9, 12, 75
globalisation, 21
Glöckner, Olaf, 96–7
Goldberg, Amos, 72–3, 82, 152, 157

Goldhagen debate, 35n54
Gordon, Michelle, 12
Goschler, Constantin, 41–2
Grant, Linda
   The People on the Street: A Writer's View of Israel, 47
graphic narrative, 173–9
Grass, Günter
   'Was gesagt werden muss' ('What Needs to be Said'), 37n80
Great Britain, 2, 4–5, 6–11
   and Balfour Declaration, 6–7, 32n21
   and colonialism, 3, 5
   and divided loyalties, 178
   and the Holocaust, 11–13
   and Israel, 7, 8
   and Palestine, 6–11
   and Sykes-Picot agreement, 32n21
   see also British Mandate; *Honourable Woman, The*; *Ishmael's Oranges*; *Promise, The*; *We Are All Made of Glue*
Greene, Toby, 7–8
Grossman, David, 70n85
Grünberg, Harri, 112
guilt, 42, 44, 58, 98, 165
   and *Balagan*, 49
   and *Das war der gute Teil des Tages*, 99, 103–4
   and *Wo samstags immer Sonntag ist*, 110–11
   and *Zerbrochenes Deutsch: Zweimal Berlin-Haifa*, 58

Habermas, Jürgen, 13
Hadassah hospital, 149–50, 151
   and convoy attack, 147, 156
Haganah, 155
Hajaj, Claire, 28–9, 113–14, 121, 122–3, 125–32, 139

Hamas, 1, 61
Hannas Reise (*Hanna's Journey*) (film, 2013), 99
Harwood, Sarah, 120, 134
Hayot, Eric, 26
heart transplant *see* organ donation
Hepperle, Sabine, 15
Herero and Nama genocide, 43
Herrmann, Meike, 14, 41
Hiller, Mischa, 133
Historikerstreit, 111
Hjorth, Ronnie, 121
Hochberg, Gil Z., 4, 23, 152
Holm, Nicolas, 102
Holocaust, 3, 5, 178
  and *Balagan*, 44–54
  and Britain, 10–13
  and comparative approach, 71–4, 89–90
  and cultural memory, 41–2
  and *Das war der gute Teil des Tages*, 99–105
  and education, 50–1, 67n43
  and Germany, 9, 13–14, 16, 98
  and guilt, 17–19
  and *The Honourable Woman*, 134
  and humour, 116n35
  and *Ishmael's Oranges*, 127, 128
  and Israeli culture, 47, 116n33
  and Memorial Day, 12
  and memory, 22–3, 27–8
  and as metaphor, 71, 73–4, 75, 84, 86
  and the *nakba*, 72–4
  and Palestinian culture, 12–13, 50–2, 67n43
  and *The Promise*, 75–8, 82–3
  and rebirth myth, 25
  and victimhood, 42–3
  and *We Are All Made of Glue*, 83–9
  and *Wenn ich dich vergesse, Jerusalem*, 149, 150–1, 152–4, 155–8
  and *Wo samstags immer Sonntag ist*, 108–9, 110–12
  and *Zerbrochenes Deutsch: Zweimal Berlin-Haifa*, 55–63
Honourable Woman, The (TV miniseries, 2014), 29, 113–14, 121, 122, 123–4, 132–9
Hughes, William, 145–6
human rights, 9, 121–2
humour, 28, 97, 98
  and *Das war der gute Teil des Tages*, 99–105
  and Germany, 90, 113, 116n35
  and Israel, 90, 95–6
  and Palestine, 96
  and *Wo samstags immer Sonntag ist*, 105–13
  see also jokes
Huntington, Samuel, 146
Hussein, Cherine, 149
Huyssen, Andreas, 11, 71
hybridity, 128, 129, 131, 135–6, 138

identity, 23–4, 42–3, 60–1, 148
imperialism *see* colonialism
Intifadas *see* First Intifada; Second Intifada
Irgun, 8, 78–9, 81
Ishmael's Oranges (Hajaj), 28–9, 113–14, 121, 122–3, 125–32, 139
Islam, 20; *see also* Muslims
Islamophobia, 25
Israel, 1–2, 3–4
  and anti-Semitism, 9–10
  and *Balagan*, 44–54
  and Britain, 7, 8
  and coexistence, 147–8
  as contemporary signifier, 19–30
  and creation, 4–5
  and *Das Herz von Jenin*, 158–64

and *Das war der gute Teil des Tages*, 99–105
and disrupted familial relationality, 113–14
and family metaphor, 120–3, 124
and Germany, 14–19, 27–8, 43–4
and *The Honourable Woman*, 132–9
and humour, 96
and *Ishmael's Oranges*, 125–30
and minority groups, 169n56
and *The Novel of Nonel and Vovel*, 173–4, 177–9
and *The Promise*, 75, 76–83
and security discourse, 43, 55, 59, 60, 104
and *We Are All Made of Glue*, 84–5, 87–9
and *Wenn ich dich vergesse, Jerusalem*, 148–58
and *Wo samstags immer Sonntag ist*, 105–13
and *Zerbrochenes Deutsch: Zweimal Berlin-Haifa*, 55–63
see also Jews
Israeli Defense Force (IDF), 59–60
Israeli Palestinians, 47–8, 51, 54, 63
   and *Das Herz von Jenin*, 159
   and *The Promise*, 80, 81, 82
   and shared state, 147

Jaeger, Kinan, 43
Jenin, 160, 161–4, 172–3
Jews, 1–2, 3–4
   and *Balagan*, 46–54
   and blood/organ donation, 145–6
   and British Mandate, 6, 7
   and *Das Herz von Jenin*, 159–61, 162–4
   and *Das war der gute Teil des Tages*, 99–100, 101–5
   and *The Honourable Woman*, 132–9
   and identity, 23–4
   and *Ishmael's Oranges*, 122–3, 125–32
   and *The Novel of Nonel and Vovel*, 173–9
   and Palestinian relations, 141n30
   and *The Promise*, 75–83
   and relational memories, 89–90
   and right to return, 61–2
   and stereotypes, 19–20, 108–9
   and territorial rights, 72
   and victimhood, 20–1, 26
   and *We Are All Made of Glue*, 83, 84–5
   and *Wenn ich dich vergesse, Jerusalem*, 149, 150–8
   and *Wo samstags immer Sonntag ist*, 107, 108–12
   and *Zerbrochenes Deutsch: Zweimal Berlin-Haifa*, 55–63
   see also anti-Semitism; Ashkenazi Jews; Holocaust; Mizrahi Jews; Zionism
jokes, 108–9, 110
Jones, Andrew, 75
Joronen, Mikko, 174–5
Jureit, Ulrike, 42, 43

Karim, Sameena, 130
Karmi, Ghada, 147
Kashua, Sayed, 95
Keret, Etgar, 95
Khalidi, Walid, 155
Khalili, Laleh, 20
Khoury, Elias, 156
Kindertransport, 127, 134
King David Hotel bombing, 78–9
kinship, 29, 52–3, 121
   and blood/organ donation, 145–6, 151–2, 164
   and ethnicity, 124
   and *Ishmael's Oranges*, 125–32
   and metaphor, 139–40
   see also disrupted familial relationality

Kloke, Martin, 16
Klug, Brian, 2, 25
Knesset, 8
Kosminsky, Peter, 28, 64, 73–83, 89–90, 92n17, 92n23
Kotef, Hagar, 148
Kuwait, 128–9

Labour Party (UK), 7, 10
Lakoff, George, 133
Larsen, Jonas, 100
Lavy, George, 19
Lawson, Tom, 11
Levy, Daniel, 11, 84
Lewycka, Marina, 28, 64, 73–4, 83–90
libidinal relationality, 97, 98, 178
    and *Das war der gute Teil des Tages*, 99–105
    and *The Promise*, 80–2
    and *Wenn ich dich vergesse, Jerusalem*, 154–5
    and *Wo samstags immer Sonntag ist*, 109–10, 111
Lionis, Chrisoula, 95, 107
Lisle, Debbie, 98, 100, 106
literature, 23–4, 25, 26–7, 33n30; see also *Das war der gute Teil des Tages*; *Ishmael's Oranges*; *The Novel of Nonel and Vovel*; *We Are All Made of Glue*; *Wenn ich dich vergesse, Jerusalem*; *Wo samstags immer Sonntag ist*; *Zerbrochenes Deutsch: Zweimal Berlin-Haifa*
Livingstone, Ken, 10
Lloyd, David, 178
Lockman, Zachary, 23, 150
Luxembourg Agreement, 15

Maayan, David
    Arbeit macht frei vom Toitland Europa (*Work Liberates from Deathland Europe*), 45, 48, 49, 50–4, 63

Maayan, Madi Smadar, 48, 50, 52
Mamdani, Mahmood, 153
Martin, Rod, 102
Masalha, Nur, 72, 85, 126
Mbembe, Achille, 17–18
McClintock, Anne, 120, 128, 135
McCormack, Donna, 160, 162
McGreal, Chris, 145
memory, 27–8, 41–2, 72–3
    and comparative memory, 22, 45, 72
    and German memory culture, 14, 25, 42–3, 49
    and multidirectional memory, 22–3, 43, 72, 78
    and palimpsestic memory, 22, 76, 77, 84
    see also *Balagan*; relational memories
Merkel, Angela, 17
mess (*balagan*), 47–8
metaphors, 40n115, 87–9
    and Holocaust, 71, 73–4, 75, 84, 86
    and kinship, 28–9, 139–40
Middle East see Israel; Palestine
Milton-Edwards, Beverley, 8
Mintz, Lawrence E., 96
miscegenation, 124, 128, 129, 131, 135–6, 138
Mizrahi Jews, 46, 96, 109–10, 113
Morreall, John, 96
Muslims, 18, 24–5; see also British Muslims

nakba (catastrophe), 25, 28
    and *Balagan*, 46, 47, 50, 51–2, 54
    and Holocaust, 72–4
    and *Ishmael's Oranges*, 125–6, 127, 128, 132
    and *The Promise*, 76–8, 80
    and *We Are All Made of Glue*, 83–9
    and *Wenn ich dich vergesse, Jerusalem*, 152–4, 155–8
National Socialism see Nazism

nationalism, 120, 121–2
Nazism, 5, 43, 48
   and colonialism, 14
   and FRG, 15, 16
   and GDR, 13, 14–15
   see also Holocaust
neo-Nazism, 9
Niven, Bill, 14
Nolte, Ernst, 13
normalisation, 14, 16, 45, 111–13, 172
Novel of Nonel and Vovel, The (graphic narrative, 2009), 30, 165, 173–9

Ó Dochartaigh, Pól, 17, 44, 151
Occupied Palestinian Territories *see* East Jerusalem; Gaza Strip; West Bank
Ofer, Dalia, 46–7
one-state solution, 147–8, 164
Ophir, Adi, 122
organ donation, 29, 140, 145–6, 147, 148
   and *Das Herz von Jenin*, 158–64
Orientalism, 5, 6, 19, 97
   and stereotypes, 24, 117n42
Orthodox Jews, 162–4, 169n56
Oslo Accords (1993), 21, 99, 147, 149, 165
othering, 24–5, 104–5
Ottoman Empire, 6, 32n21
Oz, Amos, 101
Ozacky-Lazar, Sarah, 50–1

Palestine, 2, 3–4, 5
   and *Balagan*, 44–54
   and British imaginary, 6–11
   and coexistence, 147–8
   as contemporary signifier, 19–20
   and *Das Herz von Jenin*, 158–64
   and *Das war der gute Teil des Tages*, 99–105
   and disrupted familial relationality, 113–14
   and family metaphor, 120–3, 124
   and Germany, 14–19
   and the Holocaust, 12–13
   and *The Honourable Woman*, 132–9
   and humour, 96
   and *Ishmael's Oranges*, 125–32
   and *The Novel of Nonel and Vovel*, 173–9
   and *The Promise*, 74–83
   and *We Are All Made of Glue*, 83–9
   and *Wenn ich dich vergesse, Jerusalem*, 148–58
   and *Wo samstags immer Sonntag ist*, 105–12
   and *Zerbrochenes Deutsch: Zweimal Berlin-Haifa*, 55–6, 58–63
   see also British Mandate; *nakba*; Palestinians
Palestinians, 1–2, 3–4
   and *Balagan*, 44–54
   and blood/organ donation, 145–6
   and *Das Herz von Jenin*, 159–64
   and *Das war der gute Teil des Tages*, 104–5
   and Holocaust knowledge, 50–2, 67n43
   and *The Honourable Woman*, 132–9
   and identity, 23–4
   and *Ishmael's Oranges*, 122–3, 125–32
   and Jewish relations, 141n30
   and othering, 24–5
   and *The Promise*, 74–83
   and relational memories, 89–90
   and right to return, 61–2
   and self-determination, 4, 5, 15, 46
   and stereotypes, 20–1
   and *The Novel of Nonel and Vovel*, 173–9
   and *We Are All Made of Glue*, 83–9
   and *Wenn ich dich vergesse, Jerusalem*, 148–58
   and *Wo samstags immer Sonntag ist*, 106–7, 112–13
   and *Zerbrochenes Deutsch: Zweimal Berlin-Haifa*, 55–63
   see also Palestine

palimpsest, 22, 76–7
Pappé, Ilan, 72, 123, 128, 132
partition, 3, 31n11, 88, 131, 154–5
Pearce, Andy, 11
Pearce, Caroline, 14, 101, 102, 111
Perry, Ruth, 122, 131–2
philo-Semitism, 17, 18, 44, 62
philo-Zionism, 44, 59, 62
Piterberg, Gabriel, 150
Plan Dalet, 155
pogroms, 61, 127
Pollock, Griselda, 75–6, 77, 84
postcolonial amnesia, 8, 12
post-Zionism, 128, 129
Promise, The (TV miniseries, 2011), 28, 64, 73–83

Rabin, Yitzhak, 149
Reinhart, Tanya, 104
relational memories, 73–4, 89–90, 178
    and *The Promise*, 74–83
    and *We Are All Made of Glue*, 83–9
relational turn, 2, 23
relationality, 2–3, 4
    and coexistence, 140
    and critical, 21–30
    and memories, 63–4
    and *The Novel of Nonel and Vovel*, 176, 179
    see also displaced relationality; disrupted familial relationality; future relationality; libidinal relationality; relational memories
reparations, 43, 103, 109, 117n40; *see also* Luxembourg agreement
resistance, 8, 20, 130, 150, 157
    and *Das Herz von Jenin*, 160–1
    and *The Honourable Woman*, 139
    and Jewish underground, 149, 154
responsibility, 105–13, 111
reunification, 14, 16–17, 18, 27, 41, 45

Rich, Dave, 9
right of return, 61–2, 70n85
Rogers, Robert, 56
romance, 97
    and across-the-divide trope, 96, 103, 123, 145, 154
    and *Das war der gute Teil des Tages*, 99–100, 101–2, 103, 104
    and *Ishmael's Oranges*, 122–3, 126–32
    and *The Promise*, 74–83
    and *Wenn ich dich vergesse, Jerusalem*, 154–5
Rose, Jacqueline, 177–8
Rosenfeld, Gavriel D., 103
Rothberg, Michael, 14, 22–3, 43, 72, 78, 89, 90
Rovit, Rebecca, 54
Rovner, Adam, 7
Russell, Emily, 145, 160, 161, 164

Sabra and Shatila massacre, 130
Sa'di, Ahmad H., 129
Said, Edward, 25, 100–1, 104
    and coexistence, 147–8, 152, 159
    and filiation and affiliation, 124
    and Jewish–Arab relations, 123, 125
    Orientalism, 6
Salcedo, Doris
    Shibboleth, 3
Sansour, Larissa, 30, 165, 173–9
Sarsar, Saliba, 130
satire, 102–3
Scarfe, Gerald, 10
Schoeps, Julius H., 97
Schuhmann, Antje, 16
Schütte, Helmuth, 110
second generation, 42
    and *Balagan*, 46
    and *Zerbrochenes Deutsch: Zweimal Berlin-Haifa*, 55

Second Intifada, 3, 10, 21
   and *Das war der gute Teil des Tages*, 99, 104
   and Germany, 17
   and Jenin, 161
   and two-state solution, 147
   and victimhood, 20
   and *Zerbrochenes Deutsch: Zweimal Berlin-Haifa*, 55, 60
sentimentalism, 164–5
separation, 3–4, 24
September 11 2001 *see* 9/11
settler-colonialism, 3–4, 31n12, 62
Shah, Naz, 10
Sharp, Lesley A., 162
Shih, Shu-mei, 26, 73
Shohat, Ella, 2, 127, 146
Silverman, Maxim, 22, 72, 76, 77, 87
Sommer, Doris, 103, 104
Song Hwee Lim, 25
Sonne, Werner, 29, 140, 146–7, 148–58
Sontag, Susan, 84, 126
Spurr, David, 104–5
Stam, Robert, 2
Stav, Shira, 52, 157
Steir-Livny, Liat, 102
stereotypes, 19–20, 24, 180n10
   and *Das Herz von Jenin*, 160–1, 162
   and *Das war der gute Teil des Tages*, 100, 104
   and Orientalism, 117n42
   and *Wo samstags immer Sonntag ist*, 106, 108–9
Stern gang, 8
Stone, Dan, 12
Styron, William
   Sophie's Choice, 86
suffering, 72–3, 84, 85, 89–90; *see also* Holocaust; *nakba*
Suleiman, Elia, 176

superhero narratives, 174, 175, 176, 177
Sznaider, Natan, 11, 84

Tawil-Souri, Helga, 21
third generation
   and *Das war der gute Teil des Tages*, 101, 103–4, 105
   and *Wo samstags immer Sonntag ist*, 109, 110
   and *Zerbrochenes Deutsch: Zweimal Berlin-Haifa*, 55, 56, 57
Thompson, Carl, 98, 101
Timm, Angelika, 15
Torpey, John, 43
transplants *see* blood donation; organ donation
travel writing, 96, 98, 101, 114n5; *see also Das war der gute Teil des Tages*; *Wo samstags immer Sonntag ist*
tribalism, 130–1
Tuchman, Barbara, 6
TV drama, 26–7; *see also Honourable Woman, The*; *Promise, The*
two-state solution, 3, 147

Ullrich, Peter, 98
United Kingdom (UK) *see* Great Britain
United Nations partition plan, 3, 154
United States of America (USA), 4, 10, 71, 137, 174
universal humanity, 158–64
Unsere Mütter, unsere Väter (*Generation War*) (TV miniseries, 2013), 56
Urry, John, 100

Van Teeffelen, Toine, 79, 87, 121, 133
Veiel, Andres, 27–8, 42, 44–54, 63, 66n22
Vetter, Marcus, 29, 140, 146, 147, 158–64, 172–3

victimhood, 20–1, 26, 44
  and *Balagan*, 46
  and comparative approach, 72–3
  and Holocaust, 42–3
  and *The Honourable Woman*, 133
  and Nazism, 64n7

Walser, Martin, 49, 66n32
Warriors (TV drama, 1999), 74
Warwick Research Collective, 25
We Are All Made of Glue (Lewycka), 28, 64, 73–4, 83–90
Wenn ich dich vergesse, Jerusalem (*If I Forget You, Jerusalem*) (Sonne), 29, 140, 146–7, 148–58
West Bank, 3, 9, 148
  and *Das Herz von Jenin*, 159, 160, 161
  and *The Honourable Woman*, 132–3
  and *The Novel of Nonel and Vovel*, 175–7
  and *The Promise*, 75
  and *We Are All Made of Glue*, 88
  and *Zerbrochenes Deutsch: Zweimal Berlin-Haifa*, 61, 62
  see also Jenin
West Germany *see* Federal Republic of Germany
Weston, Kath, 146, 154

Where the Desert Meets the Sea (Sonne), 29, 140, 146–7, 148–58
Wir weigern uns Feinde zu sein (*We Refuse to Be Enemies*) (documentary, 2011), 67n43
Wo samstags immer Sonntag ist (*Where Saturday Is Always Sunday*) (Flohr), 28, 90, 95–6, 105–13
Wolff, Fabian, 17, 96
world literature, 25, 26
World War II, 5, 25, 42; *see also* Holocaust; Nazism
Wright, Timothy, 157, 161

Yablonka, Hanna, 153
Yad Vashem, 50, 110
Younes, Anna-Esther, 18

Zandberg, Eyal, 103–4, 109, 110
Zerbrochenes Deutsch: Zweimal Berlin-Haifa (*Broken German: Two Times Berlin-Haifa*) (Dentler), 27–8, 44, 45, 55–63, 75
Zionism, 7, 9, 10, 43–4
  and *Ishmael's Oranges*, 123
  and Plan Dalet, 155
  and *We Are All Made of Glue*, 85
  see also Irgun; philo-Zionism; post-Zionism
Zreik, Raef, 4

EU representative:
Easy Access System Europe
Mustamäe tee 50, 10621 Tallinn, Estonia
Gpsr.requests@easproject.com

www.ingramcontent.com/pod-product-compliance
Lightning Source LLC
Chambersburg PA
CBHW051123160426
43195CB00014B/2323